AUGUSTINE:

DE FIDE ET SYMBOLO

INTRODUCTION, TRANSLATION, COMMENTARY

by

E.P. MEIJERING

J.C. GIEBEN, PUBLISHER

AMSTERDAM 1987

ISBN 90 70265 78 8
Printed in The Netherlands

AUGUSTINE: *DE FIDE ET SYMBOLO*

CEBO C. DE BRUIN
XVI LUSTRA COMPLENTI
D.D.D.
AUCTOR

CONTENTS

PREFACE

"The doctrine of the Trinity is not closed. It can be neither discarded nor accepted in its traditional form. It must be kept open in order to fulfil its original function- to express in embracing symbols the self-manifestation of the Divine Life to man." This statement made by Paul Tillich (*Systematic Theology III,* p 314) applies to all elements of traditional Christian thought as they are expressed in the Creed.

Augustine's reflections on the Creed are the thoughts of a sublime mind about a common belief. If the present study can show that these reflections can still help us to find a meaning in what we inherited from the past, the author's efforts will not have been in vain.

I want to thank my colleague and friend Professor J.C.M. van Winden for his very thorough correction of the original manuscript, especially of the translation.

The book has been dedicated to Professor C.C. de Bruin on the occasion of his eightieth birthday. I admire his knowledge of the history of Christian thought and share his critical reverence towards it.

Ridderspoorlaan 103
Oegstgeest / The Netherlands

E.P.M.

INTRODUCTION

We are fairly well informed concerning the date and the circumstances of the *De fide et symbolo:* It is a discussion of the contents of the Creed which Augustine, still a presbyter, gave before the bishops at an African Synod at Hippo Regius (in October 393). In this discussion the Creed, which has to be memorized, is, as Augustine tells us himself, not reproduced in its exact wording, although the facts stated in the Creed are discussed (see *Retractationes* 1,17: . . . in quo (sc. libro) de rebus ipsis ita disseritur, ut tamen non fiat verborum illa contextio, quae tenenda memoriter competentibus traditur).

When one tries to find out which Creed Augustine is using in this piece of writing one has the choice between the following Creeds (cf. A. Hahn, *Bibliothek der Symbole und Glaubensregeln der alten Kirche,* Breslau 1897, pp 38ff, J.N.D. Kelly, *Early Christian Creeds,* New York 1972[3], p 102, P.C. Eichenseer, *Das Symbolum Apostolicum beim heiligen Augustinus mit Berücksichtigung des dogmengeschichtlichen Zusammenhangs,* St. Ottilien 1960, pp 100f):

[1]) *Vetus Romanum* (see J.N.D. Kelly, *op. cit.*, p. 102):

Credo in Deum Patrem omnipotentem, et in Christum Jesum filium eius unicum, dominum nostrum qui natus est de Spiritu sancto et Maria virgine, qui sub Pontio Pilato crucifixus est et sepultus, tertia die resurrexit a mortuis, ascendit in caelos, sedet ad dexteram Patris, unde venturus est iudicare vivos et mortuos, et in Spiritum Sanctum, sanctam ecclesiam, remissionem peccatorum, carnis resurrectionem.

[2]) *Confession of Milan* (see J.N.D. Kelly, *op. cit.*, p. 173):

Credo in Deum Patrem omnipotentem, et in Jesum Christum, filium eius unicum, dominum nostrum, qui natus est de Spiritu sancto et Maria virgine, passus est sub Pontio Pilato, crucifixus et sepultus, tertia die resurrexit a mortuis, ascendit in coelum, sedet ad dexteram Patris, inde venturus est iudicare vivos et mortuos, et in Spiritum sanctum, sanctam ecclesiam, remissionem peccatorum, carnis resurrectionem.

[3]) *North African Creed* (P.C. Eichenseer, *op. cit.*, p. 105, n. 128):

Credo in Deum Patrem omnipotentem, universorum creatorem. Credo et in Filium eius Jesum Christum, Dominum nostrum, qui natus est de

Spiritu sancto ex virgine Maria, crucifixus est sub Pontio Pilato et sepultus, descendit in infernum, tertio die a mortuis resurrexit, in caelum ascendit, et in dextera Patris sedet, inde venturus est iudicare vivos et mortuos. Credo et in Spiritum sanctum, remissionem peccatorum, carnis resurrectionem ert vitam aeternam, per sanctam ecclesiam.

The choice between these Creeds as the background of the *De fide et symbolo* is made difficult by the fact that Augustine seems not to stick to one specific symbol in explaining "the symbol":
In *Sermones* 212, 213 and 214 he uses the Confession of Milan. This is clear from the almost litteral quotations given in *Sermo* 213:
213,1,1: Credo in Deum Patrem omnipotentem
213,2,2: et in Jesum Christum Filium eius unicum, Dominum nostrum. Qui conceptus est de Spiritu sancto natus ex virgine Maria
213,3,3: Passus est sub Pontio Pilato, crucifixus mortuus et sepultus
213,4,4: Tertia ... die resurrexit a mortuis ascendit in caelum, sedet ad dexteram Patris, inde venturus est iudicare vivos et mortuos
213,6,6: et in Spiritum sanctum
213,7,7: sanctam ecclesiam
213,8,8: remissionem peccatorum
213,9,9: carnis resurrectionem (iste iam finis est).

There are slight differences with the Confession of Milan ("qui conceptus est de Spiritu sancto natus ex virgine Maria" instead of "qui natus est de Spiritu sancto et Maria virgine",- "mortuus" is added,- "inde venturus iudicaturus" instead of "inde venturus est iudicare", but none of these alterations appear in the *Vetus Romanum* or the North African Creed). The fact that "passus est" appears in this Sermon and that it uses "in caelum" and not "in caelos" points towards the Confession of Milan and not the *Vetus Romanum.* The North African Creed can be ruled out, since there is no reference to the descent to the underworld and no other peculiarities of this Creed appear.
Whether in *Sermo* 215 Augustine follows the North African Creed, as P.C. Eichenseer (*op. cit.,* p 105) suggests, is not entirely clear. He does say (215,1): salutis est regula nos credere in Deum Patrem omnipotentem, universorum creatorem, but there is no reference to the descent to the underworld. It seems that he does reproduce the following words of this Creed: Credo in Spiritum sanctum, remissionem peccatorum, carnis resurrectionem et vitam aeternam, per sanctam ecclesiam, see 215,8 and 9: Credamus et in Spiritum sanctum ... Per ipsum remissionem accipimus peccatorum, per ipsum resurrectionem credimus carnis, per ipsum vitam speramus aeternam ... quasi supplementum quoddam addi-

tum, ut diceretur, Per sanctam Ecclesiam. On balance it seems most likely that the North African Creed is followed in this sermon.

So it is likely that two of the three Creeds quoted above are followed by Augustine in the *Sermones* 212-215, viz., the Confession of Milan and the North African Creed. In trying to find out which Creed he follows in the *De fide et symbolo* we shall isolate from the text of this work those words which seem to stem from a Creed; the following picture then emerges:

2,3: Credentes itaque in Deum Patrem omnipotentem, nullam creaturam esse quae ab omnipotente non creata sit, existimare debemus. Behind this sentence lie the words of the Creed (which were explained in 2,2): Credo in Deum Patrem omnipotentem (we here suppose that the plural is caused by the fact that Augustine is addressing the members of the Synod who adhere to the Creed).

3,3: Credimus etiam in Jesum Christum Filium Dei, Patris unigenitum, id est unicum Dominum nostrum. The words "credimus etiam" and the explanation "id est unicum" are caused by the context, so this leaves: et in Jesum Christum, Filium Dei, Patris unigenitum, Dominum nostrum.

4,8: (credentes in eum Dei Filium), qui natus est per Spiritum sanctum ex virgine Maria

5,11: (Credimus itaque in eum) qui sub Pontio Pilato crucifixus est, et sepultus.

5,12: Credimus etiam illum tertio die resurrexisse a mortuis, behind this obviously lies: tertio die resurrexit a mortuis.

6,13: Credimus in coelum ascendisse, behind this lies: ascendit in coelum.

7,14: (Credimus etiam quod) sedet ad dexteram Patris.

8,15: Credimus etiam inde venturum convenientissimo tempore, et iudicaturum vivos et mortuos, behind this lies: inde venturus et iudicaturus vivos et mortuos.

9,16:...adiungitur confessioni nostrae ... Spiritus sanctus, behind this lies: credo et in Spiritum sanctum.

10,21: (Credimus et) sanctam ecclesiam (utique catholicam).

10,22: (Ideo credimus et) remissionem peccatorum.

10,23: (Et ideo credimus et) carnis resurrectionem. This reference to the resurrection of the flesh seems to be the end of the Creed which Augustine is explaining. What is said in 10,24 about eternal life is an explanation of this belief in the resurrection of the flesh and is not presented as an explanation of words taken from the Creed.

If we now put together the words which seem to have been drawn from the Creed we arrive at the following text:

"Credo in Deum Patrem omnipotentem, et in Jesum Christum, Filium Dei, Patris unigenitum, Dominum nostrum, qui natus est per Spiritum sanctum ex Maria virgine, qui sub Pontio Pilato crucifixus est et sepultus. Tertio die resurrexit a mortuis, ascendit in caelum, sedet ad dexteram Patris, inde venturus et iudicaturus vivos et mortuos, et in Spiritum sanctum, sanctam ecclesiam, remissionem peccatorum, carnis resurrectionem."

This reconstructed "Creed" is a purely hypothetical one which as such does not exist. The question is: with which of the three Creeds quoted above does this hypothetical "Creed" show the greatest similarity? The North African Creed can be ruled out, since the Father is merely called "omnipotens" and not "creator universorum", since there is no reference to the descent to the underworld, since the reference to the holy church is not at the end, and since there is no separate reference to eternal life. So the choice is between the *Vetus Romanum* and the Confession of Milan. This choice is made difficult by the fact that Augustine does not quote literally, and that these two Creeds show such great similarity to one another. So one must ask from which of these two Creeds the hypothetical "Creed" shows the smallest divergence. On balance this seems to be the *Vetus Romanum:*
The "passus est" which is added in the Confession of Milan is absent in 5,11; this seems more important than the fact that in the present treatise Augustine uses (in accordance with the Confession of Milan and at variance with the *Vetus Romanum*) "Jesum Christum" and not "Christum Jesum", and "in caelum" instead of "in coelos". Looking at the differences between our reconstructed hypothetical "Creed" and the *Vetus Romanum* the following additional observations can be made:
Christ as the Son is called "unigenitus", to which the explanation "unicus" is given (3,3). One might expect the reverse to occur, that firstly the "unicus" of the Creed be given and that this then be explained as "unigenitus". Augustine is here obviously influenced by the Nicene Creed (cf. *infra*, 61).
Augustine says in connection with the second coming of Christ "venturus et iudicaturus vivos et mortuos" instead of "venturus est iudicare vivos et mortuos" as given in the Vetus Romanum. This could be caused by the fact that in his text he inserts "convenientissimo tempore": the moment of the second coming is thus clarified, and the meaning of the judgement of the living and the dead is explained in the next sentences. So here there is in fact a reference to two activities, hence the juxtaposition instead of the supposition.
Nothing can be said in this matter with absolute certainty. What seems

certain is that Augustine does not follow the North African Creed in the *De fide et symbolo,* and that it seems more likely that he follows the *Vetus Romanum* than the Confession of Milan. Augustine obviously inserted the words from the Creed into his argument in the way which suited him best. Given that the two Creeds from which the words could have been taken are so similar, it is impossible to determine with certainty from which of the two Creeds Augustine is drawing. We can provide no more than probable explanations.

In the present study we shall firstly translate the text and then try to analyse the various sections of the translated text. In our analysis Augustine's own writings will provide the background, where possible, primarily those treatises which were written before or around the date of the *De fide et symbolo.* However, later writings will also be used, as will be the writings of other Christian and Pagan authors when this seems necessary and enlightening. This method marks the similarity and the difference between the present study and Eichenseer's great and important book on Augustine's use of the Apostolic Creed. Eichenseer tries to find out how the Creed functions in Augustine; we try to analyse (the background of) the thoughts expressed in the *De fide et symbolo.* In following this method and in asking this question we hope to do some of the work which Eichenseer could not accomplish within the limits of his work (see *op. cit.,* p VII: "Die Untersuchung zu jedem einzelnen Artikel bemühte sich herauszuarbeiten, welcher Glaubensinhalt hier in den ersten Zeiten des Christentums seine bestimmte Ausprägung erfahren hat. Dabei lag das Hauptgewicht auf der Auslegung Augustins, und zwar besonders auf jenen Texten, in denen der Kirchenvater kommentierend oder predigend oder argumentierend einen Artikel auswertet. Nicht möglich war es jedoch, eine Eingruppierung in die theologische Gesamtschau Augustins vorzunehmen , weil dazu Arbeiten notwendig geworden wären, die den Rahmen einer Dissertation gesprängt hätten.") The similarity with Eichenseer's book is that we, too, deal with the major articles of the Christian faith as they were explained by Augustine ; the difference is that we do so by singling out the *De fide et symbolo* and by trying to show how far this piece of writing is representative of Augustine's theology.

For the Latin text we made use of the one prepared by J. Zycha in the CSEL XXXXI (SECT. V, PARS III). This text shows few variances with the one given by the the Benedictines (*Migne,* PL 40, pp 181ff) which is also reproduced by J. Rivière in *Oeuvres de Saint Augustin, IX, Exposés généraux de la foi. De fide et symbolo-Enchiridion. Texte, Traduction, Notes*, Paris 1947.

CONTENTS OF THE "DE FIDE ET SYMBOLO"

I. Introduction. The function of the Symbol and of reflections about the Symbol (1,1).

II. Part I. Faith in God the Father (2,2-2,3a).

1) In His omnipotence God the Father created formless matter from nothing and granted forms to it (2,2).
2) The Father created all things through His Word (Truth, Power and Wisdom) (2,3a).

III. Part II. Faith in God the Son (2,3b-8,15).

1) The Son is God's unchangeable and eternal, generated Word (2,3b-3,3).
2) Unlike the human words which cannot fully reveal the human mind, God's Word can truly reveal the Father (3,4).
3) Refutation of the Sabellian and the Arian doctrine about the Son (4,5).
4) The meaning and purpose of the incarnation of the Son (4,6).
5) God is Being, the opposite of God is non-being (4,7).
6) When the Son assumed manhood through the virgin Mary, this means that manhood in its totality was assumed and not only the human body (as the Apollinarians claim) (4,8).
7) Refutation of the Manicheans' denial of the reality of Christ's birth (4,9).
8) Refutation of the Manicheans' claim that birth from a woman's womb is unworthy of Christ (4,10).
9) Christ's crucifixion, death and burial (5,11).
10) Christ's resurrection (5,12).
11) Christ's ascension to heaven and a brief discussion of the quality of risen bodies (6,13).
12) Christ's sitting at the right hand of the Father (7,14).
13) Christ's second coming as the Judge of the living and the dead (8,15).

IV. Part III. Faith in God the Holy Spirit and expositions on the Trinity (9,16-9,20).

1) The Holy Spirit is fully God, just like the Father and the Son. Father, Son and Spirit are one God (9,16).
2) The inadequacy of images of the Trinity taken from the realm of creation (9,17).
3) Expositions by ecclesiastical writers on the Father and the Son (9,18).

4) The Holy Spirit as the divinity and love of the Father and the Son (9,19).
5) God is an incorporeal reality and as such can only be known by believers who have cleansed their hearts (9,20).

V. Part IV. Belief in the holy church, the forgiveness of sins and the resurrection of the flesh (9,21-10,24).
1) Love of one's neighbour presupposes a communion (9,21).
2) This communion is the holy church in which during this life sins are forgiven (9,21b-10,22).
3) The resurrection of the flesh is the final consummation of spiritual life of the homo carnalis and the homo animalis (10,23).
4) Discussion of the quality of the risen body and a proof of the rationality of belief in the resurrection (10,24).

VI. Concluding statements (10,25).

I

INTRODUCTION

Chapter 1

Introduction: Christian faith must be expressed for the benefit of believers, and it must be defended against heretics . This faith is briefly expressed in the Symbol with the intention that those who have just been reborn (baptized) may have an object of faith. Those who want to make progress need deeper insight into what is stated in the Symbol, so they need an explanation of the Symbol. This explanation is also a defence of the Christian faith against heretics, who come forward with their venomous doctrines by taking advantage of the brevity of the Symbol which leaves room for misinterpretation.

Text, Translation and Commentary:

Quoniam scriptum est et apostolicae disciplinae robustissima auctoritate firmatum, *quia iustus ex fide vivit,* eaque fides officium a nobis exigit et cordis et linguae - ait enim Apostolus, *corde creditur ad iustitiam, ore autem confessio fit ad salutem,-* oportet nos esse et iustitiae memores et salutis,

*(**1,1**) "Because it has been written and was confirmed by the strongest authority of the apostolic teaching, That the righteous one lives by faith, (Hab. 2,4 and Gal. 3,11), and this faith requires from us a service of both heart and tongue, for the Apostle says, With one's heart one believes towards righteousness, and the confession is with one's mouth towards salvation, (Rom. 10,10), for this reason we must strive after both righteousness and salvation;*

The treatise on faith and the Symbol begins with an appeal to Scripture. This must also indicate that the Symbol is based on God's words as uttered through the Prophets and the Apostles. The Biblical reference given is to an Old Testament text which is confirmed by a New Testament one (the words "scriptum est" refer to the Old Testament, this is an expression which is often used in the New Testament). This does not mean that the authority of the New Testament is greater than the authority of the Old Testament. The reason why Augustine stresses that the Apostle confirms the prophet's words is that the heretics whom he attacks in the present treatise are primarily the Manicheans: it is with them in mind that he states this apostolic confirmation of an Old Testament text. (On Augustine's views on the authority of the Bible see e.g. K. Staritz, *Augustins Schöpfungsglaube dargestellt nach seinen Genesisauslegungen,* Breslau 1931, pp

48ff, K.H. Lütcke, *"Auctoritas" bei Augustin. Mit einer Einleitung zur römischen Vorgeschichte des Begriffs,* Stuttgart 1968, especially pp 64ff, 78ff, 84ff, 128ff, 182ff, 188ff, E. König, *Augustinus philosophus. Christlicher Glaube und philosophisches Denken in den Frühschriften Augustins,* München 1970, pp 68ff, C. Walter, *Der Ertrag der Auseinandersetzung mit den Manichäern für das hermeneutische Problem bei Augustin,* München 1972, pp 105ff: Walter's study deals with Augustine's treatise *De Genesi contra Manichaeos,* which was written a few years before the present treatise). -In the stressing of faith in one's heart and the confession with one's mouth the sequence is important: one can only truly confess what one bears in one's heart,- if one confesses other things than what one bears in one's heart one does not confess, but merely speaks, cf. *In Ioann.* 26,2: De radice cordis surgit ista confessio... Hoc est enim confiteri, dicere quod habes in corde: si autem aliud in corde habes, aliud dicis,- loqueris non confiteris. (Ambrose puts it in a somewhat different way, see *In Lucam* 5,12: perfidia enim confiteri potest, credere non potest.) The reference to *Rom.* 10,10 could in the present context also be directed against the Manicheans: they hide their true intentions behind their words, they are, as Augustine calls them, "decepti deceptores" (see *infra* in this chapter).

quandoquidem in sempiterna iustitia regnaturi a praesenti saeculo maligno salvi fieri non possumus, nisi et nos ad salutem proximorum nitentes etiam ore profiteamur fidem, quam corde gestamus; quae fides ne fraudulentis calliditatibus haereticorum possit in nobis aliqua ex parte violari, pia cautaque vigilantia providendum est.

"for we, who are to reign in eternal righteousness, cannot be saved from the present evil world, unless we, too, striving after the salvation of our neighbours, profess also with our mouth the faith which we bear in our heart; and we have to take care with pious and cautious attention to prevent this faith being violated in any respect by the fraudulent machinations of the heretics."

Expression of the true faith is a precondition for the eternal reign of the Christians. Augustine says that we, too, have to express the faith which we have in our hearts, hereby meaning that we, too, must do what Paul, in *Rom.* 10,10, says should be done. This belief in the reign of the saints is also expressed in *De div. quaest. LXXXIII* 57,2 with a reference to *Apoc.* 21, where a distinction is made between eternal and temporal reign:... cum regnant iusti primo temporaliter, sicut in Apocalypsi scriptum est, deinde in aeternum in illa civitate quae ibi describitur... This is the millenarian view. In later writings Augustine modifies this millenarian view: In the present evil world the saints already reign by winning victories over the enemies (heretics), in the world to come they will reign without any enemies, see e.g. *In Ioann.* 77,3: Pacem nobis relinquit in hoc saeculo, pacem suam nobis dabit in futuro saeculo. Pacem suam nobis relinquit, in qua manentes hostem vincimus: pacem suam nobis dabit, quando sine hoste regnabimus, cf. *In Ioann.* 28,6, where *Matth.* 19,28 is quoted as the Scriptural proof of the reign of the saints: Sedebitis super duodecim sedes, iudicantes duodecim tribus Israel. In *De civ.* 20,9 the millenarian view has been abandoned explicitly and the temporal reign is relegated to the time between Christ's ascension and His second coming, cf. *Oeuvres de Saint Augustin, 10, Mélanges doctrinaux,* Paris 1952, p 735. The non-millenarian interpretation already seems to be behind the present words: In the eternal kingdom there will be no heresy any more, but heresy has to be fought in this world.- The activities of the heretics are characterized as "fraudulent machinations" (fraudulentae calliditates), cf. his reference to the Manicheans as "decepti deceptores", *Conf.* 7,2,3 (cf. e.g. Hilary of Poitiers, *De Trin.* 8,2, who says of the Arians that they are "homines mente perversi et professione fallaces, et spe inanes, et sermone viperei",- this is, of course, the usual rhetorical abuse of opponents). Augustine gives this as a general definition of a heretic: he is somebody who for the sake of temporal advantage and above all of glory and power comes forward with or follows false and new doctrines, see *De ut. cred.* 1,1:... haereticus est, ut mea fert opinio, qui alicuius temporalis commodi, et maxime gloriae principatusque sui gratia, falsas ac novas opiniones vel gignit vel sequitur. This is the traditional objection against the new doctrines of the heretics, see e.g. Irenaeus, *Adv. Haer.* 3,4,2, Tertullian, *Adv. Marc.* 1,9,1; 4,4,1-2,- a similar thirst for glory is detected by the Christians in Pagan philosophers, see J.H. Waszink's edition of Tertullian's *De anima,* p 87. - So whilst the orthodox faith has its eyes fixed on eternal salvation, the heretics only seek temporal success.

est autem catholica fides in symbolo nota fidelibus memoriaeque mandata quanta res passa est brevitate sermonis,

"Now the Catholic faith is known to the believers in the Symbol and commended to memory, in such brevity of speech as the matter permitted:"

In the Symbol is briefly contained all that is necessary to believe to obtain eternal salvation, cf. *Sermo* 212,1: Tempus est ut Symbolum accipiatis, quo continetur breviter, propter aeternam salutem, omne quod creditis, cf. Ambrose, *Explanatio Symboli* 2: Brevitas necessaria est, ut semper memoria et recordatione teneatur. The Creed should not be written down, but memorized, so it is not written on tablets, but in the hearts of the believers, see *Sermo 212,2:* Nec ut eadem verba Symboli teneatis, ullo modo debetis scribere, sed audiendo perdiscere: nec cum didiceritis, scribere, sed memoria semper tenere atque recolere, cf. again Ambrose, *Explanatio Symboli* 9: Quod enim scribis, securus quasi relegas, non quotidiana meditatione incipis recensere. Quod autem non scribis, times ne amittas, quotidie incipis recensere. Elsewhere Augustine says that the brevity of the Symbol is a necessary precondition for understanding the Christian faith, since one only has the desire to know more about a doctrine when one has a brief notion of this doctrine in one's mind, see *De Trin.* 10,1,1:... nisi breviter impressam cuiusque doctrinae haberemus in animo notionem, nullo ad eam discendam studio flagraremus, cf. *Sermo* 213,1: paucis verbis dicitur (sc. in Symbolo) unde in multum acquiratur.- In the present context the brevity functions as a means to memorize the Symbol.

ut incipientibus atque lactentibus eis, qui in Christo renati sunt, nondum Scripturarum divinarum diligentissima et spiritali tractatione atque cognitione roboratis paucis verbis credendum constitueretur, quod multis verbis exponendum esset proficientibus et ad divinam doctrinam certa humilitatis atque caritatis firmitate surgentibus.

"that for those beginners and sucklings, who have been reborn in Christ, but have not yet been strengthened by a most diligent and spiritual discussion and knowledge of the divine Scripture, would be proposed in few words for belief what had to be expounded in many words to those who are making progress and are rising up to the divine doctrine with the certain firmness of humility and love."

The beginners and sucklings are those who have just been baptized. The metaphor of milk is, of course, derived from *I Cor.* 3,3 (cf. *Hebr.* 5,12-14), cf. Ambrose, *In Epist. ad Cor. I* 3:1: Quamvis renati essent in Christo, tamen non fuit dignum tradi spiritualia; accepta enim fide, quae est velut semen spirituale, nullum fructum Deo dignum fecerunt ut perfectionis verba mererentur addiscere. The milk of the beginners is the facts of the Christian faith as they are expressed in the Bible and the Symbol, especially the fact of the incarnation of the Son of God. These facts are true and are therefore necessary nourishment. Against the Manicheans who deny that Christ assumed real flesh (see *infra,* 73), Augustine stresses the truth of Paul's preaching of the incarnation to those who are still children in Christ, see e.g. *Contra adversarium legis et prophetarum* 2,2,6: Absit ut putemus eum inaniter nec veraciter ista dixisse ... Dedit igitur parvulis parva non falsa; lactea non noxia, nutritoria non peremptoria. As long as the believer has not risen above the level of this mere faith, his nourishment is milk: it becomes bread when one acquires a deeper understanding of what one believes, see *In Ioann.* 48,1; 98,2ff, *Enchiridion* 114: Ex ista fidei confessione, quae breviter Symbolo continetur, et carnaliter cogitata lac parvulorum est, spiritaliter autem considerata atque tractata cibus est fortium... To those who understand that it is the eternal Word which became flesh, this faith becomes the road of humility: they follow the example set by Christ in the incarnation, see especially the famous section *Conf.* 7,9,13ff (cf. P. Courcelle, *Recherches sur les Confessions de Saint Augustin,* Paris 1968, pp 168ff.) Christ humiliated Himself to Man's level that Man may hear that the Word has become flesh when he is still unable to see the eternal Word as God, see e.g. *Sermo* 117,10,16: Sed ut perveniamus, si nondum possumus videre Verbum Deum, audiamus Verbum carnem: quia carnales facti sumus, audiamus Verbum carnem factum. When man has grasped the Word in the state of humility and has become humble himself, then he can rise up with the Word, see *Sermo* 117,10,17: Dignare esse humilis propter te, quia Deus dignatus est humilis esse propter eundem te: non enim propter se. Cape ergo humilitatem Christi, disce humilis esse, noli superbire ... Cum ceperis humilitatem eius, surgis cum illo. So the road of love and humility is the road upwards, since on it Man learns about the eternal Word which humiliated Itself as a man. (On Christ's humility in the state of the incarnation see further *infra,* 58).

sub ipsis ergo paucis verbis in Symbolo constitutis plerique haeretici venena sua occultare conati sunt: quibus restitit et resistit divina misericordia per spiritales viros, qui catholicam fidem non tantum in illis verbis accipere et credere, sed etiam Domino revelante intellegere atque cognoscere meruerunt. scriptum est enim, *Nisi credideritis, non intellegetis.*

"So under the cover of just the few words expressed in the Symbol most heretics have tried to hide their venom, whom the divine Mercy has resisted and resists through spiritual men, who have deserved not only to accept and believe the Catholic faith in those words, but also to understand and know it through the revelation of the Lord. For it has been written, Unless you believe you shall not understand (Is. 7,9)."

When Augustine says that the heretics take advantage of the brevity of the Symbol, he may have in mind the rule laid down by Quintilian who states that brevity can be dangerous, since it implies obscurity. It is better if too much rather than too little has been said: saying superfluous things causes "taedium", substracting necessary things is dangerous. Therefore the brevity of Sallust has to be avoided. The way between saying too much and saying too little is to say as much as is necessary and is enough, see *Inst. or.* 4,2,44-45: Non minus autem cavenda erit quae nimium corripientes omnia sequitur obscuritas, satiusque est aliquid narrationi superesse quam deesse. Nam supervacua cum taedio dicuntur, necessaria cum periculo subtrahuntur. Quare vitanda est etiam illa Sallustiana ... brevitas... media haec tenenda sit via dicendi quantum opus est et quantum satis est. The implication of this is of course, that heresies are (at least partly) caused by the brevity of the Symbol. In the present context Augustine states this only as a fact and says that divine Mercy provided spiritual men, i.e. ecclesiastical writers, in order to fight heresy. This could already be interpreted in a positive way, since heresy obviously caused them to think more profoundly about the Symbol and to receive from the Lord a deeper understanding of it. Elsewhere Augustine goes much further and in a sense welcomes heresies, see *In Ioann.* 36,6: God permitted the heresies to be numerous, lest the believers would always remain on the level of receiving only milk. The heretics did not rightly understand the divinity of Christ and therefore put very difficult questions to the believers. Therefore the church needed spiritual men who not only read in the gospel about the divinity of Christ, but also understood it and could fight the arms of the devil with the arms of Christ and who in speaking out in defence of the true divinity of Christ could prevent others from perishing: Multi haeretici abundant, et ad hoc Deus eos abundare permisit, ne semper lacte nutriamur, et in bruta infantia remaneamus. Quia enim non intellexerunt quomodo commendaretur divinitas Christi, sapuerunt sicut voluerunt: non autem recte sapiendo, fidelibus catholicis quaestiones molestissimas intulerunt, coeperunt exagitari et fluctuare corda fidelium. Iam tunc necessitas facta est spiritalibus viris, qui aliquid secundum divinitatem Domini nostri Jesu Christi non solum legerant in Evangelio, sed etiam intellexerant, ut contra arma diaboli Christi arma proferrent: et de Christi divinitate adversus falsos fallacesque doctores, quantis possent viribus, apertissima conflictatione pugnarent, ne cum ipsi tacerent, alii perirent, cf. *Conf.* 7,19,25: Improbatio quippe haereticorum facit eminere, quid Ecclesia tua sentiat et quid habeat sana doctrina. Oportuit enim haereses esse ut probati manifesti fierent inter infirmos. This is the traditional explanation of the function of heresies, see e.g. Tertullian, *De praescr. haer.* 4,6: Et ideo haereses quoque oportebat esse ut probabiles quique manifestarentur, for further examples from Tertullian's writings see J.H. Waszink's edition of the *De anima,* pp 114f,- cf. Hilary of Poitiers, *De Trin.* 2,22: Commendat autem fidei huius integritatem et evangelica auctoritas et apostolica doctrina et circumstrepentium undique haereticorum otiosa fraudulentia. This view on the function of heresies as it is expressed by orthodox writers can be summarized as follows: temporal heresies function to the benefit of the lasting orthodoxy.- When Augustine says that the spiritual men not only accepted and believed the Catholic faith, but also understood it, this means that faith precedes understanding, as is also stated in the famous text *Is.* 7,9: Nisi credideritis, non intelligetis. This is an important tenet to Augustine which he elaborates with great circumspection (cf. for the following: R.E. Cushman, Faith and Reason in the Thought of Augustine, *Church History* (19) 1950, pp 271ff, especially p 283 (in connection with the incarnation) and pp 289ff (in connection with the incarnation and humility), and G. Madec, Notes sur l'intelligence augustinienne de la foi, *Révue des études augustiniennes* (17) 1971, pp 140ff). He accuses the Manicheans of promising reason and of holding the Catholic faith in contempt, see e.g. *De ut. cred.* 1,2, where he says that this is the reason why he followed the Manicheans for nine years: their promise of reason: Quid enim me aliud cogebat, annos fere novem, spreta religione quae mihi puerulo a parentibus insita erat, homines illos sequi ac diligenter audire: nisi quod nos superstitione terreri, et fidem nobis ante rationem imperari dicerent, se autem nullum premere ad fidem, nisi prius discussa et enodata veritate, see further 9,21ff. But they in fact do the opposite: they claim with temerity what should be sought diligently, see *De Gen. contra Manichaeos* 1,2,3, cf. *De Gen. ad litt. lib. imp.* 1,1, *De Gen. ad litt.* 1,19,38-39; 1,20,40; 7,1,1; 12,1,1. In *Sermo* 43,3,4ff Augustine expresses his thoughts on the relation between faith and reason in a very subtle way which can be regarded as representative for his ideas on this matter. Firstly, he stages a controversy between himself and an opponent: his own view is that faith precedes reason, his opponent's view is the opposite. He then seeks a man through whom God can judge between them: Dicit mihi homo, Intelligam ut credam, respondeo, Crede ut intelligas. Cum ergo nata inter nos sit controversia talis quodam modo, ut ille mihi dicat, Intelligam ut credam; ego ei respondeam, Imo crede ut intelligas: cum hac controversia veniamus ad iudicem, neuter nostrum praesumat pro sua parte sententiam. Quem iudicem inventuri sumus? Discussis omnibus hominibus, nescio utrum meliorem iudicem invenire possimus quam hominem per quem loquitur Deus. This man, through whom God speaks, appears to be the prophet who says, Nisi credideritis non intelligetis (*Sermo* 43,6,7). This response of the prophet puts an end to the controversy by showing that both are right in a certain respect: Augustine admits that his own words in his sermon are meant to make his hearers believe, but they cannot believe unless they understand these words. One should understand in order to believe and believe in order to understand. But this is not meant in the sense of a constant interaction between faith and understanding: one should understand the human words in order to believe God's Word, and one should believe God's Word in order to understand It, *Sermo* 43,7,9: Nam utique modo quod loquor, ad hoc loquor, ut credant qui nondum credunt: et tamen nisi quod loquor intelligant, credere non possunt. Ergo ex aliqua parte verum est quod ille dicit, Intelligam ut credam; et ego qui dico,sicut dicit propheta, Imo crede ut intelligas: verum dicimus, concordemus. Ergo intellige, ut credas: crede ut intelligas. Breviter dico quomodo utcumque sine controversia accipiamus. Intellige ut credas, verbum meum; crede ut intelligas Verbum Dei (cf. G. Madec's correct summary of the argument, *op. cit,* p 142: L'exégète et le prédicateur peuvent dire au fidèle: "Intellige ut credas verbum meum", mais le fidèle entend la suite: "Crede ut intelligas Verbum Dei"); cf. also *Epist.* 120,1,3: Si igitur rationabile est (sc. praeceptum "Nisi credideritis non intelligetis") ut magnam quaedam, quae capi nondum potest, fides praecedat rationem, procul dubio quantalacumque ratio, quae hoc persuadet, etiam ipsa antecedit fidem, and further *Epist.* 120,2,8. So Augustine's differentiated views on the relation between faith and reason avoid the two extreme errors which he detects in the Manicheans: their arrogant claim that reason must precede faith and their stupid practice of making irrational claims which they cannot prove (on the anti-Manichean line of Augustine's views on this matter see also F.E. van Fleteren, Authority and Reason, Faith and Understanding in the Thought of Saint Augustine, *Augustinian Studies* (4) 1973, pp 33ff).- Since the Symbol contains the main truths revealed in the Bible, it contains the words of God, and therefore the Symbol must be believed first of all. The explanation given to the Symbol must be given in human words, and these words must first of all be understood in order to lead to a deeper understanding of the Symbol. Augustine has no illusions about the number of people who reach this level of faith with understanding: it is only a minority. The majority merely believes, see e.g. what he says of the Trinity, *De Gen. a.l.* 7,2,3: Nos enim credimus naturam atque substantiam, quae in Trinitate creditur a multis, intelligitur a paucis, omnino esse incommutabilem, and *Conf.* 13,11,12: Trinitatem omnipotentem quis intelliget? Et quis loquitur non eam, si tamen eam? Rara anima quaecumque de illa loquitur, scit quod loquitur.

sed tractatio fidei ad muniendum symbolum valet; non ut ipsa pro symbolo gratiam Dei consequentibus memoriae mandanda et reddenda tradatur,

"But the discussion of faith has the power to protect the Symbol, not in order that this discussion instead of the Symbol should be committed and given to the

memory of those who receive God's grace,"

The explanation is not committed to memory, only the Symbol is. The explanation is added. Augustine's views, just quoted, on the number of people who reach the level of faith with understanding may be another reason why this discussion is not committed to memory: faith is enough to acquire God's grace, understanding is not a necessary precondition of receiving grace, since otherwise only a small minority even of the believers would be saved. (J. Rivière, *op. cit.*, p. 20, note 3, suggests that behind this statement may also lie the distinction between the "traditio" and the "redditio symboli" which are part of the (pre-)baptismal liturgy, see on this matter further P.C. Eichenseer, *op. cit.,* pp 140ff).

sed ut illa quae in symbolo retinentur, contra haereticorum insidias auctoritate catholica et munitiore defensione custodiat.

"but that this discussion may protect with the authority of the Catholic church and with a stronger defence those matters which are retained in the Symbol against the plots of the heretics."

The discussion of faith must lead to a deeper understanding of faith. This deeper understanding is also based on the authority of the Catholic church. Closely connected with the relation between faith and understanding is the relation between authority and faith. In the present context the understanding of faith (given in the discussion of the Symbol) is based on the authority of the Catholic church. The natural order is, according to Augustine, that authority precedes reason, see *De mor. eccl. cath.* 1,2,3: Naturae quidem ordo ita se habet, ut cum aliquid discimus, rationem praecedat auctoritas (the reason why he reverses this order in the *De mor.* is that he wants to render a service to those who reverse the order themselves, *ibid.:* Sed quoniam cum iis nobis res est qui omnia contra ordinem, et sentiunt, et loquuntur, et gerunt, nihilque aliud maxime dicunt, nisi rationem prius esse reddendam, morem illis geram, quod fateor in disputando vitiosum esse suscipiam). But, as is the case with the relation between faith and understanding, Augustine expresses his thoughts on the relation between faith (understanding) and authority with circumspection. One needs, Augustine argues, in order to learn, both authority and reason, authority precedes "tempore", reason precedes "re". Authority seems more suitable for the ignorant multitude, reason for those who are learned,- but since one becomes learned after being ignorant, only authority can open the door to those who want to learn the great and hidden good things. Once one has entered this door one discovers that these things are reasonable, see *De ordine* 2,9,26: Ad discendum item necessario dupliciter ducimur, auctoritate atque ratione. Tempore auctoritas, re autem ratio prior est . . . Itaque tanquam bonorum auctoritas imperitae multitudini videatur esse salubrior, ratio vero aptior eruditis, tamen quia nullus hominum nisi ex imperito peritus fit . . . evenit ut omnibus bona magna et occulta discere cupientibus non aperiat nisi auctoritas ianuam. Quam quisque ingressus sine ulla dubitatione vitae optimae praecepta sectatur per quae cum docilis factus fuerit, tum demum discet et quanta ratione praedita sint ea ipsa quae secutus est ante rationem . . . (cf. *De vera religione* 24,45).- In the present context this means that the authority of the Catholic church declares the Symbol to contain the core of divine revelation, faith is based upon this revelation, but it seeks further revelation from the Lord through ecclesiastical writers, *viz.,* a deeper understanding of faith. This deeper understanding is received in the defence of faith against the heretics who are, in the present treatise, in the first place the Manicheans, and then the Apollinarians, the Arians and Sabellians. By following the ecclesiastical writers in his defence of the faith he avoids the mistake made by the heretics: he does not come forward with novelties, but he presents himself as the true traditional Christian.

II

PART I
(2,2 - 2,3a)

FAITH IN GOD THE FATHER

Chapter 2

Introduction: He attacks the Manicheans who deny that God created the world from nothing and say that He created it from matter. In teaching this they deny God's omnipotence and make matter co-eternal with God, i.e. make matter God. Augustine, too, says that heaven and earth were formed from unformed matter, but according to him this unformed matter was created by God. It received the possibility to be formed out of God and therefore was to a certain degree good. The most beautiful species of all things is in God. God created all things through His Word which He generated out of Himself.

Text, Translation and Commentary:

(2,2) Conati sunt enim quidam persuadere Deum Patrem non esse omnipotentem; non quia hoc dicere ausi sunt, sed in suis traditionibus hoc sentire et credere convincuntur. cum enim dicunt esse naturam quam Deus omnipotens non creaverit, de qua tamen istum mundum fabricaverit, quem pulchre ordinatum esse concedunt, ita omnipotentem Deum negant, ut non eum credant mundum potuisse facere, nisi ad eum fabricandum alia natura, quae iam fuerat et quam ipse non fecerat, uteretur;

"For some have tried to persuade us that God the Father is not almighty; not that they have dared to say this, but it can be proved in their teachings that this is their sentiment and belief. For when they say that there is a nature which the almighty God has not created, from which He nevertheless created this world, which they concede to have been beautifully ordered, they deny that God is almighty in such a way that they do not believe Him to have been able to create the world without using for its fabrication another nature which already existed, and which He Himself had not made,"

The word "for"(enim) at the beginning of this sentence implies that the heretics, i.e. the Manicheans, are attacked and not the Platonists (whose doctrine of creation from chaotic matter shows similarity with the doctrine quoted here): a refutation of the heretics' objections against the Symbol was promised at the end of the previous chapter.- So the Manicheans try to persuade the Catholics that God the Father is not almighty. They do not say this openly, but it is the clear implication of their doctrine of creation from pre-existent matter. They call the world "good", but matter, from which the world has been created, is evil (see on this subject H.-C. Puech, *Le Manichéisme. Son fondateur-sa doctrine,* Paris 1949, pp 73ff, on the Manichean criticism of the story of creation given in the first chapters of the book Genesis see also F.C. Baur, *Das manichäische Religionssystem nach den Quellen neu untersucht und entwickelt,* Tübingen 1831, pp 354ff). The Manichean doctrine is quoted in *Contra Faustum* 21,1 as being that there are two principles, viz., God and matter, God being the good principle, matter the evil one, but Augustine also says there that the Manicheans deny explicitly that matter is God: Est quidem quod duo principia confitemur, sed unum ex his Deum vocamus, alterum Hylen . . . Sic et cum duo principia doceo, Deum et Hylen, non idcirco videri iam debeo tibi duos ostendere deos. An quia vim omnem maleficam Hylae assignamus, et beneficam Deo, ut congruit, idcirco nihil interesse putas, an utrumque eorum vocamus Deum? The Biblical background of this Manichean doctrine is on the one hand the realm of darkness spoken of in *Gen. 1:2* and on the other hand *John 1:4:* Quod factum est in ipso vita est. The Manicheans drew from this latter text the conclusion that there is also something which has not been made in Him, and that is death,- so they introduce two principles, cf. Ambrose, *De fide* 3,6,42: Obiciunt enim Manichaei: Si quod in ipso factum est, vita est: est ergo aliquid quod in ipso factum non sit, et mors sit; ut duo impie inducant principia.- Augustine is well aware of the difference between the Marcionites and the Manicheans in this respect: the Manicheans admit that the Creator is good, but deny that he is the god spoken of in the Old Testament; the Marcionites deny that the Creator is good, and say that this evil creator is the god spoken of in the Old Testament, see e.g. *Contra advers. leg. et proph.* 1,1,1: Non enim soli Manichaei legem prophetasque condemnant, sed et Marcionistae . . . Iste autem . . . detestatur Deum mundi fabricatorem (this is the Marcionite position) cum Manichaei quamvis librum Geneseos non accipiant, atque blasphement, Deum tamen bonum fabricasse mundum, etsi ex aliena natura atque materia, confiteantur. Ambrose has obviously much less time for any subtleties in the Manichean position on this matter and simply makes them say that the devil is the creator of man's flesh, see *De fide* 2,13,119: Dicat et Manichaeus: Ego auctorem carnis nostrae diabolum credo.

(Here evil matter is not co-eternal with God, but it has been created by an evil principle, i.e. the devil).- The Manicheans do not deny explicitly the omnipotence of the Creator, but, according to Augustine, the consequence of their doctrine is that God is not almighty. In *Conf.* 7,5,7 Augustine tells us that before his conversion he held views on this matter which show similarity with the Manichean views. He tells *inter alia* that he asked himself, why, if God created a good world from evil matter, He was unable to change it into a good one, whilst nevertheless being almighty: an unde fecit ea, materies aliqua mala erat, et formavit atque ordinavit eam, sed reliquit aliquid in illa quod in bonum non converteret? cur et hoc? an inpotens erat totam vertere et commutare, ut nihil mali remaneret, cum sit omnipotens? (This view also shows some similarity with Plato's doctrine in the *Timaeus* that the Demiurge created the world as good as possible from chaotic matter, see *Timaeus* 30A (**I**), cf. J. Blic, Platonisme et christianisme dans la conception augustinienne de Dieu Créateur, *Recherches de science religieuse* (30) 1940, pp 172ff). Augustine here expresses the traditional objections made by early Christian writers against the doctrine of a creation from matter, see e.g. Irenaeus, *Adv. Haer.* 2,10,2, *Epid.* 4, Athenagoras, *Leg.* 4 and 15, and especially Tertullian's treatise against Hermogenes, cf. J.H. Waszink, Observations on Tertullian's Treatise against Hermogenes, *Vigiliae Christianae* (9), 1955, pp 129-147, on this subject in general see G. May, *Schöpfung aus dem Nichts, Die Entstehung der Lehre von der creatio ex nihilo,* Berlin-New York 1978.

carnali scilicet consuetudine videndi fabros et domorum structores et quoslibet opifices, qui, nisi adiuventur parata materia, ad effectum suae artis pervenire non possunt;

"because they are accustomed to seeing with their bodily eyes carpenters and builders of houses and all kinds of artisans who cannot carry out their craft without the aid of appropiate materials;"

It is typical of the human craftsmen to apply their craft to already existing matter (and to be in this sense helped by matter to make what they want to make), see e.g. *Conf.* 11,5,7, where it is denied that God creates in this human way: Quomodo autem fecisti caelum et terram et quae machina tam grandis operationis tuae? Non enim sicut homo artifex formans corpus de corpore arbitratu animae valentis imponere utcumque speciem ... et imponit speciem iam existenti et habenti ut esset, veluti terrae aut lapidi aut ligno aut auro aut id genus rerum cuilibet, cf. *Sermo* 214,2. On Augustine's views on the doctrine of creation see also E. Gilson, *Introduction à l'étude de Saint Augustin,* Paris 1929, pp 241ff, P.C. Eichenseer, *op. cit.,* pp

163ff, C. Tresmontant, *La Métaphysique du christianisme et la naissance de la philosophie chrétienne. Problèmes de la création et de l'anthropologie dès origines à Saint Augustin,* Paris 1961, pp 145ff, K. Kremer, Das Warum der Schöpfung: "quia bonus vel/et quia voluit?" Ein Beitrag zum Verhältnis von Neuplatonismus und Christentum an Hand des Prinzips "bonum est diffusum sui", *Parusia. Studien zur Philosophie Platons und zur Problemgeschichte des Platonismus. Festgabe für Johannes Hirschberger herausgegeben von* Kurt Flasch, Frankfurt/M. 1965, pp 241ff.

ita intellegunt fabricatorem mundi non esse omnipotentem, si mundum fabricare non posset, nisi eum aliqua non ab illo fabricata natura tanquam materies adiuvaret.

"in this way they conceive the Creator of the world not to be almighty, if He could not fabricate the world without being helped by some nature, as matter, not fabricated by Him."

He who needs help cannot do what he wants to do, but God's omnipotence implies that He can do what He wants to do, cf. the definition given in *De civ.* 21,7,1 (to which Augustine undoubtedly adhered during all periods of his life): qui certe non ob aliud vocatur omnipotens nisi quoniam quidquid vult potest (cf. Athanasius, *Contra Gentes* 28).- Important in this context is that God's omnipotence is not in conflict with God's goodness: if God could not make what is good, then God would have no power; if He could make what is good but actually did not (want to) make it, God would be envious, so since He is both almighty and good, He made all things very good, see *De Gen. a.l.* 4,16,27: Sed bona facere si non posset, nulla esset potentia: si autem posset nec faceret, magna esset invidentia. Quia ergo est omnipotens et bonus, omnia valde bona fecit. (Envy is also excluded from God in Plato's often quoted statement in the *Timaeus* 29E (**II**), cf. Irenaeus, *Adv. Haer.* 3,41, Athanasius, *De Inc.* 3, *Contra Gentes* 41,-further examples are given by Ch. Kannengiesser, *Athanase d'Alexandrie, Sur l'Incarnation du Verbe,* S.C. 199, Paris 1973, pp 270f, note 1). God's will and God's power are in fact identical, see e.g. *Conf.* 7,4,6: voluntas enim et potentia Dei Deus ipse est, and *De Gen. a.l.* 6,15,26ff. This is, of course, the answer to the famous objection against Providence, clearly expressed by the Epicureans (and echoed by many), that evil in the world proves that either God is not good, because He lets it happen, or that He is weak, since He cannot put an end to it (see Lactance, *De ira Dei* 13,19 where Epicure is quoted as saying: Deus . . . aut vult tollere mala et non potest, aut potest et non vult, aut neque vult neque potest; si vult et non potest, inbecillis est, quod in deum non cadit; si potest et non vult, invidus, quod aeque alienum a deo; si neque vult neque potest, et invidus et inbecillis est, ideo nec deus; si vult et potest, quod solum deo convenit, unde ergo sunt mala? aut cur illa non tollit?,-see also the Marcionites as they are quoted by Tertullian, *Adversus Marcionem* 2,5ff (cf. J. Gager, Marcion and Philosophy, *Vigiliae Christianae* (26) 1972, pp 53ff). Augustine goes to great lengths to show that the fact that God permits sin and evil is no proof that He is not good or not almighty, since this permission is just and therefore also good, see e.g. *Ench.* 96, *Conf.* 7,3,5, *Sermo* 214,3ff, *De nat. et grat.* 49,57, *Contra Faustum* 26,4f, *De civ.* 5,10.- As God's will and God's power are identical, so are God's power and God's being, and in this respect God differs from man, see *In Ioann.* 20,4: Homo aliud est quod est, aliud quod potest. Aliquando enim et est homo, et non potest quod vult, aliquando autem sic est homo ut possit quod vult: itaque aliud est esse ipsius, aliud posse ipsius . . . Deus autem cui non est alia substantia ut sit, et alia potestas ut possit, sed consubstantiale illi est quidquid eius est, et quidquid est, quia Deus est, non alio modo est et alio modo potest, sed esse et posse simul habet quia velle et facere simul habet. So the identical nature of God's will and God's power must prove that God is not unjust and that there is a righteous Providence, the identical nature of God's being and God's power must prove that God differs from man.- In dealing with God's omnipotence Augustine is confronted with traditional questions to which he gives traditional answers: God cannot die, change, err, become miserable, be defeated,- the reason being that He wants to be the opposite of these negative actions which are contrary to His being. Thus His "impotence" in this respect does not contradict His power, but confirms it, see e.g. *Sermo* 214,4: Deus omnipotens non potest mori, non potest mutari, non potest falli, non potest miser fieri, non potest vinci . . . Volens enim est Deus quidquid est; aeternus ergo, et incommutabilis, et verax, et beatus, et insuperabalis volens est: est autem omnipotens, ergo quidquid vult potest. Et ideo quod non vult, esse non potest, qui propterea dicitur omnipotens, quoniam quidquid vult potest, cf. Origen, *Contra Celsum* 3,70 (**III**) (see on this the explanatory notes given by H. Chadwick, *Origen: Contra Celsum, Translated with an Introduction and Notes,* Cambridge 1965, pp 175 and 281) and Ambrose, *De fide* 1,2,14: Et ideo bonum Deum, sempiternum, perfectum, omnipotentem, verum debemus credere . . . quia sine his Deus non est. Non potest enim bonus non esse, qui Deus est cum in natura Dei plenitudo bonitatis sit: neque ex tempore Deus potest esse qui fecit tempora: neque potest imperfectus Deus esse; qui enim minor est, imperfectus utique est, cui desit aliquid, quo maiori possit aequari.-Interesting is Augustine's answer to the question of whether God can alter the past: God can change the being of something, but a precondition is that it exists. In this sense God can make die something which begins to exist at its birth, see *Contra Faustum*

26,5: Potest enim facere ut aliquid non sit quod erat, tunc enim facit ut non sit, quando id esse invenerit de quo fiat: velut cum aliquem, qui coepit esse nascendo facit non esse moriendo. But one cannot say that God causes something not to be which does not exist (any longer). The past is no longer; this is a truth which God cannot make false, since God is not contrary to the truth. Therefore God cannot alter the past: Quis autem dicat ut id quod iam non est, faciat non esse? Quidquid enim praeteritum est, iam non est . . . Sententia quippe qua dicimus aliquid fuisse, ideo vera est quia illud de quo dicimus iam non est. Hanc sententiam Deus falsa, facere non potest, quia non est contrarius veritati. Behind this lies the following idea: God is the Creator of time. The past is one of the tenses. God has made time in such a way that the past is no longer. God would contradict His own creation if He altered a past which He Himself caused not to exist any longer. Then God would be inconsistent. (On God's omnipotence and natural laws see also *infra,* 154).

ac si omnipotentem Deum fabricatorem mundi esse concedunt, fateantur necesse est ex nihilo eum fecisse quae fecit. non enim aliquid esse potest, cuius creator non esset, cum esset omnipotens,

"And if they concede that the almighty God is the fabricator of the world, they must confess that what He made He made from nothing. For there could be nothing of which He were not the Creator, since He is almighty;"

Firstly, it was argued that if God was helped by an already existent matter He cannot be almighty. Now the same thought is developed from the opposite angle: If God is almighty (which the Manicheans on the one hand seem to concede by saying that there is a nature which the almighty God did not create, but which can be shown to be a fraudulent concession, see *supra,*25), then there can be nothing which He did not create (cf. K. Staritz, *op. cit.* p 73). This also implies that there can be no evil matter: all that is, is inferior to the Highest Good, but since it is created by the Highest Good, it is good, cf. *Contra advers. leg. et proph.* 1,4,6: Intelligat utique Deum facere bona posse, bonis autem a se factis egere non posse: unde nec faciendis eguit, qui facis non eget. Sed summe bonus fecit omnia, sibi quidem imparia, sed tamen bona.

quia etsi aliquid fecit ex aliquo, sicut hominem de limo, non utique fecit ex eo, quod ipse non fecerat, quia terram, unde limus est, ex nihilo fecerat.

"for although He made something from something else, e.g. man from dust, He

certainly did not make it from that which He Himself had not made, for He had made the earth, from which dust comes, from nothing."

The Old Testament text (*Gen.* 2:7) that God created man from dust seems to contradict Augustine's doctrine that God creates from nothing. The Manicheans themselves do not make this objection, for they criticize this statement in the story of creation for a different reason: In *De Gen. contra Man.* 2,7,8 Augustine quotes them as saying that God should have created man from a better and heavenly substance, since man as he now is has been created from an earthly pollution: Dicunt enim: Quare de limo fecit Deus hominem? . . . an defuerat ei melior et caelestis materia, unde hominem faceret, ut de labe terrena tam fragilem mortalemque formaret? This is in line with the Manichean claim that creation is from evil matter, and that this fact is the cause of man's mortality. Augustine's reply to this is that man's mortality is caused by damnation after man's sin. Man was destined to death after his sin. Although God created man from earthly dust, He neverteless made him such that he would not be subjected to corruption, if he, by keeping God's commandment, had not wanted to sin: Dicimus enim tabidum et fragile et morti destinatum corpus humanum post peccatum esse coepisse. Non enim in nostro corpore isti exhorrescunt nisi mortalitatem quam damnatione meruimus. Quid autem mirum, aut difficile Deo, etiamsi de limo istius terrae hominem fecit, tale tamen corpus eius efficere, quod corruptioni non subiaceret, si homo praeceptum Dei custodiens peccare noluisset? The same idea lies behind what is said in the present chapter: evil in the world and in man cannot be explained by any principle independent of the Creator. Man, as he has been created, is good until the Fall, and all evil has been caused by the Fall.

et si ipsum coelum et terram, id est mundum et omnia, quae in eo sunt, ex aliqua materia fecerat, sicut scriptum est, *qui fecisti mundum ex materia invisa,* vel etiam *informi,* sicut nonnulla exemplaria tenent, nullo modo credendum est illam ipsam materiam, de qua factus est mundus, quamvis informem, quamvis invisam, quocumque modo esset, per se ipsam esse potuisse tanquam coaeternam et coaevam Deo;

"And if He had made that very heaven and earth, which is the world and all that is in it, from some matter, as it is written, Who hast made the world from invisible matter (Sap. Sal. 11,18), or also from formless matter, as some transcripts have it, in no way may one believe that just that matter from which the world was made, be it formless, be it invisible, or however it may be, could have been by virtue of itself, as though it were co-eternal and co-eval with God;"

The text *Sap. Sal.* 11,18 again seems to contradict the doctrine of creation from nothing. (On Augustine's use of this text see A.M. la Bonnardière, *Biblia Augustiniana, A.T. Le Livre de la Sagesse,* Paris 1970, pp 87ff and p 295.) What is said by Augustine in the present context is a brief statement of his well-known doctrine of creation and formation, which is that the chaotic matter spoken of in *Gen.* 1,2 was created by God from nothing and that the world was created from this chaotic matter (see on this subject e. g. the explanatory note given by A. Solignac, *Oeuvres de Saint Augustin, 14, Les Confessions, VIII-XIII,* pp 599ff, A.H. Armstrong, Spiritual or Intelligible Matter in Plotinus and Saint Augustine, *Plotinian and Christian Studies,* ch. VII, pp 277-283, B. Altaner, Augustin und Origenes, *Kleine Patristische Schriften,* Berlin 1967, pp 246ff (who detects primarily the influence of Basil and Hilary), E. zum Brunn, Le dilemme de l'être et du néant chez Saint Augustin. Dès premiers dialogues aux Confessions, *Recherches augustiniennes* (6) 1969, pp 45ff), see e. g. *Conf.* 12,3ff; 12,39,40ff; 13,33,48, *De Gen. contra Man.* 1,3,5; 1,5,9ff, *De Gen. a.l. lib. imp.* 3,9ff, *De Gen. a.l.* 1,13,27ff; 2,11,24; 5,5,13, *Sermo* 214,2. In the present chapter the formless matter spoken of in *Sap. Sal.* 11,18 and *Gen.* 1:2 is the formless state of all corporeal reality. This is clear from the fact that heaven and earth are called "the world and all that is in it" and that this is referred to as one creation. In the *Confessions* he prefers another explanation, *viz.,* that heaven in this stage of creation is the name of that spiritual or intellectual creation which always beholds the face of God (the beholding of the face of God is the activity which gives form to the spiritual reality), earth is that of unshaped matter, see J.C.M. van Winden, The Early Christian Exegesis of "Heaven and Earth" in Genesis 1,1, *Romanitas et Christianitas. Studia J.H. Waszink . . . oblata,* Amsterdam/London 1973, pp 377ff. In the present chapter Augustine does not discuss the question of the temporal sequence in these stages of creation, a sequence which is denied by him, see e.g. *Conf.* 13,33,48: de nihilo enim a te, non de te facta sunt, non de aliqua non tua vel quae antea fuerit, sed de concreata, id est simul a te creata materia, quia eius informitatem sine ulla temporis interpositione formasti, nam cum aliud sit caeli et terrae materies, aliud caeli et terrae species, materiem quidem de omnino nihilo, mundi autem speciem de informi materia, simul tamen utrumque fecisti, ut materiam forma nulla mora intercapedine sequeretur. (Similarly he does not discuss in the present chapter the objections made by the Manicheans against the arbitrariness in the choice of the moment of the beginning of creation, this is discussed in the well-known passage *Conf.* 11,10,12ff and further e. g. *Contra advers. leg. et proph.* 1,3,4f, where the question is raised by opponents of the Biblical story of creation why the beginning in which God made heaven and earth did not occur much earlier, since that would have been better: Si mundus iste bonum aliquid est, cur non olim ex initio ab eo factum est quod melius fuit? Augustine denies that there is time before creation, therefore God could not have been idle for countless ages and could not "suddenly" have changed to becoming active, cf. on this subject E.P. Meijering, *Augustin über Schöpfung, Ewigkeit und Zeit. Das elfte Buch der Bekenntnisse,* Leiden 1979, pp 40ff).- Now Augustine digresses to a slightly different subject. Firstly he had argued that although the Manicheans dare not say openly that God the Father is not almighty, this is the clear implication of their doctrine of creation from matter. Now he argues that such matter would be co-eternal with God: if the invisible or formless matter existed by itself, it would be co-eternal with God, see also *Contra advers. leg. et proph.* 1,2,3: Deus igitur nec coepit esse, nec desinet: sed opera eius quaedam incipientia certo fine esse desistunt, sicut tempora et temporalia, quaedam incipientia permanebunt, sicut ipsa sanctorum hominum quam percepturi sunt vita aeterna. So Augustine is by no means convinced by the Manicheans' claim (see e.g. *Contra Faustum* 21,1, *supra,* 26) that they do not teach that there are two gods, since they say that they do not regard matter as God,- according to Augustine, it is obvious that an uncreated and eternal matter is God. This is again the traditional argument against uncreated matter, see especially Tertullian, *Adversus Hermogenem* 4-6, and the explanatory notes given by J.H. Waszink, *Tertullian, The Treatise against Hermogenes,* A.C.W. 24, London 1956, pp 109ff.

sed quemlibet modum suum, quem habebat, ut quoquo modo esset et distinctarum rerum formas posset accipere, non habebat nisi ab omnipotente Deo, cuius beneficio est res non solum quaecumque formata, sed etiam quaecumque formabilis. inter formatum autem et formabile hoc interest, quod formatum iam accepit formam, formabile autem potest accipere.

"but whatever way of being it had, in order to be able to be in some way and to be able to receive the forms of distinctive things, it only had this way of being from the almighty God, through whose good will not only everything that has been formed but also everything that can be formed exists. Now the difference between what has been formed and what can be formed is this, that what has been formed has already received its form, what can be formed can receive it."

The "materia invisa" or "informis" spoken of in *Sap. Sal.* 11,18 is interpreted as "materia formabilis", i.e. as matter which can receive a form (see on this also E. König, *op. cit.,* p 113 and A.M. la Bonnardière, *op. cit.,* pp 88ff). Augustine often speaks of the "materia formabilis", see e.g. *De lib. arb.* 2,17,45, *De vera rel.* 18,35ff, *Contra Faustum* 20,14; 21,4, *Contra adv. leg. et proph.* 1,11,14ff, *De natura boni* 18, *De Gen. a.l. lib. imp.* 15,51. He presents his doctrine on this matter in a clearly anti-Manichean way, since he stresses two aspects of the "materia formabilis": it has been created by God (this is said in the present chapter as well, where it says that God's beneficium, good will, is the cause of this matter), and it is good, though less good than the "materia formata", see e. g. *De vera rel.* 18,36: Quapropter etiam si de aliqua informi materia factus est mundus, haec ipsa facta est omnino de nihilo. Nam et quod nondum formatum est, tamen aliquo modo ut formari possit inchoatum est, Dei beneficio formabile est: bonum est enim esse formatum. Nonnullum ergo bonum est et capacitas formae. Whilst this doctrine is anti-Manichean, Augustine says *disertis verbis* that he has no objections to the philosophers' doctrine of matter, except to the fact that it is co-eternal with God, see e. g. *Contra Faustum* 20,14: Hylen namque Graeci, cum de natura disserunt, materiam quandam rerum definiunt, nullo prorsus modo formatum, sed omnium corporalium formarum capacem ... verum in hoc errant quidam Gentilium quod eam tanquam coaeternam Deo coniungunt, cf. *De natura boni* 18,- this is, of course, a reference to the well-known doctrine of matter as "receptaculum", see J. Pépin, *Théologie cosmique et théologie chrétienne,* 1964, p 25, pp 53ff, J.C.M. van Winden, *Calcidius on Matter,* Leiden 1959, pp 172ff.

sed qui praestat rebus formam, ipse praestat etiam posse formari, quoniam de illo et in illo est omnium speciosissima species incommutabilis,

"But He who grants form to things, also grants the possibility of being formed, because from Him and in Him is the most beautiful, unchangeable form of all things;"

Whilst the human craftsman can only apply his form to matter which he did not make himself (see *supra,* 27), God the Creator applies His form i.e. His Wisdom, to matter which He Himself had made in such a way that it could receive forms, cf. *In Ioann.* 1,17: Sapientia Dei, per quam facta sunt omnia, secundum artem continet omnia antequam fabricaret omnia. But there is also another difference between the human craftsman and God the Creator: God has the most beautiful species of all things in Himself and not outside Himself, see e. g. *De div. quaest. LXXXIII* 46,2: Has autem rationes ubi arbitrandum est esse nisi in ipsa mente Creatoris? Non enim extra se quidquam positum intuebatur, ut secundum id constitueret quod constituebat. (Earlier in 46,2 he had said that the words "formae" and "species" are literal translations of the Greek, "rationes" not literal but a legitimate one). Augustine is here in line with the Middle Platonic doctrine that Ideas are the eternal thoughts of God, see on this subject the literature quoted by W.Theiler in the Preface to *Die Vorbereitung des Neuplatonismus,* Berlin/Zürich 1964[2], the explanatory note in *Oeuvres de Saint Augustin, 10, Mélanges doctrinaux,* Paris 1952, pp 726f (J.A. Beckaert), H.A. Wolfson, *The Philosophy of the Church Fathers,* Cambridge 1956, p 257, J.H. Waszink, Bemerkungen zum Einfluss des Platonismus im frühen Christentum, *Vigiliae Christianae* (19) 1965, pp 139ff). But the human craftsman does not hold the form in himself, but the divine Art works through the human artists, they imitate the divine Art, see *De div. quaest. LXXXIII* 78: Ars illa summa omnipotentis Dei per quam ex nihilo facta sunt omnia, quae etiam sapientia eius dicitur, ipsa operatur etiam per artifices, ut pulchra atque congruentia fiant . . . quae ipsos numeros et ipsam convenientiam longe artificiosius universo mundi corpori impressit . . . quam cum artifices homines easdem figuras corporum et formas in suis operibus imitantur. (A similar view of art is presented by Plotinus, see A.H. Armstrong, Plotinus. Man and Reality, *The Cambridge History of Later Greek and Early Medieval Philosophy,* Cambridge 1970[2], pp 233f and K. Flasch, Ars imitatur naturam. Platonischer Naturbegriff und mittelalterliche Philosophie der Kunst, *Parusia,* pp 270ff). This "most beautiful form", as it is called in the present chapter, is, since it is also called "sapientia" (as appears from *De div. quaest. LXXXIII* 78), identical with Christ. Until the end of his life Augustine identified Christ with the ideas in God's mind, see *Retractationes* 1,3,2, where he criticizes himself for having identified the Kingdom of God with the realm of ideas, but still identifies Christ with the Ideas: Nec Plato quidem in hoc erravit, quia esse mundum intelligibilem dixit . . . Mundum quippe ille intelligibilem nuncupavit ipsam rationem sempiternam atque incommutabilem qua fecit Deus mundum. Quam qui esse negat, sequitur ut dicat, irrationabiliter Deum fecisse quod fecit. (See on this matter R.M. Markus, Alienatio. Philosophy and Eschatology in the Development of an Augustinian Idea, *Studia Patristica* (9), Berlin 1966, pp 431f. It appears that Augustine's self-criticism is much milder than H. Dörrie suggests to be the case, see his paper, Was ist "spätantiker Platonismus"? Überlegungen zur Grenzziehung zwischen Platonismus und Christentum, *Theologische Rundschau* (N.F.)(36) 1971, p 294.) Therefore he can say that it is "from God and in God", as he also says about Christ in 3,4: Deus vero cum Verbum genuit id quod est ipse genuit . . . de se id ipso id quod est ipse.

et ideo ipse unus est, qui cuilibet rei non solum, ut pulchra sit, sed etiam ut pulchra esse possit adtribuit.

"and therefore He Himself is the only one to give to anything not only that it is beautiful, but also that it can be beautiful."

The Manichean position (as quoted in the beginning of this chapter) is that God gave beauty to the world, but that evil matter remained an obstacle. Augustine's position is that the world's beauty, as it is, has as its *only* cause God: God made the world beautiful and created a matter which could become beautiful. (The reason why the world, also in Augustine's view, is less beautiful than God is not that evil matter remains an obstacle, but that a cause is superior to what is caused, see *infra,* 44).

quapropter rectissime creditur omnia Deum fecisse de nihilo; quia etiam si de aliqua materia factus est mundus, eadem ipsa materia de nihilo facta est, ut ordinatissimo Dei munere prima capacitas formarum fieret ac deinde formarentur quaecumque formata sunt.

"Therefore it is most rightly believed that God has made all things from nothing, even if the world has been made from some matter, this same matter has itself been made from nothing so that through the most orderly work of God firstly the possibility to receive forms was created and that hence all things were formed that have been formed."

This sentence sums up the doctrine of creation which he contrasts with the Manichean one: God has not (as the Manicheans claim) made a world, which to some degree can be called beautiful, from a chaotic, evil matter, but in His goodness God has created matter which had the possibility to be formed by God, and from it God formed everything He formed. This possibility to be formed is also expressed by Augustine by means of the image of seeds: formless matter, as created by God, are the seeds of the whole creation, see e. g. *De Gen. contra Man.* 1,7,11: Quemadmodum si semen arboris considerantes dicamus ibi esse radices, et robur, et ramos, et fructus, et folia; non quia iam sunt, sed quia inde futura sunt: sic dictum est, In principio fecit Deus caelum et terram, quasi semen caeli et terrae, cum in confuso adhuc esset caeli et terrae materia; sed quia certum erat inde futurum esse caelum et terram, iam et ipsa materia caelum et terra appellata est. (This doctrine already appears in the Greek Fathers, see e.g. Basil, *Hexaem.* 2,3 (**IV** cf. M.L. Colish, *op. cit.* p. 203 ff.).

.hoc autem diximus, ne quis existimet contrarias sibi esse divinarum scripturarum sententias, quoniam et omnia Deum de nihilo fecisse scriptum est et mundum esse factum de informi materia.

"Now we have said this lest anybody should believe that the statements made in the divine Scriptures contradict each other, because it is written both that God made all things from nothing and that the world was made from formless

matter."

Here he wants to exclude the idea that *Gen.* 1,1-2 (which in Augustine's interpretation teaches creation from nothing) and *Sap. Sal.* 11,18 (which teaches creation from formless matter) contradict each other. In Augustine's view *Sap. Sal.* 11,18 is in line with *Gen.* 1,2 and therefore with *Gen.* 1,1. So here Augustine is concerned with the Manichean misinterpretation of two Old Testament texts; usually he is concerned with the Manichean claim that the Old Testament and the New Testament, especially Paul, provide conflicting doctrines, see e. g. *Conf.* 7,21,27, where he says, looking back on his Manichean times: Itaque avidissime arripui venerabilem stilum spiritus tui, et prae caeteris apostolum Paulum; et perierunt illae quaestiones in quibus mihi aliquando visus est adversari sibi, et non congruere testimoniis legis et prophetarum textus sermonis eius. See further *De mor. eccl. cath.* 1,16-18; 1,24-34, cf. P. Courcelle, *Recherches sur les Confessions de Saint Augustin,* pp 177f.

(2,3a) Credentes itaque in Deum Patrem omnipotentem, nullam creaturam esse, quae ab omnipotente non creata sit, existimare debemus.

"So when we believe in God, the almighty Father, we must hold the view that there is no creature which has not been created by the Almighty."

This is the conclusion drawn from the argument developed in the previous paragraph: God's omnipotence implies that He needs no help in the act of creation, i.e. that He created from nothing,- if there were anything which were not created by Him, then He would not be almighty.

III

PART II
(2,3b - 8,15)

FAITH IN GOD THE SON

Chapter 3

Introduction: This chapter explains the article of the Symbol which expresses faith in Jesus Christ, the Father's only-begotten Son. Human words are intended to reveal the speaker's mind, similarly the Father's creative Word reveals the Father. But there is a great difference between human words and the divine Word: human words perish whilst they are spoken, the divine Word remains unchangeable what It is, also in the act of the incarnation. Furthermore, human words are created by men, and they are unable to reveal completely the speakers' minds, whereas the divine Word is not created, but generated, and therefore is able to reveal the Father in the most reliable way.

Text, Translation and Commentary:

(2,3b) et quia *omnia per Verbum* creavit, quod Verbum et *Veritas* dicitur, et *Virtus* et *Sapientia Dei,* multisque aliis insinuatur vocabulis quibus nostrae fidei Jesus Christus Dominus commendatur, liberator scilicet noster et rector Filius Dei

"And because He created all things through His Word, which Word is also called Truth (John 14:6), and Power and Wisdom of God (I Cor. 1:24), and together with many other words is intimated to us, with which the Lord Jesus Christ is commended to our faith, viz., our Liberator and Ruler, the Son of God,"

(We read „vocabulis quibus" instead of "vocabulis qui"). What Augustine here provides is common thought and language in early Christian writers, caused by the "speaking of God" in *Genesis* 1 and by *John* 1,1. Verbum is, of course, the translation of the Greek "*logos*"; Augustine says somewhere that this word can be translated both by "verbum" and by "ratio", in the context of the doctrine of creation he prefers "verbum", see *De div. quaest. LXXXIII* 63: In principio erat Verbum. Quod graece logos dicitur, latine et rationem et verbum significat. Sed hoc loco melius verbum interpretamur, ut significetur non solum ad Patrem respectus, sed ad illa etiam quae per Verbum facta sunt operativa potentia. Ratio autem, etsi nihil per illam fiat, recte ratio dicitur.- In an allusion to *John* 14:6 Augustine only picks up the word "Truth", and leaves out the words "Way" and "Life". It is understandable why he does not give the word "Way" in this context, but it is a little strange that the word "Life" is not given here, since, according to Augustine, Christ was in His divinity Truth and Life, and in the manhood He assumed He was the Way, see *In Ioann.* 34,9: Manens apud Patrem Veritas et Vita: induens se carnem, factus est Via. In *Sermo* 141,1 he says that the philosophers have an idea about an eternal truth in which all "rationes" of created things are contained, but they do not know how to reach this truth: veritatem fixam, stabilem, indeclinabilem, ubi sunt omnes rationes rerum omnium creatarum, viderunt quidem, sed de longinquo viderunt, sed in errore positi: et idcirco ad eam tam magnam et ineffabilem et beatificam possessionem qua via perveniretur, non invenerunt, cf. the well-known section *Conf.* 7,9,13ff where he says that the Platonists know about God's eternal Word but not about Its incarnation. It is this creative and eternal Word which Augustine is envisaging in the present context by calling It God's Truth, Wisdom and Power. When Augustine explains *John* 1,4 (in illo vita erat), he says that this life is some "ratio" in the divine Wisdom, see *In Ioann.* 1,16: Facta est terra, sed ipsa terra quae facta est, non est vita, est autem in ipsa Sapientia spiritaliter ratio quaedam qua terra facta est, haec vita est. So not only the word "Truth", but also the word "Life" would have suited the present context, but not the word "Way" which is applied by Augustine to the state of the incarnation which will be discussed later on (see *infra*, 56ff). (On Christ as God's Power and especially as God's Wisdom see *infra*, 50). The words "Liberator" and "Ruler" not only apply to Christ as God's creative Word, but also often to the incarnate and risen Christ. The fact that Augustine mentions these titles already in the present context in which the incarnation and exaltation of Christ are not yet discussed could have an anti-Manichean aim: The Creator of the Old Testament and the Redeemer of the New Testament is one God. This is made clear *disertis verbis* elsewhere when Augustine states that in the act of redemption we give ourselves back to our origin, if our origin did not remain there would be no place to which we can go back, see *Conf.* 11,8,10; . . . ad veritatem stabilem ducimur . . . reddentes nos, unde sumus. et ideo principium, quia, nisi maneret, cum erraremus, non esset quo rediremus, cf. *De vera rel.* 55,113: unum Deum . . . a quo discessimus, cui dissimiles facti sumus, a quo perire non permissi sumus: principium ad quod recurrimus, see on this subject: W. Theiler, Antike und christliche Rückkehr zu Gott, *Forschungen zum Neuplatonismus,* Berlin 1966, pp 313ff (see also *infra,* 56ff).

-non enim Verbum illud, per quod sunt omnia condita, generare potuit nisi ille, qui per ipsum condidit omnia-

"-for only He could generate that Word through which all things were created, who created all things trough It,-"

Creation of all things through the Word is a miracle which can only be wrought by an almighty God. The generation of this Word must be an even greater miracle. According to Augustine things can come into being in three ways: from the originator, from something else, from nothing. Man can generate a son from himself, he can make something from something else, but since he is not almighty he cannot create from nothing, -God is almighty, so He could generate the Son from Himself, make the world from nothing and man from dust, see *De actis cum Fel. Man.* 2,18: . . . accipe quomodo intelligas Deum omnipotentem factorem. Omnia quae fiunt, et quod quisque facit, aut de se est, aut ex aliquo, aut ex nihilo. Homo quia non est omnipotens, de se filium facit, ex aliquo sicut artifex ex ligno arcam . . . Ex nihilo autem, ex eo quod prorsus non est facere ut sit, nullus hominum potest. Deus autem quia omnipotens est, et de se filium genuit, et ex nihilo mundum fecit, et ex limo hominem formavit: ut per istas tres potentias ostenderet effectionem suam in omnibus valentem. (See on this subject further *infra,* 58.)

(3,3) credimus etiam in Jesum Christum Filium Dei, Patris unigenitum, id est unicum, Dominum nostrum.

"we also believe in Jesus Christ, the Son of God, the Father's only-begotten one, i.e. only one, our Lord."

The word given in the Symbol "unicus" is used as an explanation of "unigenitus" with which Augustine works in the present treatise and which he uses both against the Arians and the Manicheans, see *infra,* 59ff, on "unigenitus" and "unicus" see also *supra*, 11. (Cf. for the following also P.C. Eichenseer, *op. cit.,* pp 200ff). "Unigenitus" could here have been caused by the Nicene Creed, cf. 4,6: Naturalis ergo Filius de ipsa Patris substantia unicus natus est, id est existens quod Pater est, Deus de Deo, Lumen de Lumine (cf. *infra*, 61).

quod tamen Verbum non sicut verba nostra debemus accipere, quae voce atque ore prolata verberato aere transeunt nec diutius manent quam sonant;

"But we must not interpret this Word in the same way as we interpret our words which, having been expressed by voice and mouth strike the air and pass by and do not remain for longer than they sound;"

The Son is immediately identified with the Word spoken of in the previous chapter. In the Symbol the reference to the only- begotten Son belongs to the doctrine of redemption in the incarnation. Augustine also treats it in the context of the doctrine of creation, possibly partly in order to stress that the Redeemer is the Creator (see *supra,* 39).- Augustine draws a clear distinction between perishable human words which strike the air and God's eternal Word, see e. g. *Conf.* 11,6,8, *In Ioann.* 1,8; 14,7; 29,4. It is usual to make this observation on the difference between God's Word and our words (which is, in fact, the difference between the unchangeable being and changeable becoming), see e.g. Athanasius, *Contra Gentes* 40 (V), cf. *Contra Arianos* 2,35, Ambrose, *De fide* 4,9,101: Amentes homines, quasi non intelligant, quid intersit inter prolativum sermonem, et in aeternum permanens Dei Verbum ex Patre natum: natum utique, non prolatum: in quo non composita syllaba, sed plenitudo divinitatis aeternae est, et vita sine fine, cf. 4,7,72 (on the Stoic background see M.L. Colish, *The Stoic Tradition from Antiquity to the Early Middle Ages* II, Leiden 1985, pp. 181-198). To Augustine, this is not only important in order to exclude the possibility that the Son is (as the Arians say) a creature, but also in connection with his doctrine of creation: God's creative Word cannot have been a temporal one, i.e. a word spoken in time, since in that case there would have been time and movement before the creation of the world, see *Conf.* 11,6,8: si ergo verbis sonantibus et praetereuntibus dixisti (sc. deus) ut fieret caelum et terra, atque ita fecisti caelum et terram, erat iam creatura corporalis ante caelum et terram, cuius motibus temporalibus temporaliter vox illa percurreret, cf. *De Gen. a.l.* 1,9,15. But it is Augustine's view that time was created with the world and that therefore there was no time before the world, see *Conf.* 11,13,15.- The eternity of the Son consists of the fact that He has been generated in an eternal way, not that He is generated in an eternal way. If He were eternally generated, He would never have been generated and therefore not be the Son, see *De div. quaest. LXXXIII* 37: Melior est semper natus quam qui semper nascitur. Quia qui semper nascitur, nondum est natus, et numquam natus est aut natus erit, si semper nascitur. Aliud est enim nasci, aliud natum esse. Ac per hoc numquam filius, si numquam natus: filius autem quia natus, est semper filius: semper igitur natus.

manet enim illud Verbum incommutabiliter. nam de ipso dictum est, cum de Sapientia diceretur, *in se ipsa manens innovat omnia.*

"for that Word remains unchangeably, for it is this Word that is spoken of when it is said of Wisdom, Remaining in itself It renews all things (Sap. Sal. 7,27)."

The text *Sap. Sal.* 7,27 (see A.M. la Bonnardière, *op. cit.,* pp 157ff, 283f) is quoted in support of the general tenet that God is unchangeable, see e.g. *De nat. boni* 24, *De Trin.* 2,8,14, and in connection with the Son: the Son's unchangeability leads to the specific doctrine that the Son remained in the act of the incarnation what He was, *viz.,* God. This generally accepted tenet has in Augustine also an anti-Manichean aim: In the Manichean doctrine of redemption a part of God is corrupted even without assuming flesh, whilst Christ assumes flesh without being changed into flesh and without deteriorating, see *De act. cum Fel. Man.* 2,9: Verbum caro factum est, assumendo carnem, non mutatum in carnem: assumpsit enim humanitatem, non amisit divinitatem . . . non tamen in illa carne ipse deterior factus, sed caro in illo melior facta est. Pars vero Dei vestri, nulla carne assumta . . . descendit ut teneretur, ligaretur, pollueretur, et turpius quam ligabatur purgaretur. (See also *supra,* 39 on the idea that the Creator is the Redeemer.) On the unchangeability of the Son in the act of the incarnation see further *Sermo* 186,2,2: Confitendum est igitur, eum qui Filius Dei erat, ut de virgine Maria nasceretur, assumpta forma servi filium hominis factum quod erat manentem quod non erat assumentem: esse incipientem quo minor est Patre, et semper manentem in eo quod unum sunt ipse et Pater, cf. *De Trin.* 2,5,9, *De doct. christ.* 1,13,12, *Epist.* 137,3,10, and the famous lines in the "Mirabile Mysterium": id quod fuit permansit, et quod non erat assumpsit, see further Gregory Nazianzen, *Oratio* 39,13 (**VI**), Hilary of Poitiers, *De Trin.* 3,16: Non amiserat quod erat, sed coeperat esse quod non erat. Non de suo destiterat, sed quod nostrum est acceperat, (see on this subject L. Bron, Saint Grégoire de Nazianze et l'antienne "Mirabile Mysterium" des landes de la circoncision, *Ephemerides Liturgicae* (58) 1944, pp 17f.

verbum autem Patris ideo dictum est, quia per ipsum innotescit Pater. sicut enim verbis nostris id agimus, cum verum loquimur, ut noster animus innotescat audienti et quidquid secretum in corde gerimus, per signa huiusmodi ad cognitionem alterius proferatur, sic illa Sapientia, quam Deus Pater genuit, quoniam per ipsam innotescit dignis animis secretissimus Pater, Verbum eius convenientissime nominatur.

"Now It is called the Word of the Father for this reason that the Father becomes known through It. For as it is our intention with our words when we speak the truth that our mind becomes known to him who listens and that whatever secret we have in our heart is brought out through signs of this kind to the understanding of somebody else: in this way that Wisdom which God the Father generated, because the most hidden Father makes Himself known to minds which are worthy of it, is most conveniently called His Word."

Human words must express the human minds, so Christ as the Word reveals the Father. Again this is a generally used comparison (see e.g. Athanasius, *Contra Arianos* 2,35 (**VII**), Ambrose, *De fide* 4,7,72: Verbum hoc nostrum ... a sensu nostro et mente non discrepat et quae interiori tenemus affectu, ea tamquam operantis verbi testificatione signamus) and Augustine often refers to it, see e.g. *De doct. christ.* 1,13,12: cum loquimur, ut id quod animo gerimus, in audientis animum per aures carneas illabatur fit sonus verbum quod corde gestamus, et locutio vocatur, and *In Ioann.* 37,4. The restriction which Augustine makes, *viz.*, "when we speak the truth", refers to the fact that when men lie they do not reveal what is in their hearts, see the quotations given *supra,* 16, and *infra,* 48. (The correctness of this restriction can be disputed, see *infra,* 49).- God's revelation is restricted to souls which are worthy of it: This is stated more extensively in *De div. quaest. LXXXIII* 53,2: As the Father of Truth God does not deceive, but He does distribute according to merit, those who deserve to be deceived He deceives through other creatures (in this context the robbery of silver and gold by the Jews when they left Egypt is used as an example): Quapropter Deus quidem per seipsum neminem decipit, est enim Pater Veritatis . . . dignis tamen digna distribuens . . . utitur animis pro meritis et dignitatibus . . . Quapropter cum et Aegyptii deceptione digni essent . . . factum est ut iuberet Deus . . . ut vasa aurea et argentea . . . et peterent ab Aegyptiis non redditituri et acciperent quasi reddituri (on the interpretation of this story see W.C. van Unnik, Irenaeus en de Pax Romana, *Kerk en Vrede. Feestbundel voor Prof. dr J. de Graaf,* Baarn 1976, pp 211ff). So when men do not receive God's revelation they only have themselves and not God to blame (this could be directed against Manichean determinism; see also *infra,* 164 f).

(3,4) Inter animum autem nostrum et verba nostra, quibus eundem animum ostendere conamur, plurimum distat. nos quippe non gignimus sonantia verba, sed facimus; quibus faciendis materia subiacet corpus. plurimum autem interest inter animum et corpus.

"But our mind and our words with which we try to show this very mind, are very different from each other. For we do not generate audible words, but make them; and for this making of words the body is the matter at our disposal. But there is a very great difference between mind and body."

The difference between human mind and human words is caused by the fact that human words are not, as the divine Word or Wisdom is, generated, but that they are created. God generates what is equal to Himself, see *De div. quaest. LXXXIII* 50: Deus quidem genuit, quoniam meliorem generare non potuit (nihil enim Deo melius) generare debuit aequalem, but God creates what is inferior to Him, see e. g. *De vera religione* 18,35: Quare mutabilia sunt? Quia summe non sunt. Quare non summe sunt? Quia inferiora sunt eo a quo facta sunt. Quis ea fecit? Qui summe est, *De div. quaest. LXXXIII* 28: omne autem efficiens maius est quam id quod efficitur, for further examples see E.P. Meijering, *Augustin über Schöpfung, Ewigkeit und Zeit,* p 23.- When Augustine speaks of the body at our disposal when we speak, he thinks, of course, of tongue and mouth, see e. g. *Conf.* 11,3,5. The speaking of words with our body is an image taken from the realm of art: similarly the artist uses matter in order to give form to what he sees in his mind, but he cannot shape a product which is equally beautiful as the art which is in his mind, see *De Gen. contra Man.* 1,8,13: Prorsus noverat (sc. artifex) intus in animo (sc. bonum), ubi ars ipsa pulchrior est quam illa quae arte fabricantur (a similar view is found in Plotinus, *Enneads* 5,8,1,15-21, who says that not the art in the mind of the artist is expressed in matter, but something inferior to it **(VIII)**, cf. K. Flasch, *op. cit.*, pp 249f). As the Creator God transcends the human artist because He creates from nothing,-but the divine Word does not transcend the human words because It is created from nothing whilst human words are not,- It transcends the human words because It is generated from God's being. God needs no matter in generating the Word, the human mind is helped and hindered by the human body when it wants to express its thoughts in words (on the obedience or disobedience of the body to the mind see *infra,* 141ff). The similarity between speaking and creating is also expressed with the words "formabile" and "formatum": when man creates he creates from something which can be formed, similarly a word is in our mind "formabile" before it has been formed, see *De Trin* 15,15,25: quiddam illud mentis nostrae quod de nostra scientia formari potest, etiam priusquam formatum sit, quia iam ut ita dicam, formabile est. Augustine hastens to add that the generation of God's eternal Word is not like this,but, as we have seen (*supra,* 34), God's creating activity can be compared with this, the difference being that the "formabile" was also created by God.

deus vero cum Verbum genuit, id quod est ipse genuit, neque de nihilo neque de aliqua iam facta conditaque materia, sed de seipso id quod est ipse.

"But when God generated the Word, He generated what He is Himself, neither from nothing nor from some matter which was already made and created, but from Himself that which He is Himself.

The Arian doctrine which will be attacked in the next chapter is here already briefly opposed; according to the Arians, the Son was created from nothing and is God's most outstanding creature (see *infra*, 53). Augustine wants to exclude right from the beginning that the second way of God's creative activity, *viz.*, creation from a created "materia formabilis" (see *supra*, 34) applies to the generation of the Son.

hoc enim et nos conamur, cum loquimur, si diligenter consideremus nostrae voluntatis adpetitum, non cum mentimur, sed cum verum loquimur.

"For we, too, try to do this when we speak, when we pay close attention to the intention of our will, not when we lie, but when we speak the truth."

The comparison between man's words and God's Word is that both reveal the mind, but man can only try to express adequately what is in his mind. When man lies he does not try to do this, since in that case there is a clear and conscious difference between what man has in mind and what he expresses in his words, see *De mendacio* 3,3: ille mentitur qui aliud habet in animo et aliud verbis vel quibuslibet significationibus enuntiat. Unde etiam duplex cor dicitur esse mentientis, id est, duplex cogitatio: una rei eius quam veram esse vel scit vel putat, et non profert; altera eius rei quam pro ista profert sciens falsam esse vel putans, cf. *Sermo* 133,4; 23,5. This restriction, that when man lies he does not try to imitate God and reveal what is in his mind, seems only partly to the point in the present context: God's Word reveals God's being in a reliable way, a lie does not reveal what man really has in mind. So far Augustine is right in making this restriction. But he also deals with a slightly different matter: since man in expressing his thoughts needs the help of his body, i.e. of his tongue and his mouth, he cannot adequately express his thoughts, since his body to a certain degree prevents him from doing so. Now it is obvious that it is equally difficult to verbalize a lie which one has in mind as it is to verbalize a truth.- The words "intention of will" (appetitus voluntatis) are of Aristotelian background and seem to be a translation of "*boyleytikè orexis*", see Aristotle, *Eth. Nic.* 3,3,11131,9-13 (**IX**), cf. K.A. Neuhausen, *De voluntarii notione platonica et aristotelea*, Wiesbaden 1967, pp. 120f and A. Dihle, *The Theory of Will in Classical Antiquity*, Univ. of Calif. Press, 1982, pp. 132ff. Augustine does not, of course, suggest that there is also such an intention of will in God, when He generates the Word (the difference between God and men being that God is completely successful in following the intention of His will, and that men are only partly successful). Augustine explicitly denies that the generation of the Son is caused by God's will, see *De Trin.* 15,20,38: . . . ridenda est dialectica Eunomii . . . qui cum non potuisset intelligere nec credere voluisset, unigenitum Dei Verbum per quod facta sunt omnia, Filium esse natura, hoc est, de substantia Patris genitum; non naturae vel substantiae suae sive essentiae dixit esse Filium, sed filium voluntatis Dei, accidentem scilicet Deo volens asserere voluntatem qua gigneret Filium: videlicet ideo quia nos aliquid aliquando volumus quod antea non volebamus. Augustine then goes on to quote with approval a theologian who countered this Eunomian argument that the alternative "by God's will or against God's will" does not apply to the Son, as it does not apply to God's very divinity, since God is what He is by nature, cf. Athanasius, *Contra Arianos* 3,59ff, Ambrose, *De fide* 4,9,102f: Subtexunt aliam impietatem, proponentes utrum volens an invitus generaverit Pater . . . Sed mihi in sempiterna generatione praecedit nec velle nec nolle: ergo nec invitum dixerim nec volentem; quia generatio non in voluntatis possibilitate est, sed in iure quodam et proprietate paterni videtur esse secreti. Nam sicut bonus Pater non aut ex voluntate est, aut necessitate, sed super utrumque, hoc est, natura, ita non generat ex voluntate aut necessitate Pater (almost the same argument is given by Athanasius, *Contra Arianos* 3,62). If the generation of the Son were caused by God's will in the sense that God wanted to have something which He did not yet possess, this would be in conflict with God's perfection (cf. A. Dihle, *op. cit.,* p 142).

quid enim aliud molimur, nisi animum ipsum nostrum, si fieri potest, cognoscendum et perspiciendum animo auditoris inferre? ut in nobis quidem ipsi maneamus nec recedamus a nobis et tamen tale indicium, quo fiat in altero nostra notitia, proferamus, ut, quantum facultas conceditur, quasi alter animus ab animo, per quem se indicet, proferatur.

"For what else do we strive for, if not to make our mind known and visible, if possible, to the mind of our listener? So that on the one hand we remain in ourselves and do not recede from ourselves and yet on the other hand produce such an indication that knowledge of ourselves becomes apparent in somebody else, so that, as far as possible, our mind, as it were, brings forward a second mind

through which it can reveal itself;"

Augustine wants to make it clear that with their words men try to create, so to speak, a second mind which can be grasped and understood, but he also concedes that this is not entirely possible. This concession implies a good deal of scepticism about rhetoric (cf. *infra,* 48. Cf. for the following: U. Duchrow, "Signum" und "superbia" beim jungen Augustin, *Révue des études augustiniennes* (7) 1961, pp 369ff, R.M. Markus, St. Augustine on Signs, *Phronesis* (2) 1957, pp 81f, C.P. Mayer, *Die Zeichen in der geistigen Entwicklung in der Theologie des jungen Augustinus I,* Würzburg 1969, II, 1974, and the long explanatory note given by P. Godard in *Oeuvres de Saint Augustin,* 11, pp 563ff). For this scepticism see e.g. *De cat. rud.* 2,3 where he complains that he cannot make somebody else understand what he understands himself, because he sees something in his mind with the swiftness of a lightning, whilst the words are slow and very dissimilar: Totum enim quod intelligo volo ut qui me audit intelligat; et sentio me non ita loqui ut hoc efficiam: maxime quia ille intellectus quasi rapida coruscatione perfundit animum, illa autem locutio tarda et longa est, longeque dissimilis, cf. the brief expanatory note given by G. Combès and M. Farges in *Oeuvres de Saint Augustin, 11,* p 549. Augustine denies that the generation of God's Word is similar to this expression of human thoughts, see e.g. *In Ioann.* 1,10. But the speaking of words which must make known the mind is a suitable illustration of the divine generation in another way: mind remains what it is and at the same time goes out to somebody else and makes itself known, similarly God remains unchangeable in the revelation of the Word both in the generation and the incarnation, see e.g. *De doct. christ.* 1,13,12: Sicuti cum loquimur ut id quod animo gerimus in audientis animum per aures carneas illabatur, fit sonus verbum quod corde gestamus et locutio vocatur, nec tamen in eundem sonum cogitatio nostra convertitur, sed apud se manens integra, formam vocis qua se insinuet auribus, sine aliqua labe suae mutationis assumit: ita Verbum Dei non commutatum, caro tamen factum est, ut habitaret in nobis;- *In Ioann.* 14,7: Quomodo enim tu verbum quod loqueris in corde habes, et apud te est, et ipsa conceptio spiritalis est (nam sicut anima tua spiritus est, ita et verbum quod concepisti, spiritus est, nondum enim accepit sonum ut per syllabas dividatur, sed manet in conceptione cordis et in speculo mentis): sic Deus edidit Verbum, hoc est genuit Filium, see further *In Ioann.* 37,4; 69,4, *Sermo* 119,7; 187,3; 288,3f.- Human mind brings forward, so to speak, a second mind through which it reveals itself: Christ is not, of course, a second God besides the Father, but just like the Father He is fully God, and it is in this sense that the comparison between the mind and the word, which, so to speak, becomes a second mind, is suitable. The word "quasi", so to speak, again indicates that the words are inferior to the thoughts of mind.

id facimus conantes et verbis et ipso sono vocis et vultu et gestu corporis, tot scilicet machinamentis id, quod intus est, demonstrare cupientes, quia tale aliquid proferre non possumus; et ideo non potest loquentis animus penitus innotescere, unde etiam mendaciis locus patet.

"we try to do this with words, the very sound of voice, with the expression of face, with bodily gestures, wanting to show what is inside us with so many means, because we cannot produce such a thing, and therefore the mind of the speaker cannot become completely known, hence there is also room for lies."

In *De doct. christ.* 2,2,3 he deals with signs which must indicate one's feelings, and then, too, he indicates that this is not entirely possible: Data vero signa sunt quae sibi quaeque viventia invicem dant ad demonstrandos, quantum possunt, motus animi, vel sensa, aut intellecta quaelibet. In the *Confessions* he describes how as a baby he tried to make his feelings known with expressions of face and with gestures before he could utter words, and then, too, he stresses that this was not entirely possible, see 1,6,8: itaque iactabam membra et voces, signa similia voluntatibus meis, pauca quae poteram qualia poteram: non enim erant verisimilia, 1,8,13: ... ego ipse mente, quam dedisti mihi, deus meus, cum gemitibus et vocibus variis et variis membrorum motibus edere vellem sensa cordis mei, ut voluntati pareretur, nec valerem quae volebam omnia nec quibus volebam omnibus. So Augustine also expresses some scepticism about the possibility to make one's feelings known with gestures. The fact that the quotations given from the *Confessions* apply to a little child is of no importance, for age does not matter when one deals with spontaneous gestures. With this scepticism Augustine diverges to a certain degree from the rhetorical tradition in which it is stressed that gestures obey the mind and do reveal the mind, see e.g. Quintilian, *Inst. or.* 11,65f: ... de gestu prius dicam qui et ipse voci consentit et animo cum ea simul paret ... Quippe non manus solum, sed nutus etiam declarant nostram voluntatem et in mutis pro sermone sunt, et saltatio frequenter sine voce intelligitur atque adficit, et ex vultu ingressuque perspicitur animorum (cf. U. Duchrow, *op. cit.*, p 372).- This scepticism about man's ability to express his thoughts makes it understandable why Augustine shows a keen interest in the question of whether in eternal life in the risen bodies men can read each other's thoughts: If in this life we can recognize many thoughts in each other's eyes, then in the life to come no thought will be hidden, since the whole body will be ethereal, see *De div. quaest. LXXXIII* 47: si ergo multi motus animi nostri nunc agnoscuntur in oculis, probabile est quod nullus motus animi latebit, cum totum fuerit corpus aethereum, in cuius comparatione isti oculi caro sunt. So what is only partly possible in this life will be entirely possible in the life to come.- There is also another connection between the eyes and the risen body: the risen body has a heavenly substance, the substance of fire comes nearest to this (see *infra,* 156). With reference to Plato Augustine says that as the lower gods could take away from the light of the eyes the burning, so the Highest God can take away from the bodies their corruptibility, see *De civ.* 13,18: si dii minores ... potuerunt, sicut dicit (sc. Plato) ab igne removere urendi qualitatem lucendi relinquere quae per oculos emicaret, itane Deo summo concedere dubitabimus ... ut de carne hominis, cui donat immortalitatem ... detrahat tarditatem? The reference is to Plato, *Timaeus* 41A/B (see on this text *infra*, 155) and to 45B (X). (This reference seems to have been taken from Cicero's translation of the *Timaeus*, a passage which is now lost, see P. Courcelle, *Les lettres grecques en occident. De Macrobe à Cassiodore*, Paris 1948, pp 157f). So if God can change on earth the quality of the highest substance, which is clear from the nature of the eyes, then God can in heaven change the quality of an earthly substance and give it a substance which shows similarity with the substance of the eyes. The eyes now reveal the mind to a certain degree, the risen bodies will reveal it completely, so man's inability to reveal his thoughts completely will be overcome in eternal life.- When Augustine says that there is room for lies, since words, gestures and facial expressions do not completely reveal what one has in mind, he means that man can take advantage of the fact that it is not possible to reveal adequately one's thoughts and can say things which he knows not to be a true expression of his real thoughts. One may, of course, object to this that on the one hand gestures can hide the truth one knows, but that on the other hand they can be in accordance with the lie one tells (otherwise liars would easily give themselves away, cf. *supra*, 45).

deus autem Pater, qui verissime se indicare animis cognituris et voluit et potuit, hoc ad se ipsum indicandum genuit, quod est ipse qui genuit: qui *Virtus* etiam eius et *Sapientia* dicitur, quia per ipsum operatus est et disposuit omnia. de quo propterea dicitur, *Adtingit a fine usque ad finem fortiter, et disponit omnia suaviter.*

"But God the Father who in complete truth both wanted and could make Himself known to minds which were to know Him, generated, in order to make Himself known, that which is He Himself who generated: He is also called His Power and Wisdom (I Cor. 1,24), because through Him He has wrought and or-

dered all things; for this reason it is said about Him: He touches with strength from one limit to the other and orders all things beautifully (Sap. Sal. 8,1)."

Whilst human words are inferior to human mind, God's Word is God's being,- on God's power and will to generate such a Word see *supra,* 40. Through Christ as Power God has wrought all things, through Christ as Wisdom He ordered them. On Christ as God's creative Power and Wisdom see further *supra,* 38ff and the interesting observations he makes on this in *Contra Secundinum* 10: When higher things decline towards lower ones, towards sin, force (vis) imitates Power and fallacy Wisdom, when these higher things return again, magnanimity imitates Power and instruction Wisdom,- this is caused by the fact that all things were created through God's Power and Wisdom: Quoniam vere virtus et sapientia Dei est, per quam facta sunt omnia propterea in his quae facta sunt cum superiora ad inferiora declinant, ubi est omne peccatum et omne quod dicitur malum, vis imitatur virtutem, et fallacia sapientiam: cum vero ea quae declinaverunt recurrunt, et redeunt, magnanimitas virtutem, doctrina sapientiam imitatur. So the creation through Power and Wisdom has both a positive and a negative resemblance in the actions of men. This statement has an anti-Manichean aim: evil has no substance, but evil is the abuse of the possibilities granted by God the Creator, good is the return to those possibilities.- In the present context the creation through Power and Wisdom has another aim: Unlike human words which perish in the air, i.e. disappear in creation (see *supra,* 41), God's Word is the Cause of creation.- On Augustine's use of *Sap. Sal.* 8,1 see the detailed expositions given by A.M. la Bonnardière, *op. cit.* pp 170ff and 285f.

Chapter 4

Introduction: The doctrine of the Son is defended against heretics, the Son is not identical with the Father (as the Sabellians teach), and He is not an outstanding creature (as the Arians teach)(5). The famous text *Proverbs* 8,22 ("The Lord created Me in the beginning of His ways") which the Arians use as a Scriptural confirmation of their doctrine, does, according to Augustine, not refer to the eternal generation of the Son, but to His incarnation. Christ is called the "first-born" because of His incarnation, He is called the "only-begotten" because of His eternal generation (6a). In His eternal being the Son is equal to the Father (cf. *Ex.* 3,14), as the only real being, God has non-being as the only opposite (a statement obviously made against Manichean dualism)(6b-7). In the act of the incarnation, man in his entirety was assumed by the Word, this seems to be stated especially against the Apollinarians (8). The Manicheans try to deny the real manhood of Christ by using *John* 2,4 ("What have we to do with each other, woman, My hour has not yet come") which, according to them, implies that Christ did not regard Mary as His mother and therefore also contradicts His birth. This argument is refuted (9). There is no reason to fear, as the Manicheans do, that the Word was defiled in Mary's womb (10).

Text, Translation and Commentary:

(4,5) Quamobrem unigenitus Filius Dei neque factus est a Patre, quia, sicut dicit evangelista, *Omnia per ipsum facta sunt,* neque ex tempore genitus, quoniam sempiterne Deus sapiens sempiternam secum habet sapientiam suam; neque inpar est Patri, id est in aliquo minor, quia et apostolus dicit, *Qui cum in forma Dei esset constitutus, non rapinam arbitratus est esse aequalis Deo.*

"Therefore the only-begotten Son of God has neither been made by the Father, for as the evangelist says, All things have been made through Him (John 1,3), nor has His generation a beginning in time, for the eternally wise God has eternal Wisdom with Him, nor is He unequal to the Father, i.e. inferior in any way, for also the Apostle says, Who, being in the form of God, did not regard being equal to God as a robbery (Phil. 2,6)."

The Arians are obviously attacked here (on Augustine and the Arians see also M. Simonetti, S. Agostino e gli Ariani, *Révue des études augustiniennes* (13) 1967, pp 55ff). Augustine repeatedly attacks their doctrine that the Son was made, i.e. was a creature (see e.g. *In Ioann.* 1,11: Exeat nunc nescio qui infidelis Arianus, et dicat, quia Verbum Dei factum est) and their doctrine that the Son's generation has a beginning in time and that therefore the Father is prior to the Son in time (see e.g. *Sermo* 117,4,6: Ausi sunt enim quidam (as is clear from the previous sentence this applies to the Arians) dicere, Maior est Pater Filio, et praecedit in tempore: id est, maior est Filio Pater et minor est Patre Filius, et a Patre in tempore praeceditur. Et sic disputant: Si natus est, utique erat Pater antequam Filius illi esset natus, cf. *In Ioann.* 37,6. See for this Arian argument e.g. Athanasius, *Contra Arianos* 3,67, but there the Arians are quoted as saying that women did not have sons before they gave birth to them, to which Athanasius replies that fathers are fathers by nature. Arius' position on this matter is not entirely clear. On the one hand he does say that the Son was not before He was generated, but on the other hand he also says something quite different, *viz.*, that He was generated in a timeless way before all things, see the quotation given by Athanasius, *De Synodis* 16 **(XI)**. So Arius denies that the Son is co-eternal with the Father, but he does not say (as Augustine suggests) that the Son's generation has a beginning in time, i.e. took place in time, cf. G.C. Stead, The Platonism of Arius, *The Journal of Theological Studies* (15) 1964, pp 26f. Similarly Athanasius puts his finger on what is, according to him, the only consequence of the Arian doctrine that the Father is prior to the Son: then there must have been a time when the Son was not, see *Contra Arianos* 1,11ff. The orthodox position is clear: there is a sharp difference between eternal generation on the one hand and creation which has a beginning in time on the other hand. Therefore the Son has been eternally generated. The Arian position is ambiguous: the Son is a creature who once was not, but He was also generated before all times.- The Son can have no beginning in time, since the Father is eternally wise and has His Wisdom eternally with Himself: this argument will be developed in *De Trin.* 7,1-3 (it is briefly summarized in 15,7,12,cf. 6,1, see further *De div. quaest. LXXXIII* 16 and 23, *De doct. christ.* 1,8,8). Augustine's argument runs as follows: The Father cannot become wise by generating the Son, in that case the Son would make the Father wise and even cause the Father's being (since in God wisdom and being are identical), but the Son is generated as Wisdom from Wisdom as He is generated as Light from Light, see *De Trin.* 7,1,2: Quapropter quae causa illi est ut sapiens sit, ipsa illi causa est ut sit; proinde si sapientia quam genuit causa illi est ut sapiens sit, etiam ut sit ipsa illi causa est. Quod fieri non potest nisi gignendo eum aut faciendo. Sed neque genitricem, neque conditricem Patris ullo modo quisquam dixerit sapientiam. Quid enim insanius? Ergo et Pater ipse sapientia est; et ita dicitur Filius sapientia Patris quomodo dicitur lumen Patris. As Augustine says himself (*De Trin.* 6,1,1) the core of this argument appears already in other anti- Arian writers, see e.g. Athanasius, *Contra Arianos* 1,14;19;24;25;2,32; 3,63, *De Decr. Nic. Syn.* 15 (cf. E.P. Meijering, *Athanasius: Contra Gentes, Introduction, Translation and Commentary,* Leiden 1984, p 134 and the explanatory note given by J.-A. Beckaert in *Oeuvres de Saint Augustin,* 10, p 708).- Christ as God's creative Wisdom and Power must also exclude the idea that God is almighty through any arbitrary power, see *De Gen. a.l.* 9,17,32: Neque enim potentia temeraria, sed sapientiae virtute omnipotens est. In the act of creation God's eternal Wisdom is at work, not a sudden rash exhibition of power (cf. the opposition to a sudden moment of creation, *supra,* 33). This was also a kind of a compromise between two extreme positions which were both unacceptable to Augustine (and the orthodox Christians in general): The Manichean interpretation of the Old Testament that an evil god decided at an arbitrary moment to create a world and the position of a majority of Pla-

tonists that the world is eternal (and has God as its eternal Cause).- God's Power and Wisdom are identical, so there can be no question that there is more than one co-eternal Son of God (as there are many sons of God through adoption), see *De Trin.* 6,1,2: Nam illud non est formidandum, ne cogamur multos filios Dei dicere, praeter adoptionem creaturae, coaeternos Patri, si magnitudinis suae genitor est, et bonitatis, et aeternitatis, et omnipotentiae. Huic enim calumniae facile respondetur, sic non effici, quia multa nominata sunt, ut ille multorum filiorum coaeternorum sit Pater; quemadmodum non efficitur ut duorum sit, cum dicitur Christus Dei virtus et dei sapientia. Eadem quippe virtus et sapientia, et eadem sapientia quae virtus est.

hac igitur fide catholica et illi excluduntur, qui eundem dicunt Filium esse, qui Pater est, quia et hoc Verbum apud deum esse non posset nisi apud Patrem Deum, et nulli est aequalis qui solus est;

"So by this Catholic faith they, too, are excluded who say that the Son is the same as the Father, because this Word, too, could not be with God, if It were not with God the Father, and he who is alone is equal to nobody;"

This is obviously aimed at the Sabellians who declare the Father and the Son to be identical, see e.g. *Sermo* 183,5,7: Sabellianum audi. Ipse est Filius qui est et Pater. The Word, Augustine argues, can only be with God, if It is (as Son) with the Father, this must exclude the idea (to which also the Sabellians strongly object) that there are two gods, but the fact that the Son is with the Father also excludes the idea that there is one God completely on His own (cf. J. Rivière, *op. cit.,* p 29, note 2).

excluduntur etiam illi, qui creaturam esse dicunt Filium, quamvis non talem, quales sunt caeterae creaturae. quantamcumque enim creaturam dicant, si creatura est, condita et facta est;

"and equally they are excluded who say that the Son is a creature, albeit not like other creatures. For however great a creature they may call Him, if He is a creature, He is a creature which was created and made;"

It was normal to condemn at the same time both the Sabellians who declare the Father and the Son to be identical and the Arians who teach that they are different beings, see e.g. Hilary of Poitiers, *De Trin.* 1,17, Ambrose, *De fide* 1,1,6ff. This suggests that the orthodox position stands midway between these errors (which must imply that it is in fact the true one, see e.g. Augustine, *In Ioann.* 37,6: In errore Sabellianorum unus est solus, ipse est

Pater qui Filius: in errore Arianorum, alius est quidem Pater, alius Filius, sed ipse Filius non solum alius, sed etiam aliud est: tu in medio quid? Exclusisti Sabellianum, exclude et Arianum. Pater, Pater est, Filius, Filius est: alius, non aliud, quia, Ego et Pater, inquit, unum sumus . . . Cum audit, sumus, abscedat confusus Sabellianus; cum audit, unum, abscedat confusus Arianus: gubernet catholicus inter utrumque fidei suae navigium, quoniam cavendum est in utroque naufragium. (Similarly Hilary of Poitiers argues that the Arians and Sabellians fight each other and thereby render a service to the church, see *De Trin.* 7,4-7; 1,26).- The Arians call the Son a creature, but a creature which is not like other creatures, see the quotation given from Arius by Hilary, *De Trin.* 6,5: creaturam Dei perfectam, sed non sicuti unum de creatura; facturam, sed non sicuti caeterae facturae, and by Athanasius, *Contra Arianos* 2,19: **(XII)**. Like the other anti-Arian writers Augustine refuses to take seriously the restriction that Christ as a creature is unlike the other creatures and only focuses on the fact that they call Him a creature, cf. Athanasius, *Contra Arianos* 2,19 **(XIII)** and *De Syn.* 16 (cf. G.C. Stead, Rhetorical Method in Athanasius, *Vigiliae Christianae* (30) 1976, p 129), Hilary of Poitiers, *De Trin.* 4,11; 6,18. As the restriction in connection with the beginning of the Son was not taken seriously, in the sense that the orthodox regarded the Arian assertion that the Logos was created before all times as worthless because of the other assertion that "*èn pote hote oyk èn ho Hyios*", so the restriction that the Son is unlike other creatures is not taken seriously, because in the eyes of the orthodox a creature (of whatever quality) is a creature and as such not divine.

nam idem est condere, quod creare, quamquam in latinae linguae consuetudine dicatur aliquando creare pro eo, quod est gignere; sed graeca discernit. hoc enim dicimus creaturam quod illi "*ktisma*" vel "*ktisin*" vocant; et cum sine ambiguitate loqui volumus, non dicimus, creare, sed, condere. Ergo si creatura est Filius, quamlibet magna sit, facta est.

"for "to produce" is the same as "to create"; although in Latin we may have the habit to use the word "to create" instead of the word "to generate", in Greek there is a distinction. For we call that a creature what they call "ktisma" or "ktisis". And when we want to speak without uncertainty we do not say "to create", but "to produce". So if the Son is a creature, however great, as this creature He has been made."

Augustine obviously wants to suggest that the Arians, by calling Christ a creature ("creatura"), use a word which could also, because of a not unusual but inaccurate use of the Latin language, be understood as implying "generation",- the word which the orthodox use in this context (see the quotation given by Hilary of Poitiers from the Arian doctrine in *De Trin.* 6,5: Hunc Deum genuisse Filium unigenitum ante omnia saecula, cf. Ambrose, *De fide* 1,16,100f, who suggests that according to the Arians there is no difference between "generare" and "creare". (For examples of this use of "creare" in the sense of "gignere", "procreare", "parere" see *Th.l.l. IV,* pp 1157ff). But Augustine had already made it clear that the "generation" which the Arians have in mind has a beginning in time and therefore ought to be rejected in connection with the eternal Son. According to Augustine, the Arians mean by the word "creature" that the Son was like all other things produced by God, and (that they only) suggest fraudulently that this word could imply the right notion of "generation". According to Augustine, such a fraud is impossible in Greek, and with regard to the language this may be true, but it is interesting to see that Athanasius, too, accuses the Arians of a similar fraud: when the Arians say that the Son came into being through the will of God, they say something which, when it is said by the orthodox, could be interpreted in a correct way (a concession which Athanasius is forced to make by the fact that authors whose orthodoxy he did not doubt did say this, see e.g. Justin Martyr, *Dial.* 61,1, see further H.A. Wolfson, *The Philosophy of the Church Fathers,* p 224), but since the heretics' words are suspect, they must be unmasked as implying the same as when they state that the Son is a creature, see *Contra Arianos* 3,59 where Athanasius quotes the Arians as saying: **(XIV)**, and then goes on to say: **(XV)**. (In the present context Augustine says that "to create" (creare) and "to produce" (condere) are identical and that both words imply the same as "to make" (facere), hence his conclusion: Ergo si creatura est Filius, quamlibet magna sit, facta est, but elsewhere he says that in Scripture "to make" (facere) means to make something from nothing, whilst "to create" (creare, condere) can mean to make something from something else, see *Contra adv. leg. et proph.* 1,23,48 and *De mor. eccl. cath.* 2,7,9). (Athanasius makes a similar observation on the word *ktizein*: it can mean "to renew", "to recreate" things which already exist, see *Contra Arianos* 2,46 **(XVI)**). Augustine makes, as we have seen, no effort to take into account all aspects of the Arians' view on Christ, but when he quotes as the Arian doctrine that Christ is a creature, he must know that they mean that Christ was created (perhaps: "generated") from nothing and not from something else, cf. Hilary of Poitiers, *De Trin.* 4,11: Memorant namque (sc. Ariani) Dei Filium neque ex aliqua subiacente materia genitum esse, quia per eum creata omnia sunt.

nos autem in eum credimus, per quem facta sunt omnia, non in eum, per quem facta sunt cetera; neque enim aliter hic accipere possumus omnia, nisi quaecumque sunt facta.

"But we believe in Him through whom all things have been made, not in Him through whom the other things have been made: for we can here take "all things" only to mean "whatever has been made"."

The Arians also say that all things have been made through the Son, see the quotation given by Hilary, *De Trin.* 6,5. But since they call Christ a perfect creature unlike the other creatures (see *supra*, 53) Augustine draws from this the conclusion that, according to them, "the other creatures" were made through Him who is the most perfect creature (this consequence is not a distortion of the Arian views). If all things were made through the Word, then the Word Itself was not made, cf. his objections against the Arians in *In Ioann.* 1,12: Evangelista dicit: In principio erat Verbum, et tu dicis: In principio factum est Verbum. Ille: Omnia per ipsum facta sunt, dicit, et tu dicis quia et ipsum Verbum factum est. Poterat dicere Evangelista: In principio factum est Verbum, sed quid ait? In principio erat Verbum. Si erat, non est factum, ut ista omnia per ipsum fierent, et sine ipso nihil, cf. Hilary of Poitiers, *De Trin.* 2,17: Ergo si nihil sine illo est per quem universa coeperunt, et infinitum est per quem quod est omne sit factum.- Elsewhere Augustine says that if the Word were made, It would have had to be made through another Word, see *In Ioann.* 1,11: Si et Verbum Dei ipsum factum est, per quod aliud Verbum factum est? The same argument is used by Athanasius, who develops it ad infinitum, see *Contra Arianos* 2,24; 2,26, *De Decr.* 8, and by Irenaeus against the Gnostic doctrine of the *aeones* as mediators, see *Adv. Haer.* 2,6,3; 2,20,1. (This is the wellknown argument of the *sorites*, see on this J.H. Waszink's edition of Tertullian, *De anima*, pp 113f).

(4,6) Sed quoniam *Verbum caro factum est et habitavit in nobis*, eadem Sapientia, quae de Deo genita est, dignata est etiam in hominibus creari. quo pertinet illud: *Dominus creavit me in principio viarum suarum;*

"But because the Word became flesh and dwelt amongst us, (John 1,14), the same Wisdom which was generated from the Father regarded it worthy of Itself to be created also amongst men. This is referred to in that text, The Lord created Me as the beginning of His ways (Prov. 8,22),"

In the previous chapter it was rejected that the Word was created, now it is made clear that the famous text *Prov.* 8,22 which the Arians quote in support of their doctrine does not contradict what has been said by Augustine but that it applies to the incarnation. The word "fieri" and "creare" can be used for the Son (as is the case in *John* 1,14 and *Proverbs* 8,22) in connection with the incarnation. (On *Proverbs* 8,22 which played such an important part in the Arian controversy, see C.F. Burney, Christ as the APXH of Creation, *Journal of Theological Studies* (27), 1926, pp 170ff, J.H. Waszink, *Tertullian's Treatise against Hermogenes,* pp 131ff, E. Evans, *Tertullian's Treatise against Praxeas,* London 1948, pp 220ff, M. Tetz, Zur Theologie des Markell von Ankyra I. Eine markellinische Schrift "De Incarnatione et contra Arianos", *Zeitschrift für Kirchengeschichte* (75) 1964, pp 258ff). As A.M. la Bonnardière, *Biblia Augustiniana, A.T. Le Livre des Proverbes,* Paris 1975, pp 171f (cf. p 208) indicates, Augustine quotes in all his works *Proverbs* 8,22 only three times. La Bonnardière takes this as a clear proof of the limited information Augustine had about Arianism. We regard the fact that one of the writings in which this verse is quoted and interpreted is the present one, as an indication of the deliberately traditional character of this piece of writing (cf. *infra,* 111): Augustine quotes in this context a Biblical text which used to be quoted here, but which he himself hardly uses in his other writings (perhaps because he was not entirely sure about the correctness of the interpretation given to it by the orthodox).

viarum enim eius principium caput est ecclesiae, quod est Christus hominem indutus, per quem vivendi exemplum nobis daretur, hoc est via certa, qua perveniremus ad Deum.

"for the beginning of His ways is the Head of the Church, which is Christ having assumed the form of Man, so that through Him an example of life might be given to us, which is a certain way through which we can reach God."

Proverbs 8,22 is here obviously interpreted in the light of *Col.* 1,17f **(XVII)**.

This is furthermore combined with *John* 14,6, which Augustine, as we have seen (*supra,* 39) interprets as referring to Christ's manhood, whilst the words "Truth" and "Life" refer to His divinity; a similar interpretation is given by Hilary of Poitiers, *De Trin.* 12,45: Ac primum, quia Christus sapientia est, videndum est an ipse sit initium viae operum Dei. Nec, ut opinor, ambigitur. Ait enim: Ego sum via, et: Nemo vadit ad patrem nisi per me . . . Ergo in viarum initium in opera Dei creatur, quia et via est et deducit ad Patrem. It was usual to refer *Prov.* 8,22 to the act of the incarnation, see e.g. Athanasius, *Contra Arianos* 2,47; 50; 51; 53; 61; 66; 67; 74,

Ambrose, *De fide* 3,7,46ff (who also interprets the text in the light of inter alia *Col.* 1,18 and *John* 14,6).

non enim redire potuimus nisi humilitate, qui superbia lapsi sumus, sicut dictum est primae nostrae creaturae: *gustate et eritis tamquam dii.*

"For it was only in humility that we who fell in pride could go back, as it was said to the first creatures of our human race, Eat and ye shall be like gods, (Gen. 3,5)."

Man has to go back to God in humility, because he turned away from God in pride. For Augustine's famous doctrine that man's Fall was caused by pride (superbia) see e.g. *De civ.* 14,13f (especially 14,13,1: Porro malae voluntatis initium quid potuit esse nisi superbia? Initium enim omnis peccati superbia est (*Eccl.* 10,15). *De Gen. a.l.* 11,5,7ff, cf. G. Bardy's expalantory note in *Oeuvres de Saint Augustin, 35, La Cité de Dieu, Livres XI-XIV,* Paris 1959, pp 534f. It is the pride to want to be more than what one has been created by God.

huius igitur humilitatis exemplum, id est viae, qua redeundum fuit, ipse Reparator noster in se ipso demonstrare dignatus est, *qui non rapinam arbitratus est esse aequalis Deo, sed semetipsum evacuavit, formam servi accipiens*, ut crearetur homo principio viarum eius, Verbum, per quod facta sunt omnia.

"So our Redeemer Himself regarded it worthy of Himself to show us an example of this humility, namely, of the way in which we have to go back, in Himself, He who did not regard the being equal to God as a robbery, but emptied Himself by taking the form of a servant (Phil. 2,6), so that the Word through which all things were made was created as a man at the beginning of His ways."

(On Augustine's important thoughts about Christ's humility see the extensive expositions given by O.Scheel in his still valuable book, *Die Anschauung Augustins über Christi Person und Werk. Unter Berücksichtigung ihrer verschiedenen Entwicklungsstufen und ihrer dogmengeschichtlichen Stellung,* Tübingen und Leipzig 1901, pp 347ff). The "Principium" in which God created all things becomes the"principium" of God's ways. This combination of *Gen.* 1,1 and *Proverbs* 8,22 shows: when He through whom all things were made becomes a creature, i.e. Man, Himself, this is an act of humility which must save man from his pride, because man must follow this example set by Christ, see e.g. *De Trin.* 8,5,7. Augustine obviously likes to reflect on this: Sometimes a doctor when he is curing a patient applies something opposite to what must be cured, e.g. something cold to what is hot, therefore God applies this humility to us when He wants to cure our pride, see *De doct. christ.* 1,14,13: Sicut etiam ille qui medetur vulneri corporis adhibet quaedam contraria, sicut frigidum calido ... quia ergo per superbiam homo lapsus est, humilitatem adhibuit (sc. sapientia sanans) ad sanandum, cf. *Sermo* 123,1. In this respect Christ's work is the opposite of what the devil does who seduces man through pride, *De Trin.* 4,10,13: Sicut enim diabolus superbus hominem superbientem perduxit ad mortem, ita Christus humilis hominem obedientem reduxit ad vitam. In his sermons Augustine exhorts his listeners to humiliate themselves in order that God may turn to them, see e.g. *Sermo* 21,2: Si extollis te, longe secedit a te: si humilias te, inclinat se ad te, 69,2; 279,6. In the *Confessions* he describes how his own pride (both as a rhetor and as a philosopher) was finally broken by Christ's humility, and how the Platonists refuse to follow the example set by Christ in the act of the incarnation (although Augustine concedes that they have correct ideas about God's Word as It has been with the Father from all eternity, see 7,9,13ff, see also *infra,* in the present paragraph. According to A. von Harnack, the humble man Jesus is the core of Augustine's christology, not the eternal Word of God, for a critical appraisal of this view see E.P. Meijering, *Die Hellenisierung des Christentums im Urteil Adolf von Harnacks,* Amsterdam/Oxford/New York 1985, pp 117ff).-When Augustine says that the Creator was created as a man in order to restore man to his original state, he expresses a traditional doctrine, see e.g. Athanasius, *De Incarnatione Verbi* 13 **(XVIII)**.

quapropter secundum id, quod unigenitus est, non habet fratres, secundum id autem, quod primogenitus est, fratres vocare dignatus est omnes, qui post eius et per eius primatum in Dei gratiam renascuntur per adoptionem filiorum, sicut apostolica disciplina commendat.

"Therefore in accordance with the fact that He is the only- begotten one, He has no brothers, but in accordance with the fact that He is the first-born, He has regarded it worthy of Himself to call His brothers all those who after and through His primacy are reborn into God's grace through being adopted as sons, as the apostolic teaching recommends, (Rom. 8,15-23, Gal. 4,5) "

This may have been directed against the Arians, since a clear distinction is made between what applies to Christ as the eternal Son and Christ who became Man on behalf of men (on the Arian doctrine of Christ as the first-born of many brethren see R.C. Gregg and D.E. Groh, *Early Aria-*

nism. A View of Salvation, Philadelphia 1981, pp 43ff), but it seems more likely that it is aimed at the Manicheans: in *Contra Secundinum Manichaeum* 5 he attacks the doctrine that Christ was in His divinity the first-born, and that His brothers are also born from the substance of the Father, and that these later born brothers are the lights in which Christ reigns: ... secundum ipsam divinitatis excellentiam vis eum primogenitum intelligi, ut illa lumina in quibus regnat fratres eius sint; non facti a Patre per ipsum, sed geniti a Patre post ipsum, ut sint ipsi postgeniti, ille primogenitus, omnes tamen de propria Patris eademque substantia. With these lights, which are His brothers, Christ was to fight the realm of darkness, see *Contra Secund. Man.* 6. Against this doctrine Augustine states the difference between "unigenitus" and "primogenitus" in almost the same words as he does in the present chapter, see *Contra Secund. Man.* 5: Itaque cum unigenitum et primogenitum eum divina testentur eloquia; unigenitum quia sine fratribus, primogenitum quia cum fratribus (cf. *Expositio quarundam propositionum ex Epistula ad Romanos* 56, on the Manicheans' doctrine on this matter see H.-C. Puech, *op. cit.,* pp 76ff). Since Augustine in the present chapter explicitly denies that men are lights by nature and states that they are illuminated by the true Light, we regard it as likely that he is attacking the Manicheans here.-Men are reborn to God's grace, this means that they are sons of God by grace and not by nature, cf. *Contra Secund. Man.* 5: Aliud est enim per Patris excellentiam esse unicum Filium Dei, aliud per misericordem gratiam accipere potestatem filios Dei fieri credentes in eum. (This is the usual way of distinguishing between Christ as the Son of God and the Christian believers as the sons of God, see e.g. Irenaeus, *Adv. Haer.* 3,20, Hilary of Poitiers, *De Trin.* 6,23,27, cf. P. Smulders, *La doctrine trinitaire de S. Hilaire de Poitiers,* Rome 1944, pp 151ff).- Elsewhere Augustine gives more speculations about "unigenitus": unlike human only sons the only begotten Son of God is not afraid to have adopted sons of God as His co-heirs, see *In Ioann.* 2,13: Unicum eundem ipsum quem genuerat, et per quem cuncta creaverat, misit in hunc mundum, ut non esset unus, sed fratres haberet adoptatos ... Non timuit ille habere cohaeredes, quia haereditas eius non fit angusta, si multi possiderint. For further examples of this interpretation of the divine "unigenitus" see *Oeuvres de Saint Augustin, 71, Homilies sur l'évangile de Saint Jean I-XVI, Traduction, Introduction et Notes par* M.-F. Berrouard, Paris 1969, pp 198f, note 5. (Ambrose gives a different interpretation of "unigenitus" and "primogenitus": "primogenitus" means that there was no son before Christ, "unigenitus" that there was no son after Him, see *De fide* 1,14,89: Legimus genitum ... Legimus primogenitum: Filium legimus unigenitum: primogenitum quia nemo ante ipsum, unigenitum quia nemo post ipsum.)

naturalis ergo Filius de ipsa Patris substantia unicus natus est, id existens, quod Pater est, Deus de Deo, Lumen de Lumine;

"So as the natural Son He has been born as the only one from the Father's very substance, existing as that what the Father is, God from God, Light from Light;"

Augustine here obviously evokes the words from the Nicene Creed (**XIX**). See on this further *supra*, 11.

nos autem non lumen naturaliter sumus, sed ab illo lumine illuminamur, ut sapientia lucere possimus; *erat* enim, inquit, *Lumen verum, quod inluminat omnem hominem venientem in hunc mundum.*

"yet we are not light by nature, but we are illuminated by that Light in order to be able to shine in wisdom. For (the Apostle) says, He was the true Light which illuminates every man who comes into this world, (John 1,9)."

This is, as we have seen, stated against the Manicheans. Elsewhere Augustine says that John the Baptist (and every man who is illuminated) is a light which is darkness if it is not illuminated, whilst Christ is the true Light which illuminates, see *In Ioann.* 2,6: . . . et homo illuminatus dicitur lux, sed vera lux illa est quae illuminat . . . Sic ergo et Ioannes erat lux, sed non vera lux: quia non illuminatus, tenebrae, sed illuminatione factus est lux, cf. 14,1: Aliud est enim lumen quod illuminat, et aliud lumen quod illuminatur . . . Lumen autem illuminans a seipso lumen est et sibi lumen est, et non indiget alio lumine ut lucere possit, sed ipso indigent caeterae ut luceant, cf. *Conf.* 7,9,13: quia hominis anima, quamvis testimonium perhibeat de lumine non est tamen ipsa lumen, sed Verbum Deus, ipse est Lumen verum, see further *De civ.* 10,3. (On Augustine's famous doctrine of illumination see further R.M. Markus, Augustine. Reason and Illumination, *The Cambridge History* etc., pp 362ff, and C.E. Schützinger, Die augustinische Erkenntnislehre im Lichte neuerer Forschung, *Recherches augustiniennes* (2) 1962, pp 17ff.)

addimus itaque fidei rerum aeternarum etiam temporalem dispensationem Domini nostri, quam gerere et ministrare nobis pro nostra salute dignatus est.

"So we add to the faith in the eternal things also the dispensation in time of our Lord which He regarded worthy of Himself to carry out and administer on behalf of our salvation."

God's saving acts in time are added to His eternal being. This addition certainly offends the philosophers (cf. *supra,* 39). The eternal God, so to speak, enters time in order to save men, cf. *Sermo* 191,1: Ipse apud Patrem, praecedit cuncta spatia saeculorum, ipse de matre in hac die cursibus se ingessit annorum . . . Ad haec atque huiusmodi sustinenda pro nobis indigna, ut liberaret indignos, and *Sermo* 214,6. In the present context "the eternal things" are the eternal generation, "the dispensation in time" is Christ's work in the incarnation culminating in the ascension to heaven. On the word "dispensatio" (a translation of the Greek *oikonomia*), see *inter* alia R. Braun, *Deus christianorum. Recherches sur le vocabulaire doctrinal de Tertullien,* 1977², pp 158ff.

nam secundum id, quod unigenitus est Dei Filius, non potest dici: fuit et erit, sed tantum, est, quia et quod fuit, iam non est, et quod erit, nondum est. ille ergo est incommutabilis sine condicione temporum et varietate.

"For in accordance with the fact that He is the only-begotten Son of God it cannot be said of Him "He was" and "He will be", but only:"He is", because what was is no longer and what will be is not yet. So He is unchangeable without existence in time and without change."

It is typical of eternity that it only is, and that there are no future and past in eternity and no change from the future via the present to the past. (Cf. for the following: G.F.D. Locher, *Hoop, eeuwigheid en tijd in de prediking van Augustinus,* Wageningen 1961, pp 36ff, E.P. Meijering, *Augustin über Schöpfung, Ewigkeit und Zeit,* pp 46f.) The following quotations (they come from all periods of Augustine's writings) may illustrate this: *De mus.* 6,11,29 where he says of eternity: ubi nullum est tempus, quia nulla mutabilitas est, *De div. quaest. LXXXIII* 17: apud Deum autem nihil deest, nec praeteritum igitur nec futurum, *Conf.* 11,11,13: non autem praeterire quicquam in aeterno, sed totum esse praesens, *De civ.* 11,6: . . . recte discernuntur aeternitas et tempus, quod tempus sine aliqua mobili mutabilitate non est, in aeternitate autem nulla mutatio est, see further *In Ioann.* 38,10; 99,5, *De div. quaest. LXXXIII* 19, *De ordine* 2,2,6, *Enarrationes in Psalmos* 2,6; 89,3,15; 101,10 (II), *Conf.* 9,10,24. So, according to Augustine, God's eternity is the "eternal now". It is not entirely clear where this thought, which was expressed by others long before Augustine, finds its origin. Plato's well-known text *Timaeus* 37E comes near, but only says that "is" should be applied to eternity not "will be" and "was", it does not say *disertis verbis* that eternity is the "eternal now" (**XX**). It is clearly expressed by Middle Platonic writers, see e.g. Numenius, *Fragments, Texte établi et traduit par E.*

des Places, S.J., Paris 1973, fr. 5 **(XXI)**. Plutarch, *De E apud Delphos* 20,393A **(XXII)** (cf. C. Andresen, *Logos und Nomos. Die Polemik des Kelsos wider das Christentum,* Berlin 1955, p 287, J. Whittaker, *God Time Being. Two Studies in the Transcendental Tradition in Greek Philosophy,* Oslo 1971, pp 27f, on this thought in Neo Platonism see W. Beierwaltes, *Plotin über Ewigkeit und Zeit. Text, Übersetzung, Kommentar,* Frankfurt/M. 1967, pp 170ff). Christian authors adopted this thought, see e.g. Athanasius, *Contra Arianos* 1,11 **(XXIII)**, cf. 2,33, *Epist. ad ep. Aeg. et Lib.* 17, Irenaeus, *Adv. Haer.* 2,16,4, Origen, *De Princ.* 2,2,1.- Future is not yet, past is no longer, both are parts of time, so the question can be asked whether time is at all when two parts of it are not, see e.g. *Conf.* 11,14,17 (similar questions are asked by Aristotle, *Phys.* IV 217b 33ff, who does not deny this question, and the Sceptic Sextus Empiricus who does deny it, *Adv. Mathem.* 10,192, cf. J.F. Callahan, *Augustine and the Greek Philosophers,* Villanova University Press 1967, pp 82ff). Augustine cannot, of course, say that time does not exist or that it is not, since it is God's creature (see ee.g. *Conf.* 11,13,15), so he says of time what he says of creation in general: it is and it is not, see e.g. *En. in Psalmos* 38,7 (for this statement on the creation in general see *Conf.* 11,4,6: creation is, but compared with God who truly is, it is not). If Augustine denied any reality to time, he would deny the reality of the incarnation (and so in fact do what the Manicheans do). But he likes to describe Christ in his incarnate state in terms of temporal categories which are excluded here from Christ's eternal being and generation, see *Encheiridion* 8: Est etiam fides et praeteritarum rerum, et praesentium, et futurarum. Credimus enim in Christum mortuum, quod iam praeteriit, credimus sedere ad dexteram Patris, quod nunc est, credimus venturum ad iudicandum, quod futurum est, cf. *De Gen. lib. imp.* 1,1,4, *De doct. christ.* 3,10,15, and *infra,* 67. Augustine does not, of course, doubt the reality of these facts. If he did he would be like the Platonists who have the right ideas about God's eternal being, but who are too proud to believe in the incarnation, see *Conf.* 7,9,14: qui autem cothurno tamquam doctrinae sublimioris elati non audiunt dicentem: discite a me, quoniam mitis sum et humilis corde. The dispensation in time does not diminish Christ's eternal divinity, but is carried out on behalf of men.

nec aliunde arbitror manare illud, quod famulo suo Moysi tale nomen suum insinuavit. nam cum ab eo quaereret, si se populus, ad quem mittebatur, contemneret, a quo se diceret esse missum, responsum dicentis accepit: *Ego sum qui sum.* deinde subiunxit, *Haec dices filiis Israhel, Qui est, misit me ad vos."*

"And I believe that for the same reason He made known to His slave Moses that

such is His name. For when He asked Him by whom he should say to have been sent, if the people to whom he was sent would treat him with contempt, he received the answer from Him saying, I am who I am, and then He added, this thou shalt say to the sons of Israel, He who is has sent me to you, (Exodus 3,14)."

The fact that in *Exodus* 3,14 only the present tense is used for God is taken as a proof that God is the eternally Being and as Scriptural confirmation of the philosophical conception of God (or the other way round: that the philosophers have taken their correct ideas about God from Scripture). Augustine refers to this text in many similar contexts, see e.g. *De vera religione* 49,97: Nihil autem praeterit in aeterno, et nihil futurum est; quia et quod praeterit esse desinit, et quod futurum est, nondum esse coepit: aeternitas autem tantummodo est: nec fuit quasi iam non sit; nec erit quasi adhuc non sit. Quare sola ipsa verissime dicere potuit humanae menti: Ego sum qui sum, see further *Sermo* 6,3,4: Quia maneo in aeternum, quia mutari non possum, *De natura boni* 19, *In Ioann.* 2,2;38,8ff, *De Trin.* 1,1,2; 5,2,3, *De doct. christ.* 1,32,35, *De civ.* 8,11 (here he suggests with some caution that Plato found his thoughts about God in these words of Moses: tanquam in eius comparatione qui vere est, quia immutablilis est, ea quae mutabilia facta sunt non sint: vehementer hoc Plato tenuit, et diligentissime commendavit. Et nescio utrum hoc uspiam reperiatur in libris eorum qui ante Platonem fuerunt, nisi ubi dictum est, Ego sum qui sum, but see the restriction made slightly earlier: . . . ut paene assentiar Platonem illorum librorum expertem non fuisse). It was quite common among early Christian writers to interpret *Exodus* 3,14 in such a philosophical way (cf. P. Munz, Ego sum qui sum, *Hibbert Journal* (50) 1950/51, p 147, G.C. Stead, *Divine Substance,* Oxford 1977, p 167), see e.g. Athanasius, *Contra Gentes* 3, *De Decr.* 22, *De Syn.* 35, Hilary of Poitiers, *De Trin.* 1,5.- In *Sermo* 6,4ff Augustine sees this theophany mentioned in *Exodus* 3 as referring to Christ and interprets it as a prefiguration of the incarnation of the eternal Son of God (cf. Ambrose, *De fide* 5,1,26). This interpretation may also be the background of what is said in the present paragraph: If this text refers to the Son, then it provides the proof that only the present tense can be used for the eternal generation and being of the Son, not the past and the future (cf. J. Rivière, *op. cit.,* p 32, note 3).

(4,7) Ex quo iam spiritalibus animis patere confido nullam naturam Deo esse posse contrariam.

"From which, I trust, it is already clear to spiritual minds that there can be no nature opposite to God."

In this paragraph the attack on Manichean dualism is resumed and brought to a conclusion. Spiritual minds are those who have learned to understand the faith in the Creator as expressed in the Creed. They understand that if God is the only eternal Being there can be no nature, i.e. no being which is opposite to Him, so there can be no eternal matter from which the world was created (cf. *supra,* 25ff). And in the previous paragraphs they have received the real reason why the Creator wanted to redeem mankind, a reason which is totally different from the Manicheans' accounts of the fight between the Father of Light and the realm of darkness, in which God proved to be vulnerable.

si enim ille est et de solo Deo proprie dici potest hoc verbum - quod enim vere est, incommutabiliter manet, quoniam quod mutatur, fuit aliquid, quod iam non est, et erit, quod nondum est- nihil habet Deus contrarium.

"For if He is, and this word can only be used for God in the proper sense (for what truly is remains unchangeable, because what changes was something which it is no longer and will be what it is not yet), then God has nothing contrary."

If the world were created from eternally chaotic matter, this matter would change from chaos to order and so become what it is not. If true being implies unchangeability, such changeable matter has no true being. If it is the opposite of God who truly and unchangeably is, then it is not. On this characterization of changeability see also *Conf.* 11,4,6: quidquid autem factum non est et tamen est, non est in eo quicquam quod ante non erat: quod est mutari atque variari. The world has been created from what is not, i.e. from nothing, by God who truly is, therefore the world has some grade of being, but even of creation (the reality of which Augustine does not doubt) it must be said on the one hand that it is, on the other hand that compared with God it is not, see *Conf.* 11,4,6: Tu ergo, Domine, fecisti ea qui es, sunt enim . . . nec ita sunt, sicut tu conditor eorum, cui comparata . . . nec sunt. (On the grades of being see *infra* in the present paragraph.)

si enim quaereretur a nobis, quid sit albo contrarium, responderemus nigrum; si quaereretur, quid sit calido contrarium, responderemus frigidum; si quaereretur, quid sit veloci contrarium, responderemus tardum, et quaecumque similia. cum autem quaeritur, quid sit contrarium ei quod est, recte respondetur: quod non est.

"For if one asked us what is opposite to white, we would answer: black, if it was asked what is the opposite to warm, we would answer:cold, if it was asked what is opposite to quick, we would answer: slow, and whatever similar things. But when it is asked what is the opposite to what is, it is rightly answered: what is not."

The opposites which are used as analogies for the difference between the Highest Being and what is not at all, all have some degree of being, whilst the opposite to God, the truly Being, has no being at all, it is marked by the total absence of being, i.e. goodness. This applies to what the Manicheans call evil matter: this evil matter does not exist, since it is the very opposite of being and existing. Whilst in the present paragraph Augustine opposes black and white (which both to a certain degree are), he explains the darkness spoken of in *Gen.* 1,2 (which the Manicheans interpret as evil matter) in a different way, *viz.,* as the absence of light, see *De Gen. contra Manichaeos* 1,4,7: . . . solent dicere: Unde erant ipsae tenebrae super abyssum, antequam faceret Deus lumen? Quis illas fecerat vel genuerat? aut si nemo fecerat vel genuerat eas, aeternae erant tenebrae. Quasi aliquid sint tenebrae: sed, ut dictum est, lucis absentia hoc nomen accepit, cf. 1,9,15. The qualification of evil as non-being not only opposes the Manichean doctrine of matter, but also the idea that God created evil, see *De Gen. a.l. lib. imp.* 5,23-25, cf. 1,3: God has created all things very good, evil is either sin or the punishment of sin: Ecce autem omnia quae fecit Deus, bona valde: mala vero non esse naturalia, sed omne quod dicitur malum, aut peccatum esse aut poenam peccati. It is important to note that the complete absence of goodness and being is typical of evil, not of creation, which has received grades of being from the Creator, see the general remark in *De natura boni* 19: Omnis enim mutatio facit non esse quod erat: vere ergo ille est qui incommutabilis est; caetera quae ab illo facta sunt, ab illo pro suo modo esse acceperunt. As the truly being God is good, everything that receives being from Him is good, *ibid.:* Ei ergo qui summe est, non potest esse contrarium nisi quod non est: ac per hoc sicut ab illo est omne quod bonum est, sic ab illo est omne quod naturaliter est; quoniam omne quod naturaliter est, bonum est. Omnis itaque natura bona est, et omne bonum a Deo est: omnis ergo natura a Deo est. See on this matter further P. Courcelle, *Recherches sur les Confessions de Saint Augustin,* pp 107ff, 124ff, who explains Augustine's thoughts against the background of Plotinus and Ambrose. The relation between Plotinus' and Augustine's thoughts about evil has been redefined by J.M. Rist, Plotinus and Augustine on Evil, *Atti del convegno internazionale sul tema: Plotino e il Neoplatonismo in Oriente e in Occidente,* Rome 1974, pp 495ff, especially pp 504ff: Plotinus associates the appearance of moral evil with a weakness in the individual soul. In this respect his thought can easily be paralleled in Augustine. But in Plotinus evil is also associated with matter. Initially Augustine, too, toyed with this idea. But later on he insisted that unformed matter, too, was made by God from nothing. Even matter itself has some kind of form, and is morally neutral. According to Augustine, moral evil arises in the soul, in the will. Plotinus wishes both to make moral evil originate in the soul and to associate it with matter. Here Augustine's critique is sharp. He thinks that Plotinus is in trouble because his emanation system forces him to generate matter from what should be morally good,- and yet matter is absolute evil.- It is obvious that this is also the underlying idea in the present context: Augustine wants to make it clear that evil has nothing to do with matter and does not find in any way its origin in God.

(**4,8**) Sed per temporalem, ut dixi, dispensationem quoniam ad nostram salutem et reparationem operante Dei benignitate ab illa incommutabili Dei Sapientia natura mutabilis nostra suscepta est, temporalium rerum salubriter pro nobis gestarum adiungimus fidem, credentes in eum Dei Filium qui natus est per Spiritum sanctum ex virgine Maria.

"But since through the, as I said, dispensation in time for our salvation and restoration, a work of God's goodness, our changeable nature was assumed by that unchangeable Wisdom of God, we add the faith in temporal things, carried out redeemingly on our behalf, by believing in that Son of God who through the Holy Spirit was born out of the virgin Mary."

Having made it clear that God's being, both the Father's and the Son's, is unchangeable, Augustine stresses again (cf. *supra,* 61) the importance of the faith in the temporal things said about the Son, i.e. about the incarnation. This incarnation took place on men's behalf. The cause of the incarnation is God's goodness, as is the cause of the creation (cf. *supra*, 26f, on the anti-dualistic aim of this doctrine). When God's Wisdom assumes our changeable nature, It nevertheless remains Itself unchangeable, see *supra,* 41f. Again this could have an anti-Manichean meaning: their doctrine of salvation implies or at least could imply changeability of God, see *Conf.* 7,2,3: quid erat tibi (sc. domine) factura nescio qua gens tenebrarum quam ex adversa mole solent opponere, si tu cum ea pugnare noluisses? si enim responderetur aliquid fuisse nocituram, violabilis tu et corruptibilis fores. si autem nihil ea nocere potuisse diceretur, nulla afferretur causa pugnandi et ita pugnandi, ut quaedam portio tua et membrum tuum vel proles de ipsa substantia tua misceretur adversis potestatibus et non a te creatis naturis atque in tantum ab eis corrumperetur et commutaretur in deterius, ut a beatitudine in miseriam verteretur et indigeret auxilio, cf. *De mor. Man.* 2,12,25 (it is an argument put forward by Augustine's friend Nebridius, cf. on this argument *supra*, 42, 61, and P. Courcelle, *Recherches sur les Confessions de Saint Augustin,* p 73.)- The formulation "qui natus est per Spiritum sanctum ex virgine Maria" seems to be highly exceptional in Augustine, usually he says "de Spiritu sancto" and "de virgine Maria", see P.C. Eichenseer, *op. cit.,* pp 239ff. We are unable to give an explanation for this unusual formulation in the present context.

dono enim Dei, hoc est sancto Spiritu concessa nobis est tanta humilitas tanti Dei, ut totum hominem suscipere dignaretur in utero virginis, maternum corpus integrum inhabitans, integrum deserens.

"For through the gift of God, which is through the Holy Spirit such a great humility of such a great God has been granted to us, that He regarded it worthy of Himself to become wholly Man in the womb of a virgin, dwelling in the maternal body without impairing it and leaving it without impairing it."

The gift of the Holy Spirit is the fact that Christ was born through the Holy Spirit, as was said in the previous sentence. (On the Holy Spirit and the incarnation see further J. Verhees, Heiliger Geist und Inkarnation in der Theologie des Augustinus von Hippo, *Révue des Etudes augustiniennes* (22) 1976, pp 238ff, 246ff, and his paper, Heiliger Geist und Gemeinschaft bei Augustinus von Hippo, *Rév. Et. Aug.* (23) 1977, pp 246ff, F. Cavallera, La doctrine de Saint Augustin sur l'Esprit Saint à propos du "De Trinitate", *Recherches de theologie ancienne et médiévale* (3) 1931, pp 12f.)-On the humility of Christ in the incarnation see further *supra,* 58f.- The fact that the great gift of the incarnation is granted through the Holy Spirit is also an indication that the Son and not the Father or the Spirit incarnated Himself, nevertheless the whole Trinity is at work in the incarnation.- As Christ remained unchangeably God whilst assuming changeable manhood, He was when He dwelt in Mary's womb also in heaven. This is explained elsewhere with the analogy that many people hear the word of a man and each one hears the word in its totality, which means that the fact that one man hears the word in its totality does not prevent the word from being in its totality in many places, see *De div. quaest. LXXXIII* 42: Quomodo Christus et in utero matris fuerit et in caelis. Quomodo verbum hominis quod etsi multi audiunt, totum audiunt singuli, cf. *Epist.* 137, *Sermo* 119,6, see further the explanatory note given by G. Bardy in *Oeuvres de Saint Augustin,* 10, pp 720f, cf. also Hilary of Poitiers, *De Trin.* 2,25: Inenarrabilis a Deo originis unus unigenitus Deus in corpusculi humani formam sanctae virginis utero insertus adcrescit. Qui omnia continet et intra quem et per quem cuncta sunt, humani partus lege profertur. According to Augustine, Mary's virginity had to be preserved even at Christ's birth (and not only at His conception), since otherwise He would not have been born from a virgin and the church would falsely confess the virgin birth, see *Ench.* 34: quo si vel nascente corrumperetur eius integritas, non iam ille de virgine nasceretur, eumque falso, quod absit, natum de virgine Maria tota confiteretur ecclesia. The virgin birth was necessary in order to exclude sin from Christ's conception, *ibid.*. In *De Gen. a.l.* 10,18,33 Augustine reproduces the traditional argument by comparing Christ's birth from Mary with Adam's creation from the earth which had not yet been worked upon, cf. Irenaeus, *Adv. Haer.* 3,30-31, Tertullian, *De carne Christi* 17,3-4 (this has an anti-Marcionite aim: God the Redeemer acts in the same way as God the Creator). On Ambrose's and Jerome's views on the virgin birth see P.C. Eichenseer, *op. cit.,* pp 265ff, on the subject of the virgin birth in general see H. von Campenhausen, *Urchristliches und Altkirchliches,* Tübingen 1979, pp 63ff.-The fact that Christ assumed total manhood will now be defended against the heretics:

cui temporali dispensationi multis modis insidiantur haeretici. sed quisquis tenuerit catholicam fidem, ut totum hominem credat a Verbo Dei esse susceptum, id est corpus, animam, spiritum, satis contra illos munitus est.

"The heretics attack this temporal dispensation in many ways. But everybody who clings to the Catholic faith, so that he believes that total manhood was assumed by the Word of God, which is body, soul and spirit, is safely protected from them."

This is the simple truth which must protect the believer against the heretics, cf. *supra,* 19. This will now be further explained to those who want to make progress in understanding:

quippe cum ista susceptio pro salute nostra gesta sit, cavendum est, ne, cum crediderit aliquid nostrum non pertinere ad istam susceptionem, non pertineat ad salutem. et cum homo excepta forma membrorum, quae diversis generibus animantium diversa tributa est, non distet a pecore nisi rationali spiritu, quae mens etiam nominatur, quomodo sana est fides, qua creditur, quod id nostrum susceperit Dei Sapientia, quod habemus commune cum pecore, illud autem non susceperit, quod inlustratur luce sapientiae et quod hominis proprium est?

"For while this assumption was carried out for our salvation he must be on his guard lest when he believes that something of us is no part of this assumption, it is no part of salvation. And when man, with the exception of the form of limbs which has been attributed in a different way to the different species of living beings, only differs from the cattle in his rational spirit which is also called mind, how is a faith sound in which one believes that the Wisdom of God assumed only that part of us which we have in common with cattle, but did not assume that which is illuminated by the light of Wisdom and what is special of man?"

Behind the argument given here lies the well-known tenet: Quod non est assumptum non est sanatum, see J. Tixeront, *Histoire des dogmes de l'antiquité chrétienne II,* Paris 1924[6], p 115, cf. J. Rivière, *op. cit.,* pp 36f, note 2. Augustine here obviously has the Apollinarians in mind, this is clear from *De div. quaest. LXXXIII* 80 where the same doctrine is attacked and Apollinaris and his followers are named: Cum quidem haeretici, qui apollinaristae ex Appolinari quodam auctore suo dicti esse perhibentur, assererent dominum nostrum Jesum Christum, in quantum homo fieri dignatus est, non habuisse humanam mentem ... delectati sunt quidem ea perversitate qua ille hominem in Deo minuebat, dicens eum non habuisse mentem, hoc est rationalem animam qua homo a pecoribus secundum animum differt, cf. *In Ioann.* 23,6; 47,9, *De agone christiano* 19,21 (here the heretics are quoted as saying that Christ only had a body and a soul, so they deny that man has a *rational* soul or spirit), Augustine points out that the animals, too, have an anima, i.e. life, see *De Gen. a.l.* 3,20,30-31. He also accuses the Arians of holding this view, see *Contra serm. Arian.* 5,5: sed etiam istos, id est Arianos, in eorum disputationibus, non solum Trinitatis diversas esse naturas, sed etiam hoc sentire deprehendimus, quod animam non habeat Christus humanam; orthodox writers used to accuse the Arians of this view, cf. the quotations given by F.C. Baur, *Die christliche Lehre von der Dreieinigkeit und Menschwerdung Gottes in ihrer geschichtlichen Entwicklung I,* Tübingen 1841, p 568 note 9, for criticism made of Apollinaris see the quotations given from the Cappadocians pp 626ff. (The Manicheans are obviously not meant here, since they explicitly denied that Christ assumed human flesh, see *infra,* 73).-Time and again Augustine says that man differs in his mind from the animals, see e.g. *De lib. arb.* 1,8,18, *In Ioann.* 3,4, *De Gen. contra Man.* 2,11,16, *De Trin.* 12,1; 15,1. Interesting is Augustine's observation on the fact that in *Gen.* 3,1 the serpent is called "prudentissimus omnium bestiarum", he explains this in *De Gen. a.l.* 11,29,36f as: hoc est astutissimus, ita dictus est serpens propter astutiam diaboli. He goes on to say that he gives this explanation in order to exclude the doctrine that unrational animals can become rational beings, which leads to the absurd doctrine of the transmigration of the souls (from men into animals and vice versa): Hoc ideo commendandum putavi, ne quisquam existimans animantia rationis expertia humanum habere intellectum vel in animal rationale repente mutari, seducatur in illam opinionem ridiculam et noxiam revolutionis animarum vel hominum in bestias, vel in homines bestiarum. (This is a common concern in early Christian writers: when man is compared with animals, it applies to his behaviour, not to his nature, and this has nothing to do with the doctrine of the transmigration of the souls, see J.H. Waszink's edition of Tertullian's *De anima,* pp 391f.) The fact that the animals lack reason has as a consequence that the animals cannot share in blessed life, this is only possible for living beings with knowledge, see *De div. quaest. LXXXIII* 5: Animal quod caret ratione, caret scientia. Nullum autem animal quod scientia caret, beatum esse potest. Non igitur cadit in animalia rationis expertia ut beati sint. For the same reason animals cannot be illuminated as man can, see *In Ioann.* 1,18: Pecora non illuminantur, quia pecora non habent rationales mentes quae possint videre sapientiam, cf. 3,4 and 19,14. So the redeeming act of the incarnation is not meant for the animals, cf. J.A. Beckaert's explanatory note "Un moralisme intellectualiste" in *Oeuvres de Saint Augustin,* 10, p 704.- When Augustine defines man as a rational living being he uses, as he indicates himself, (see *De Trin.* 7,4,7: homo enim, sicut veteres definierunt, animal est rationale, cf. 15,7,11) a famous common place, see e.g. *Cicero, De leg.* 1,7,22, *De off.* 1,4,11f, Seneca, *Epist.* 121,14; 76,9, Athanasius, *Contra Gentes* 31, Eusebius, *Praep. Evang.* 7,18,3. So as a rational being man is superior to the animals. One of the proofs Augustine gives for this superiority is that man can tame animals, but the animals cannot tame man, see *De div. quaest. LXXXIII* 13: Inter multa quibus ostendi potest hominem ratione bestiis antecellere, hoc omnibus manifestum est, quod belluae ab hominibus domari et mansuefieri possunt, homines a belluis nullo modo. Behind this lies the thought that man as a rational being has a free will and as such can force the animals into a certain way of behaviour. This is in line with the idea that man's creation in God's image also implies man's power to rule over the rest of creation, see *De Gen. a.l.* 3,20,30.- For this reason Augustine also stresses that the example of humiliation set by Christ does not mean that man should debase himself to the level of animals, see *In Ioann.* 25,16:... praecipitur tibi ut sis humilis, non tibi praecipitur, ut ex homine fias pecus: ille deus factus est homo; tu, homo, cognosce quia es homo: tota humilitas tua, ut cognoscas te.- The mind, Augustine goes on to say, is illuminated by God's Wisdom: this applies in the present context to the fact that the human mind is created in God's image, see *De Gen. a.l.* 3,20,30: ... intelligamus in eo factum hominem ad imaginem Dei, in quo irrationabilibus animantibus antecellit. Id est ipsa ratio, vel mens, vel intelligentia ... satis ostendens ubi sit homo creatus ad imaginem Dei, quia non corporeis lineamentis, sed quadam forma intelligibilis mentis illuminatae. Whilst Augustine explicitly confines creation in God's image to the human mind and says that man has his body in common with the animals, the restriction he makes in this latter statement is not unimportant: the form of the limbs is different in the various species. Augustine reproduces the traditional doctrine that man's body is created in God's likeness (similitudo) because of man's erect body which can look up to heaven, see *De Gen. a.l. lib. imp.* 15,60: Caetera in eo (sc. homine) quamquam in suo genere pulchra sint, tamen cum pecoribus communia sunt, ac per hoc in homine parvipendenda. Nisi forte quod ad intuendum caelum figura humani corporis erecta est, valet aliquid etiam ut corpus ipsum ad similitudinem Dei factum credatur, ut quemadmodum a Patre illa similitudo non avertitur, ita corpus humanum a caelo non sit aversum, sicut aliorum corpora animalia aversa sunt, quia prona in alvum prosternuntur. The words "nisi forte" indicate that Augustine reproduces this doctrine here with some hesitation, the same hesitation lies behind what he says in *De div. quaest. LXXXIII* 51,4: Ergo iste spiritus ad imaginem Dei nullo dubitante factus accipitur, in quo est intelligentia veritatis: haeret enim veritati nulla interposita creatura. Caetera hominis ad similitudinem facta videri volunt; quia omnis quidem imago similis est, non autem omne quod simile est, etiam imago proprie, sed forte abusive dici potest. Sed cavendum in talibus, ne quid nimis asseverandum putetur, illa re sane salubriter custodita, ne quoniam corpus quodlibet per localia spatia porrectum est, aliquid tale credatur esse substantia Dei. So to refer the "similitudo" to man's body implies, according to Augustine, the danger of speaking and thinking about God in a corporeal way (to which he is, of course, completely opposed, see *infra,* 93). This doctrine is, however, given without any hesitation in *De Gen. a.l.* 6,12,22, cf. *De Trin.* 12,1,1: Sed sicut corpus ad ea quae sunt excelsa corporum, id est ad caelestia naturaliter erectum est; sic animus qui substantia spiritalis est, ad ea quae sunt in spiritalibus excelsa erigendus est, non elatione superbiae, sed pietate iustitiae. For the background of this doctrine see e.g. Lactance, *De ira dei* 7,4-7, cf. A. Wlosok, *Laktanz und die philosophische Gnosis. Untersuchungen zu Geschichte und Terminologie der gnostischen Erlösungsvorstellung,* Heidelberg 1960, p 182, note 7. (Tertullian says that after the Fall man was in his slavework bent down to the ground, hereby perhaps suggesting that man to some degree lost the privilege of his erect figure, see *Adv. Marc.* 2,2,6.)

(4,9) Detestandi autem etiam illi sunt, qui Dominum nostrum Jesum

Christum matrem Mariam in terris negant habuisse, cum illa dispensatio utrumque sexum, et masculinum et femininum, honoraverit et ad curam Dei pertinere monstraverit non solum quem suscepit, sed illum etiam, per quem suscepit, virum gerendo, nascendo de femina.

"But they, too, have to be detested who deny that our Lord Jesus Christ had Mary as His mother on earth, because that dispensation honoured both sexes, both the male and the female one, and proved that not only the sex which He assumed belongs to God's care, but also the one through which He assumed it, viz., by carrying a man and by being born from a woman."

After the brief attack on the Apollinarians the attack on the Manicheans is resumed (hence: etiam illi detestandi sunt, which means that those who are under attack now are not the same ones as who were attacked in the previous paragraph). The Manicheans deny (obviously *inter alia* with a reference to the story of the wedding at Cana) that Christ had a mother, thereby denying his human flesh, see *Contra Faustum* 7,2. According to the Manicheans, Christ had a body which can be compared with the dove which descended upon Christ at His baptism, see *De agone christiano* 22,24: Nec eos audiamus qui tale corpus Dominum nostrum habuisse dicunt, quale apparuit in columba quam vidit Ioannes Baptista descendentem de caelo et manentem super eum in signo Spiritus sancti (cf. G.Bardy's explanatory note in *Oeuvres de Saint Augustin,* 10, p 707).- For the reason which is given here why Christ was born a man from a woman cf. *De vera religione* 16,30: Et ne quis forte sexus a suo Creatore se contemptum putaret, virum suscepit, natus ex femina, and *Sermo* 190,2. In De div. quaest. LXXXIII 11 he gives a similar reason, but which also implies the superiority of the male sex: quia virum oportebat suscipere qui sexus honoribilior est, consequens erat ut feminei sexus liberatio hinc appareret, quod ille vir de femina natus est. Augustine draws in this context also the traditional parallel between Eve and Mary, see *Sermo* 12,12 ... et propterea undecumque Dominus noster asssumeret corpus, de sua creatura utique assumeret: sed ex femina maluit humilis, qui ad liberandam perditam creaturam venerat, quae per feminam lapsa est, cf. *Sermo* 51,2,3 and Irenaeus, *Adv. Haer.* 5,21,1: Neque enim iuste victus fuisset inimicus, nisi ex muliere homo esset qui vicit eum. Per mulierem enim homini dominatus est ab initio, semetipsum contrarium statuens homini.

nec nos ad negandam Christi matrem cogit, quod ab eo dictum est: *quid mihi et tibi est, mulier? nondum venit hora mea,* sed admonet potius, ut intellegamus secundum Deum non eum habuisse matrem, cuius maiestatis personam parabat ostendere aquam in vinum vertendo. quod autem crucifixus est, secundum hominem crucifixus est; et illa erat hora, quae nondum venerat, quando dictum est: *mihi et tibi quid est? nondum venit hora mea,* id est, qua te cognoscam. tunc enim ut homo crucifixus cognovit hominem matrem et dilectissimo discipulo humanissime commendavit.

"And we are not forced to deny that Christ had a mother by the fact that it was said by Him, Woman what have I to do with you? My hour has not yet come, (John 2,4). But this word rather admonishes us to understand that He as God did not have a mother, while He was about to show the person of His divine majesty by turning water into wine. But regarding the fact that He was crucified, He was crucified as man, and that was the hour which had not yet come, when it was said by Him, What have I to do with you? My hour has not yet come, which is: in which I shall recognize you. For then when He was crucified as man, He knew His human mother and recommended her in a most human way to His most beloved disciple (John 19,26-27)."

So, as God, Christ had no mother, while as man who was crucified He had Mary as His mother, cf. *In Ioann.* 8,9: Dominus noster Iesus Christus, et Deus erat et homo: secundum quod deus erat, matrem non habebat, secundum quod homo erat habebat. Mater ergo erat carnis, mater humanitatis, mater infirmitatis quam suscepit propter nos, cf. *Sermo* 218,10, *De vera rel.* 16,31. This distinction provides the refutation of the Manicheans' claim based inter alia on *John* 2,4 that Christ had no mother and was not born from a woman. (For the change of water into wine as a proof of Christ's divinity see also Hilary of Poitiers, *De Trin.* 3,5). When Christ was about to produce a miracle He wanted to make it clear that He did so as God who has no mother, when He was crucified as man He recognized Mary as His mother,- see again *In Ioann.* 8,9: Miraculum ergo exigebat mater, at ille tamquam non agnoscit viscera humana, operaturus facta divina, tamquam dicens: Quod de me facit miraculum, non tu genuisti, divinitatem meam non tu genuisti: sed quia genuisti infirmitatem meam, tunc te cognoscam, cum ipsa infirmitas pendebit in cruce, hoc est enim: Nondum venit hora mea, cf. *In Ioann.* 119,1, see further the explanatory note given by M.-F. Berrouard in *Oeuvres de Saint Augustin, 71, Homilies sur l'Evangile de Saint Jean,* Paris 1969, p 896. The change of water into wine (which must prove Christ's divinity) is also explained symbolically by Augustine with a typical play of words, *viz.,* that the "sapere" can mean both "to have a flavour" and "to be wise": Christ made us wine from water, i.e. wise believers from unwise unbelievers, see *In Ioann.* 8,3: ... quia et nos ex aqua eramus, et vinum nos fecit, sapientes nos fecit, sapimus enim fidem ipsius, qui prius insipientes eramus.- It was a common place in early Christian theologians to say that Christ died on the cross as man and not as God, see *e.g.* Melito of Sardes, *Homily on the Passion* 47f (**XXIV**). Irenaeus, *Adv. Haer.* 3,20,3, Ambrose, *Liber de incarnatione* 5,37, *De Spiritu sancto* 1,9,107, *Commentarius in Epist. I ad Cor.* (Migne PL 17,205), Jerome, *Symboli explanatio ad Damasum* (Migne PL 45,1717), Theodoretus, *Dialogus II* (Migne PG 83,185), Vigilius, *Contra Eutychen* 4,5.- It is interesting to see that Christ's words about His hour which has not yet come is taken by astrologers as a proof that Christ was subjected to fate, see *In Ioann.* 8,8: Dicunt enim vaniloqui et seducti seductores: Vides quia sub fato erat Christus, qui dicit: Nondum venit hora mea, cf. 104,3. Augustine answers that one should not subject to fate the Creator of heaven and stars. If fate were dependent on the stars, the Creator of the stars could not be subjected to the necessity of the stars, 8,10: nec ideo iam sub fato ponant conditorem caeli, creatorem atque ordinatorem siderum. Quia si esset fatum de sideribus non poterat esse sub necessitate siderum conditor siderum. In a similar way Augustine (in answering the Pelagian charge that His doctrine of grace is in fact a doctrine of fate) says that fate is subjected to the will of God (*Contra duas epist. Pel.* 2,5,12). But he does not reject the Pagan notion of fate if one identifies it with the will of God (*ibid.* 2,5,9), and accepts the Stoic notion of the connexio causarum if this is the will of God (*De civ.* 5,8ff). Augustine is in this context, of course, confronted with the traditional difficulty (see *e.g.* Tertullian, *De idol.* 9,3f) that at Christ's birth the magi saw a new star. Augustine's answer to this is that the Creator of heaven and earth, Christ, could show a new star at His birth just as at His death He could veil the old light of the sun, see *Sermo* 199,2,3: Ipse enim natus ex matre, de caelo terrae novum sidus ostendit, qui natus ex Patre caelum terramque formavit. Eo nascente lux nova est in stella revelata quo moriente lux antiqua est in sole velata (cf. M.L. Colish, *op. cit.*, 225ff).

(*Digression:* Augustine likes to attack astrology with the argument that the interval between the births of twins, whose lives can be totally different from each other, cannot be exactly determined, see *e.g. Conf.* 7,6,10, *De doct. christ.* 2,22,34, *De civ.* 5,2-3, cf. Ambrose, *Hexaem.* 4,14. In his *Augustin über Schöpfung, Ewigkeit und Zeit,* p 64 the author drew from this the conclusion that Augustine was unaware of the fact that astrologers did reckon with minutes and seconds and that to Augustine the most precise measurement of time was the hour (this despite the fact that Gregory of Nyssa tells us that the astrologers measure in minutes and seconds, see *Contra Fatum* (PG 45, 156B/C) (**XXV**). This statement as such is incorrect and needs further qualification. In *De div. quaest. LXXXIII* 45,2 Augustine says that the astrologers divide the Zodiac into three hundred and sixty degrees: In constellationibus autem notari partes quales trecentas sexaginta dicunt habere signiferum circulum. The movement of fifteen degrees is equal to one hour: motum autem caeli per unam horam fieri in quindecim partibus ut tanta mora quindecim partes oriantur quantum tenet una hora. This, of course, implies that one degree is equal to four minutes. Now each degree, says Augustine, is subdivided into sixty "minutes": Quae partes singulae sexaginta minutas habere dicuntur. This means that what is here called one minute is equal to what we call four seconds. Augustine then says that the astrologers do not find further subdivisions in the constellations of the stars on account of which they claim to predict the future: Minutas autem minutarum iam in constellationibus de quibus futura praedicere se dicunt, non inveniunt. This implies that Augustine looks for further subdivisions but says that they are not and cannot be applied to the movement of the Zodiac. Assuming that these "minutae minutarum" he is looking for are again sixty (but this is not said explicitly by Augustine) this smallest subdivision would be equal to one fifteenth of a second. Then Augustine says that, according to medical experts (who are more reliable than astrologers, cf. *De civ.* 5,2), the conception of twins does not extend into two minutae minutarum (which means that it takes place within what we call a fifteenth of a second): Conceptus autem geminorum quoniam uno concubio efficitur, attestantibus medicis quorum disciplina multo est certior atque manifestior tam parvo puncto temporis contigit ut in duas minutas minutarum non tendatur. Here Augustine assumes that, according to the astrologers, life began at the moment of conception,- this is what astrologers believe, according to Tertullian, *De anima* (cf. J.H. Waszink's edition p 335). It is possible that Augustine seriously believed that the conception of twins takes place within a fraction of what we call a second. But it is very difficult to understand his further claim that even the birth of twins takes place in such a way that the intervening time ought to be measured with minutae minutarum (so what we call fractions of seconds), which the astrologers do not use and cannot use in measuring the constellation of stars: Si autem ad genitales constellationes se tenere voluerint, ipsis geminis excluduntur qui plerumque ita post invicem funduntur ex utero, ut hoc temporis intervallum rursus ad minutas minutarum revertatur quas tractandas in constellationibus numquam accipiunt, nec possunt tractare. He does not, of course, claim that the birth of twins takes place within a minuta minutae (as does the conception of twins), but he claims that one needs a more precise measurement of time than a "minuta" (four seconds) in order to determine the exact interval between the births of twins. If he now says that a more precise measurement is needed he would still have to go on and subdivide that smaller unit again and so on ad infinitum. This is indeed what he argues elsewhere, *viz.*, in *Conf.* 11,15,20 (cf. *In Psalmos* 76,8; 38,7; *Sermo* 157,4): the present, the now, has no extension at all: si quid intellegitur temporis quod in nullas iam minutissimas momentorum partes dividi possit, id solum est quod praesens dicatur; quod tamen ita raptim a futuro in praeteritum transvolat, ut nulla morula extendatur, nam si extenditur, dividitur in praeteritum et futurum: praesens autem nullum habet spatium. So his argument against the astrologers runs as follows: Although they come forward with a fairly exact measurement of time (their smallest time unit being what we reckon to be four seconds), their measurement can never be exact enough, since a moment has no extension at all, whilst any unit of measurement presupposes some extension. Therefore the precise position of the stars cannot be determined at the births of twins, but then one could say that Augustine need not use the births of twins in order to prove this, since it applies to any birth. (In *De civ.* 5,5 he argues that the lives of twins whose conception took place at the same moment can be different and that lives of two people (not: twins) born at the same time are different. Here he assumes that two people can be born within the smallest unit of measurement known, but he does not discuss the exactness of this measurement). What he can prove in this context about the birth of twins is that a "minuta" of a degree (i.e. four seconds) is the most exact determination of the constellation of the stars, but that often the births of twins take place within this interval of time, so the same constellation points towards identical lives, whilst in reality the lives of twins can be very different. But it is very difficult to believe Augustine's claim that the births of twins often take place within such small intervals,- if this ever happens at all. It would be more logical to argue that no moment of birth can be exactly determined, since a moment lacks extension, and that accordingly no position of the stars corresponding with that moment can be determined exactly, and that therefore astrology is impossible. Augustine seems to offer a combination of two arguments: 1. It is impossible to explain on the basis of astrology the divergent lives of twins who are conceived and born within the smallest unit of time used by astrologers, since these divergent lives began within the same position of the stars as determined by astrologers. 2. It is impossible to determine ,with any unit of time, a moment and the corresponding position of the stars. The first argument depends on the truth of the statement that twins can be born within four seconds, the second argument holds true anyway.)

nec illud nos moveat, quod, cum ei nuntiaretur mater eius et fratres, respondit, *quae mihi mater aut qui fratres* et cetera? sed potius doceat ministerium nostrum, quo verbum Dei fratribus ministramus, parentes cum inpediunt, non eos debere cognosci. nam si propterea quisque putaverit non eum habuisse matrem in terris, quia dixit, *quae mihi mater?* cogatur necesse est et apostolos negare habuisse patres in terris, quoniam praecepit eis dicens: *nolite vobis patrem dicere in terris; unus est enim Pater vester, qui in caelis est.*

"Neither should that fact disturb us that when His mother was announced to Him, and His brothers, He answered, Who is my mother, who are my brothers?, (Matth. 12,48) and the rest, but let this rather teach us that ministry with which we offer the Word of God to our brethren that when our parents try to prevent us we should not recognize them as such. If anybody therefore believed that He did not have a mother on earth because He said, Who is my mother, he would necessarily have to deny that the Apostles had fathers on earth, because He commanded them saying, Do not call anybody your father on earth, for you have but one Father, who is in heaven (Matth. 23,9)."

To begin with, Augustine must have had difficulties with the statement that Christ had brothers, because of his belief in Mary's lasting virginity. He ignores this difficulty in the present context, but elsewhere he explains the text away by saying that in Scripture "brothers" can be relatives, see *In Ioann.* 10,2: Unde fratres Domino? Num enim Maria iterum peperit? absit. Inde coepit dignitas virginum ... Unde ergo fratres? Cognati Mariae fratres Domini, de quolibet gradu cognati. Unde probamus? Ex ipsa Scriptura. Then Augustine refers inter alia to the fact that Lot is called Abraham's brother. For further examples of this explanation see *Oeuvres de Saint Augustin,* 71, p 551 note 4. The same explanation of the meaning of "Who is my mother etc." with the help of *Matth.* 23,9 as analogy is given in *Contra Faustum* 7,2. This seemingly negative reference to Christ's relatives by Christ is obviously an old argument for those who deny Christ's birth: *Matth.* 12,48 was also used by the Marcionites (who scrapped the stories about Christ's birth from the gospel of Luke) as a proof that Christ had no mother, see Tertullian, *Adv. Marc.* 4,19,10ff and *De carne Christi* 7. Tertullian offers a similar explanation as Augustine (but without a reference to *Matth.* 23,9), see *De carne Christi 7,13:* Quale ergo erat si docens non tanti facere matrem aut patrem aut fratres, quanti dei verbum, ipse dei verbum adnuntiata matre et fraternitate desereret? Negavit itaque parentes quomodo docuit negandos: pro dei opere. Here, too, obedience to God's Word is regarded as more important than kinship.- In *Contra Adim.* 5,1 Augustine distinguishes between three ways of being a son: firstly secundum naturam, secondly secundum doctrinam and thirdly secundum imitationem,- in his reference to *Matth.* 23,9 Augustine in the present context presumably has in mind the second way as is clear from *Retract.* 1,22,3: secundum doctrinam sicut filios suos, quos evangelium docuit, Apostolus vocat (there he also criticizes himself for not having mentioned the"filius gehennae" and the "filius adoptivus").

(4,10) Nec nobis fidem istam minuat cogitatio muliebrium viscerum, ut propterea recusanda videatur talis Domini nostri generatio, quod eam sordidi sordidam putant, *quia* et *stultum Dei sapientius est hominibus* et *omnia munda mundis* verissime apostolus dicit.

"And let the thought about the internal organs of a woman not diminish this faith of ours, so that it would seem necessary to reject the idea of our Lord having been born in such a manner, for this reason that people who are themselves dirty therefore believe it to be dirty. Because most truly the Apostle not only says that God's stupidity is wiser than men (I Cor. 1,25), but also that everything is clean to those who are clean (Titus 1,15)."

The Manicheans believe the birth from a virgin's womb to be unworthy of God, since God would be polluted by it, see *Contra Faustum* 3,6: Quamvis nec sic quidem, inquit, (sc. Faustus) dignum erit, ex utero natum credere Deum, et Deum christianorum, see further *Contra Faustum* 23,10, *De Trin.* 12,5,5, *De agone christ.* 18,20. (A similar view is expressed by Marcion and his followers, see Tertullian, *Adv. Marc.* 3,11,7 where he exhorts Marcion: persequere et partus immunda et pudenda tormenta ... ut deo indigna confirmes, cf. *De carne Christi* 4. Tertullian does not deny that there is some shamefulness in procreation, conception and birth, but claims that Christ loved this very man who was carried, born and nourished in such shamefulness, see *De carne Christi* 4,3: Certe Christus dilexit hominem illum in immunditiis in utero coagulatum, illum per pudenda prolatum, illum per ludibria nutritum ... Amavit ergo cum homine etiam nativitatem, etiam carnem eius, cf. Hilary of Poitiers, *De Trin.* 2,24: Dei igitur imago invisibilis pudorem exordii humani non recusavit.- This evaluation of the internal organs (and of human body in general) seems to reflect certain Hellenistic feelings on this subject, feelings to which the Marcionites and the Manicheans showed more adherence than the orthodox, see *e.g.* Celsus' objection against the virgin birth, Origen, *Contra Celsum* 6,73 **(XXVI)** (cf. *Contra Celsum* 5,14) and what Augustine says of Porphyry, *De civ.* 10,28: contemnis enim eum (sc. Christum) propter corpus ex femina acceptum ... The Manicheans share this contempt of a birth from a woman, see the quotation given in *De agone christ.* 11,12: sunt autem stulti qui dicunt, Non poterat aliter Sapientia Dei homines liberare, nisi susciperet hominem, et nasceretur de femina et a peccatoribus omnia illa pateretur? (Cf. also the opposition against a birth of God as it is expressed by the Jew Trypho in Justin Martyr, *Dial.* 67-68). But Augustine makes it clear that some Platonists take a more positive view of the body, see *De civ.* 14,5: Non quidem Platonici sicut Manichaei desipiunt ut tamquam mali naturam terrena corpora detestentur, cum omnia elementa quibus iste mundus visibilis contrectabilisque compactus est, qualitatesque eorum Deo artifici tribuant (cf. on this subject A.H. Armstrong, Neoplatonic Valuations of Nature, Body and Intellect, *Augustinian Studies,* 1972, pp 35ff).- Augustine describes how before his conversion he held similar views on Christ's birth, see *Conf.* 5,10,20: talem itaque naturam eius nasci non posse de Maria virgine arbitrabar, nisi carni concerneretur. concerni autem et non inquinari non videbam quod mihi tale figurabam. metuebam itaque credere in carne natum, ne credere cogerer ex carne inquinatum.- When, according to the letter to Titus, to those who are clean everything is clean, it can also be said that to those who are unclean everything is unclean. In what follows Augustine formulates similarly that the conception and birth in themselves can be unclean, but that they do not pollute the Word. Here he seems to imply that these things in themselves can be unclean, but not to those who approach them with a clean mind, cf. *De Trin.* 12,5,5: fortassis quippe respondeatur haec in carnalibus habere offensionem, dum corporei conceptus partusque cogitantur. Quamquam et haec ipsa castissime cogitent, quibus mundis omnia munda sunt.

debent igitur intueri, qui hoc putant, solis huius radios, quem certe non tamquam creaturam Dei laudant, sed tamquam deum adorant, per cloacarum fetores et quaeque horribilia usquequaque diffundi et in his operari secundum suam naturam nec tamen inde aliqua contaminatione sordescere, cum visibilis lux visibilibus sordibus natura sit coniunctior: quanto minus igitur poterat pollui Verbum Dei non corporeum neque visibile de femineo corpore, ubi humanam carnem suscepit cum anima et spiritu, quibus intervenientibus habitat maiestas Verbi ab humani corporis fragilitate secretius!

"So those who hold this view ought to look at the rays of this sun which we can see, which they certainly do not praise as a creature of God but adore as God, that they are diffused everywhere through the foulness of the cloaca and whatever horrible things, and that they operate in these things according to their nature and yet do not become filthy through any pollution from there, whilst visible light is by nature closer to visible dirt: so how much less could the Word of God be polluted, which is neither corporeal nor visible, by a female body in

which it assumed human flesh with a soul and spirit through the intervention of which the majesty of the Word dwells further away from the fragility of a human body!"

Elsewhere Augustine describes the Manicheans' attitude to the sun in even more unfavourable terms: they adore the sun as God, although they know it to be a creature, see *Contra Faustum* 14,11: in sole autem et luna noverunt se servire creaturae, cf. 5,11; 20,8, *De Gen. contra Man.* 1,3,6. With a reference to *John* 8,12 (Ego sum Lux mundi) the Manicheans declare the sun to be Christ, see *In Ioann.* 34,2. So the Manicheans believe the sun which sends its rays down into filthy matter to be divine. Then it is inconsistent to oppose the incarnation of the Word because this would pollute the Word. For the argument that the rays of the sun are not polluted by the foulness of the cloaca, and even less the invisible Word by the visible body (an argument a maiori ad minus: it is a greater miracle if what is visible is not polluted by what is visible than when what is invisible is not polluted by what is visible), cf. *De agone christ.* 18,20: Nesciunt enim quodmodo substantia Dei administrans universam creaturam inquinari omnino non possit: tamen praedicant istum visibilem solem radios suos per omnes faeces et sordes corporum spargere, et eos mundos et sinceros ubique servare. Si ergo visibilia munda a visibilibus immundis contingi possunt, et non inquinari, quanto magis invisibilis et incommutabilis Veritas per spiritum animam et per animam corpus suscipiens, toto homine assumpto ab omnibus eum infirmitatibus nulla sui contaminatione liberavit. The latter part of this sentence also sheds light on what is said in the present context: the Word is separated from the body through the intervention of spirit and soul, which means that when the Word assumes manhood It observes the order of spirit-soul-body, which means that it is not subjected to the body, but governs the body through spirit and soul (cf. *infra,*141ff).- In *Sermo* 12,12,12 he also uses the sun as an analogy: as the sun illuminates the earth without being darkened by the earth, dries the water without being moistened, makes the ice melt without becoming cold, makes the mud hard without being softened, so the Word heals man without receiving any damage. The same analogy appears in Marius Victorinus, *De phys.* 19: cum solem, quem creaturam eius negare non possumus, sic immunda sordium sentinas paludium, putredines coeni, astringere videamus, ut cum vim suam per radios super haec emittat, non tamen polluatur. Quod si in his sordibus non polluitur creatura, multo minus in vivo sancto, quia corpore divinitas ipsa non polluitur. The formulation shows so much resemblance that Augustine's dependence seems clear, cf. J. Rivière, *op. cit.,* p 40 note 2. This argument seems to find its origin in Diogenes the Cynic, see Diogenes Laertius,

Vitae 6,63, it was very popular with Christian authors, see e.g. Origen, *Contra Celsum* 6,73, Athanasius, *De Inc. Verbi* 17, Eusebius, *Theophania* 3,19, Minucius Felix, *Oct.* 32,8,13, cf. H. Chadwick's translation of Origen, *Contra Celsum,* p 387 note 2, A. Olivar, Sol intaminatus, *Analecta Tarraconensia* (25) 1952, pp 209ff and (29) 1956, pp 22-23, and M. Aubineau, Le Thème du "Bourbier" dans la littérature grecque profane et chrétienne, *Recherches de science religieuse* (47) 1959, pp 210f.- Elsewhere Augustine accuses the Manicheans that whilst they oppose Christ's birth as unworthy of God, they nevertheless expose the soul, which in their view is part of God and of divine nature, to the bodies of men and animals, so they are far from being consistent, see *Contra Faustum* 3,6: Vos autem cum carnem Christi virginali utero committere horretis, ipsam divinitatem Dei, non tantum hominum, sed et canum porcorumque uteris commisistis ... et ipsam Dei partem, divinamque naturam in omnium hominum, ac bestiarum masculis seminibus et femineis uteris, in omnibus conceptibus ... ligari, opprimi, coinquinari, et nec totam postea liberari posse praedicatis.

unde manifestum est nullo modo potuisse Verbum Dei maculari humano corpore, quo nec ipsa anima humana maculata est. non enim cum regit corpus atque vivificat, sed cum eius bona mortalia concupiscit, de corpore anima maculatur.

"Hence it is clear that the Word could in no way have been polluted by the human body, by which not even the human soul itself has been polluted. For not when it governs and vivifies the body, but when it desires the mortal goods of the body, is the soul polluted by the body."

Here the argument is a minori ad maius: if the soul is not polluted by the body, a fortiori the Word which assumes the body via the soul is not polluted by the body. Not when the soul governs the body is the soul polluted, but only vice versa when the body governs the soul, and this happens when the body attracts the soul's *concupiscentia,* but this does not, of course, happen in Christ's incarnation, cf. further *infra*, 143f. In connection with the incarnation of the Word this implies that the Word only then would have been polluted by Mary's womb, if there had been any *concupiscentia* on the part of the Word (or the Holy Spirit) when Mary conceived, but this is, of course, emphatically denied by Augustine, see *Operis imperfecti contra Iulianum* 6,22: Fuit ergo in Mariae corpore carnalis materia, unde carnem sumpsit Christus: sed non in ea Christum carnalis concupiscentia seminavit. (Christians liked to attack the numerous love-affairs of Zeus, see e.g. Aristides, *Apol.* 9,6-7, Ps.-Justin, *Coh.* 2, Athenagoras, *Leg.* 20,3, Theophilus, *Ad Aut.* 1,9; 3,3; 3,8, Clement of Alexandria, *Protrept.* 2,27, Origen, *Contra Celsum* 1,17; 4,48, Eusebius, *Praep. Evang.* 2,4, Tertullian, *Apol.* 21,7f, Lactance, *Div. Inst.* 1,10, Athanasius, *Contra Gentes* 12, cf. J. Geffcken, *Zwei griechische Apologeten,* Leipzig/Berlin 1907, p 67).-So it is shown against the Manicheans that in becoming Man the unchangeable Word was not polluted by the body, because in the man Jesus the spirit was in complete control of the body, and whenever this happens no spirit (or soul) is polluted by the body. It is also shown that the Manicheans, whilst opposing the incarnation as unworthy of God, nevertheless come forward with a theory in which the soul, in their view a part of God, is subjected to and polluted by the body. So they have no right to oppose the incarnation.- (The argument about the cloaca which do not pollute the rays of the sun shows similarity with what Augustine tells us in *De ordine* 1,8,22f: Augustine's friend Licentius used to sing loudly a Psalm on the toilet, Monnica was offended by the place in which he did so and asked him to stop it. Licentius firstly asked jokingly: "But if an enemy had shut me up there, would God not hear my voice?" Later on he discussed the incident with Augustine, and then Augustine gave as his opinion that we can only turn to God and see His face if we turn away from the filth and dirtiness of our body and from the darkness into which our error has involved us: Nam illi cantico et locum ipsum quo illa offensa est et noctem congruere video. a quibus enim rebus putas nos orare ut convertamur ad Deum eiusque faciem videamus, nisi a quodam coeno corporis atque sordibus et item a tenebris quibus nos error involvit? In the same way he argues in the present context that Christ can only liberate man if He becomes Man in his totality, including the conception and birth.)

quodsi animae maculas illi vetare vellent, haec mendacia potius et sacrilegia formidarent.

"But if those wanted to avoid the pollution of the soul, they should rather fear these lies and sacrileges."

The Manicheans claim that they do not want to pollute the Word and the souls, but with their own theories they do exactly this. Similarly Augustine says of himself before his conversion when he was seeking the cause of evil, *Conf.* 7,5,7: Et quaerebam, unde malum, et male quaerebam et in ipsa inquisitione mea non videbam malum.

Chapter 5

Introduction: The death on the cross, the burial, and the resurrection of the Son are briefly explained. The discussion of this can be brief, since the cross and the burial are part of the Son's humiliation in the incarnation. This humiliation has already been discussed extensively in explaining Christ's birth.- For the death on the cross and the burial in a new tomb traditional reasons are given.

Text, Translation and Commentary:

(5,11) Sed parva erat pro nobis Domini nostri humilitas in nascendo; accessit etiam, ut mori pro mortalibus dignaretur. *humiliavit* enim *se, factus subditus usque mortem, mortem autem crucis,*

"But small was our Lord's humility on behalf of us in His birth; to this was added that He also regarded it worthy of Himself to die for mortal men. For He humiliated Himself and became obedient unto death, yea, the death of the cross (Phil. 2,8);"

Following the argument in *Phil.* 2,6ff Augustine says that the humility of death on the cross is a greater one than the one of His birth. (Tertullian puts it in a different way: Christ's birth is not more unworthy than His death, see *Adv. Marc.* 3,11,7: non erit indignior morte nativitas et cruce infantia ...) What is important to Augustine is that Christ's death was not caused by physical necessity, but that He wanted it to happen on behalf of men, see *e.g. En. in Psalmos* LXXXVII 3: Hos autem humanae infirmitatis affectus, sicut ipsam carnem infirmitatis humanae, ac mortem carnis humanae Dominus Jesus, non conditionis necessitate, sed miserationis voluntate suscepit, ut transfiguraret in se corpus suum, quod est Ecclesia, cui caput esse dignatus est (cf. Athanasius, *Contra Arianos* 3,57: **(XXVII)**,- to the Logos the opposite applies), see further *infra*, 85. (Pagans, of course, used to attack Christ's death on the cross as unworthy of God, and Christians defended it as one of Christ's saving acts, see *e.g.* Origen, *Contra Celsum* 4,14, Athanasius, *Vita Antonii* 74, *Contra Gentes* 1.)

ne quisquam nostrum, etiamsi mortem posset non timere, aliquod genus mortis, quod homines ignominiosissimum arbitrantur, horreret.

"lest anyone of us, even if he were able not to fear death, should nevertheless abhor some kind of death which men regard as most ignominious."

Not only the fact of Christ's death is to the benefit of men, but also the way in which Christ died, *viz.,* on the cross. This thought is expressed more clearly and extensively elsewhere, see *De div. quaest.* LXXXIII 25: Wisdom assumed Man in order to give an example of how to live. It is part of the correct way of life not to fear what ought not to be feared. This had to be shown by the death of that man whose form Wisdom assumed. Now there are men who, although they do not fear death itself, nevertheless fear some kind of death. But no kind of death ought to be feared by a man who lives in the right way. This had therefore to be shown by the death on the cross of that man whose form God's Wisdom assumed, for this is the most detestable and fearful kind of death: Sapientia Dei hominem ad exemplum, quo recte viveremus, suscepit. Pertinet autem ad vitam rectam ea quae non sunt metuenda non metuere. Mors autem metuenda non est. Oportuit ergo idipsum illius hominis quem Dei Sapientia suscepit morte monstrari. Sunt autem homines qui quamvis mortem ipsam non timeant, genus tamen aliquod ipsius mortis horrescunt. Nihilominus autem, ut ipsa mors metuenda non est, ita nullum genus mortis bene viventi homini metuendum est. Nihilominus igitur hoc quoque illius hominis cruce ostendendum fuit. Nihil enim erat inter omnia genera mortis illo genere exsecrabilius et formidolosius (for the Stoic background of this argument see G. Bardy's explanatory note in *Oeuvres de Saint Augustin,* 10, p 712). Amongst Christian writers, Athanasius, who discusses extensively various ways in which Christ might have died, comes quite near when he explains why Christ had to die on the cross: He endured on the cross the death inflicted by others, especially by enemies, death which they thought to be fearful, ignominious, and horrible, in order that when it had been destroyed He might be believed to be life and that the power of death be completely annihilated, see *De Inc. Verbi* 24 (**XXVIII**). Christ's death was not a necessity to Christ as death is to man (cf. *supra,* 75 on Christ and fate), but His death was a conscious act, see *In Ioann.* 31,6 (the proof is that Christ died at an earlier moment than those who were crucified with Him), 37,9: Noverat enim ipse quando deberet mori: intendit omnia quae praedicta sunt de illo, et exspectabat finiri omnia quae praedicta sunt ante eius passionem futura, ut cum impleta essent, tunc veniret et passio, dispositionis ordine, non fatali necessitate. (See on this subject more in general also B. Studer, Le Christ, notre justice, selon Saint Augustin, especially section C: La justice de Jésus qui a persévéré jusqu' à la mort, *Recherches augustiniennes* (15) 1980, pp 128ff, especially pp 136ff.)

credimus itaque in eum qui sub Pontio Pilato crucifixus est et sepultus. addendum enim erat iudicis nomen propter temporum cognitionem.

"So we believe in Him who was crucified under Pontius Pilate and buried. For the name of the judge had to be added in order to know the time at which it happened ."

In *Sermo* 214,7 Augustine gives two reasons why the name of Pontius Pilate is added: one is the reason given here which must underline the verity of these facts, the other reason is that hence Christ's humility should be commended even more: He who will come with such great power as the Judge of the living and the dead, suffered such great things under a human judge: Additur autem, sub Pontio Pilato, sive unde colligatur temporis veritas, sive unde Christi plus commendetur humilitas, quod sub homine iudice sit tanta perpessus qui iudex vivorum et mortuorum est cum potestate venturus (cf. on this subject P.C. Eichenseer, *op. cit.*, pp 279ff).

sepultura vero illa cum creditur, fit recordatio novi monumenti, quod resurrecturo ad vitae novitatem praeberet testimonium, sicut nascituro uterus virginalis. nam sicut in illo monumento nullus alius mortuus sepultus est nec ante nec postea, sic in illo utero nec ante nec postea quidquam mortale conceptum est.

"But when that burial is believed, the new tomb is mentioned in order to give testimony to Him who was to rise again to new life like the womb of the virgin to Him who was to be born. For as in that tomb no other dead man was buried either before or after, similarly in that womb neither before nor after was any mortal being conceived."

Augustine gives this traditional interpretation repeatedly, see *In Ioann.* 28,3; 120,5, *De Trin.* 4,5,9 (see M.-F. Berrouard, *Oeuvres de Saint Augustin,* 72, Paris 1977, p 573 note 24), cf. Origen, *Contra Celsum* 2,69 **(XXIX)**. Augustine amplifies this explanation by adding that nobody was buried in that tomb after Christ; this is caused by his belief in Mary's lasting virginity (see *supra*, 78).

(5,12) Credimus etiam illum tertio die resurrexisse a mortuis, primogenitum consecuturis fratribus, quos in adoptionem filiorum Dei vocavit, quos conparticipes et coheredes suos esse dignatus est.

"We also believe Him to have risen from the dead on the third day as the first born for His brethren who were to follow, whom He called to be adopted as God's sons, whom He regarded it worthy of Himself to be His coparticipants and co-heirs."

This applies to Christ as the "primogenitus" through His resurrection (to be distinguished from Christ as the "unigenitus" through His generation), see *supra*, 59f. Two quotations from the *De sermone domini in monte* (written a year after the *De fide et symbolo*) may illustrate what adoption means according to Augustine: By adoption men are called to eternal inheritance in order to be co-heirs of Christ. When men are reborn and become sons of God, they do not become so as strangers to God, but as His creatures. It was the same goodness which made men from nothing and which adopted men in order to enjoy with Him eternal life in accordance with their participation, see 1,23,78: apostolica disciplina adoptionem appellat qua in aeternam haereditatem vocamur, ut cohaeredes Christi esse possimus. Filii ergo efficimur regenaratione spirituali, et adoptamur in regnum Dei, non tamquam alieni, sed tamquam ab illo facti et creati: ut unum sit beneficium quo nos fecit esse per omnipotentiam suam, cum ante nihil essemus, alterum quo adoptavit, ut cum eo tamquam filii vita aeterna pro nostra participatione frueremur (on this participation see *infra*, 105). Two things are important in this context: God who adopts is the same as God who creates (a clearly anti-dualistic statement), and adoption reaches its final goal in eternal life. (Both motives are presupposed or briefly expressed in the present context of the *De fide et symbolo*).- Although these writings date from well before the Pelagian controversy, Augustine stresses also that the only cause of man's adoption by God is God's grace, see 2,4,16: Et quoniam quod vocamur ad aeternam haeriditatem ut simus Christi cohaeredes, et in adoptionem filiorum veniamus, non est meritorum nostrorum, sed gratiae Dei. But before the Pelagian controversy he could also express himself in terms which were less clear as far as the exclusive role of grace is concerned. In answering Porphyry's critical question of what happened to those many people who lived before Christ (see the quotation given from Porphyry in *Epist.* 102,8, cf. the similar criticism of the incarnation made by Celsus, Origen, *Contra Celsum* 4,7; 6,78) Augustine answered that the salvation of the true religion through which alone as the true one the true salvation is truly promised was never absent to anyone worthy of it, see *Epist.* 102,15 (written A.D. 408): Ita salus religionis huius, per quam solam veram salus vera veraciterque promittitur, nulli umquam defuit qui dignus fuit et cui defuit, dignus non fuit. In the *Retractationes* he feels obliged to qualify this statement by saying that he did not mean to say that this dignity of adoption was caused by human merits, but by God's call, see 2,31: non ita dixi tanquam ex meritis suis quisquam dignus fuerit, sed quemadmodum ait Apostolus: Non ex operibus, sed ex vocante dictum esse, Maior serviet minori, quam vocationem ad Dei propositum asserit pertinere. In the present context such an equivocal meaning is excluded: the words "quos participes et cohaeredes suos esse dignatus est" do not imply any inherent dignity to those who are called to Christ's heritage, the word "dignari" here means "to judge", "to declare worthy" (in this sense it is also used in 4,6 in connection with the incarnation and in 4,8 in connection with the assumption of a human body in the virgin's womb). Men are worthy of the sonship, because Christ judges, declares them to be worthy, and it is not the other way round, that because they are worthy of it Christ adopts them. (But see also *supra,* 43, where he says that God reveals Himself to those who are worthy of such revelation,- a statement which he will *not* criticize in the *Retractationes,* cf. *infra,* 165.)

Chapter 6

Introduction: This chapter briefly deals with the objection made by some Pagans that earthly bodies cannot ascend to heaven, so Christ cannot have ascended to heaven. (A lengthier exposition will be given in 10,24.) Augustine here declares that the spiritual body spoken of in I *Cor.* 15:44 does not mean a body which is transformed into spirit, but which is governed by the spirit so that it can dwell in heaven. No curious questions should be asked about how Christ's body is in heaven, it should only be believed that it is in heaven.

Text, Translation and Commentary:

(6,13) Credimus in caelum ascendisse, quem beatitudinis locum etiam nobis promisit, dicens: *erunt sicut angeli in caelis,* in illa civitate, *quae est mater omnium nostrum* Hierusalem aeterna in caelis.

"We believe Him to have ascended to heaven, which place of beatitude He also promised to us, saying, They will be like angels in heaven (Matth. 22,30), in that state which is the mother of all of us, the eternal Jerusalem in heaven, (Gal. 4,26)."

Blessedness (beatitudo) is closely connected with immortal life after the resurrection which is inaugurated by Christ and is also made credible through Christ's resurrection: if most men believe in Christs's resurrection (which seems incredible), then there is no reason for disbelief in the resurrection of the believers, see *De civ.* 22,5: Unum duorum incredibilium iam factum videmus, ut quod erat incredibile, crederet mundus: cur id quod reliquum est desperatur ut etiam hoc veniat. All men want to be happy, but not all know what happiness is, see *De Trin* 13,4,7: Cur ergo beatitudo amatur ab omnibus, nec tamen scitur ab omnibus? Both the Epicurean definition of happiness ("Beate vivere est voluptate corporis frui") and the Stoic one ("Beate vivere est virtute animi frui") are wrong, see *De Trin.* 13,4,7 (on the difference between the Epicureans and the Stoics see further *infra,* 146). The right love is the love of God, the Highest Good. In this life man needs faith for communion with God, see *De Trin.* 13,7,10. In immortal life there is complete blessedness, this immortality is given through the incarnation and resurrection of Christ, see *De Trin.* 13,9,12ff.- Similarly in the present context the blessedness of men is linked with Christ's resurrection and ascension. (See on this matter more in general R. Holte's great book, *Sagesse et Béatitude. Saint Augustin et le problème de la fin de l'homme dans la philosophie ancienne,* Paris 1962.) Eternal life in the risen body in heaven corresponds with the life of the gods as it is described by Apuleius and quoted by Augustine in *De civ.* 9,12: the gods differ from men in the highness of their place, in their eternal life and in the perfection of their nature: deos ab hominibus plurimum differentes, loci sublimitate, vitae perpetuitate, naturae perfectione (see Apuleius, *De deo Socratis* 4). Heaven is also referred to by Augustine as "sublimes sedes", see *De civ.* 11,32, and "supernae sedes", see *De civ.* 22,5.- On angelic life in heaven after the resurrection see *infra,* 150f.

solet autem quosdam offendere vel inpios gentiles vel haereticos, quod credamus adsumptum terrenum corpus in coelum. sed gentiles plerumque philosophorum argumentis nobiscum agere student, ut dicant terrenum aliquid in caelo esse non posse.

"Now some impious Gentiles or heretics are usually offended by the fact that we believe an earthly body to have been lifted up to heaven. As to the Gentiles, they very often strive to argue with us with the arguments of philosophers, so that they assert that something which is earthly cannot be in heaven."

(Cf. for the background of this argument: P. Courcelle, Propos antichrétiens rapportés par S. Augustin, *Recherches augustiniennes* (19), 1958, pp 149ff, H.I. Marrou, Le dogme de la résurrection des corps et la théologie des valeurs humains selon l'enseignement de S. Augustin, *Révue des Etudes augustiniennes* (12) 1966, pp 115ff, P.C. Eichenseer, *op. cit.,* pp 301ff, and *infra,* 153ff.) The argument referred to here is quoted in *De civ.* 13,18: Sed necesse est, inquiunt, ut terrena corpora naturale pondus vel in terra teneat vel cogat ad terram: et ideo in caelo esse non possint, cf. 22,4ff, 22,11 (on this matter see further *infra*. 153ff).- The heretics here referred to are again the Manicheans who, denying the incarnation, also deny the physical resurrection and ascension of Christ, see *De Haer.* 46: ... affirmant (sc. Manichaei) ... nec fuisse in carne vera, sed simulatam speciem carnis ludificandis humanis sensibus praebuisse, ubi non solum mortem, verum etiam resurrectionem similiter mentiretur,- cf. *De agone christ.* 25,27: Nec audiamus qui negant ipsum corpus secum levasse in caelum Dominum nostrum, and *Contra Adim.* 12,4f.

nostras enim Scripturas non noverunt nec sciunt quomodo dictum sit, *Seminatur corpus animale, surgit corpus spiritale.* Non enim ita dictum est quasi corpus vertatur in spiritum et spiritus fiat, quia et nunc corpus nostrum quod animale dicitur, non in animam versum est et anima factum; sed spiritale corpus intellegitur, quod ita spiritui subditum est, ut caelesti habitationi conveniat, omni fragilitate ac labe terrena in caelestem puritatem et stabilitatem mutata atque conversa.

"For they do not know our Scriptures, and they do not know what is meant by, An animate body is sown, a spiritual body rises, (I Cor. 15,44). This is not meant to signify that a body is changed into a spirit and becomes a spirit. For now, too, our body which is called animate was not changed into a soul and did not become a soul. But it is understood as a spiritual body, because it is subjected to the spirit in such a way that it is suitable for dwelling in heaven, since all earthly fragility and pollution have been changed and transformed into heavenly purity and stability."

In 10,24 he will provide expositions on the transformation of the risen body which could give the impression that the body is changed into spirit, an explanation which he will correct in the *Retractationes*, see *infra*, 152.- The stability of the risen body is here contrasted with the fragility of the mortal body, in *De civ.* 1,1 he speaks about the stability of the "sedes aeterna" in heaven, in *De civ.* 8,3 he refers to the Platonic ideas, causae, which live "stabiliter." So the stability of the heavenly body is its unchangeability which cannot be found in this world where everything is fluid and changeable (cf. on this idea, J.H. Waszink, *Studien zum Timaioskommentar des Calcidius I,* Leiden 1964, pp 72f, and E.P. Meijering, *Athanasius: Contra Gentes,* p 135). (This also implies that Augustine speaks about heaven and earth in a context in which he refutes the philosophers' objections against Christ's assumption in a way of which the philosophers would have approved. This is typical of his attitude towards Pagan philosophy.)- On the animate and spiritual body, and the purification of the fragile body see 10,23, *infra,* 141ff.

haec est inmutatio, de qua item dicit Apostolus: *Omnes resurgemus, sed non omnes inmutabimur.* Quam immutationem non in deterius, sed in melius fieri docet idem, cum dicit, *Et nos inmutabimur.*

"This is the change about which the Apostle speaks in the same way, We shall all rise, but not all change, (I Cor. 15,51). The same Apostle teaches that this change will not be for the worse but for the better when he says, And we shall be changed (I Cor. 15,52)."

In *Epist.* 205,14f he gives longer explanations of these texts (this letter was written much later, 420 A.D., but obviously provides the same interpretation): All shall rise, i.e. both the righteous and the unrighteous. But since a change for the better (i.e. to eternal blessedness) is envisaged not all shall be changed, but only the righteous shall change, the words "and we shall be changed" apply to them, the unrighteous shall also rise and be incorruptible, but for them it will not be a change for the better, but for the worse, since they will be eternally tormented: Ergo istam commutationem in melius sine dubitatione oportet intelligi, quia omnes et iusti et iniusti resurrecturi sunt: sed, sicut Dominus in evangelio loquitur, qui bene fecerunt in resurrectionem vitae, qui vero male egerunt in resurrectionem iudicii, iudicium appellans poenam sempiternam ... Proinde illi qui ad iudicium resurrecturi sunt non commutabuntur in illam incorruptelam, quae nec doloris corruptionem pati potest. Illa namque fidelium est atque sanctorum ... Quid sibi ergo vult ista distinctio, Et mortui resurgent incorrupti, et nos incommutabimur, nisi quia omnes incorrupti resurgent, sed ex his etiam iusti immutabuntur in illam incorruptelam cui omnino nulla possit nocere corruptio? Ac per hoc, qui in eam non commutabuntur, incorrupti quidem resurgent integritate membrorum, sed tamen corrumpendi dolore poenarum.- The Manicheans obviously claim that Paul is here envisaging a change for the worse and that this resurrection only takes place for the unrighteous, see *De agone christ.* 7,8: Et ne quisquam putet non iustis immutationem istam promitti, sed potius iniustis, et eam existimet esse poenalem (in that treatise Augustine attacks primarily the Manicheans). Later on Augustine will explain the change for the better in the sense that man will not be changed into the old "corpus animale" in which Adam was but into a "corpus spiritale" which, like the angels, can dwell in heaven, see *e.g. De Gen. a.l.* 6,24,35ff. (In early Christian literature two thoughts can be found on this subject: the state of blessedness restores the state of Adam before the Fall or it even transcends it, see A. von Harnack, *Lehrbuch der Dogmengeschichte II,* Tübingen 1909[4], pp 135f.)

sed ubi et quomodo sit in caelo corpus Dominicum, curiosissimum et supervacaneum est quaerere; tantummodo in caelo esse credendum est.

non enim est fragilitatis nostrae caelorum secreta discutere, sed est nostrae fidei de Dominici corporis dignitate sublimia et honesta sentire.

"But it is most curious and superfluous to ask where and how the body of the Lord is in heaven. One only has to believe that it is in heaven. For our fragility cannot investigate into the secrets of heaven but our faith must have high and honest feelings about the dignity of the Lord's body."

This is a somewhat surprising statement: In itself the present text aims at leading the believers further than mere faith in the facts as contained in the Symbol. It seems strange that all of a sudden the reader is asked not to go further than mere faith. The explanation of this apparent contradiction is that rational understanding of the faith is desirable and useful as long as it does not contradict but presupposes the facts as expressed in the Symbol. As soon as rational arguments contradict these facts (and cannot be easily refuted) they are a threat to faith and ought to be rejected as superfluous curiosity which does not want to subject itself to the sovereign will of God the Creator. As Augustine attributes Christ's resurrection and ascension to God's omnipotence (see *e.g. De Trin.* 13,14,18: et quid potentius quam resurgere a mortuis, et in caelum cum ipsa carne in qua est occisus ascendere) he will argue that God's omnipotence can make the believers' bodies dwell in heaven, see *infra,* 151. Rational arguments will be used by Augustine, but they must confirm faith and not contradict it. (This is the Christians' insistence on the priority of faith which infuriated Celsus, see Origen, *Contra Celsum* 1,9.) In more general terms this idea is expressed in *De div. quaest. LXXXIII* 68,2 where Augustine explains *Romans* 9,20 (O homo, tu quis es, qui respondeas Deo): the Apostle does not prohibit the putting of questions in general, but the doing so without love of God: Non enim apostolus hoc loco sanctos prohibuit a quaerendo, sed eos qui nondum sunt in charitate radicati et fundati, ut possint comprehendere cum omnibus sanctis latitudinem etc. This contrast between love and curious (striving after) knowledge goes back to *I Cor.* 8,1 (Scientia inflat, caritas autem aedificat), cf. Irenaeus, *Adv. Haer.* 2,39: Melius itaque est ... nihil omnino scientem quempiam ... credere Deo ... aut (=quam) per huiusmodi scientiam inflatos excidere a dilectione.

Chapter 7

Introduction: The "sitting at the right hand of God" should be interpreted correctly, which means that it should not be understood in a corporeal way, since in that case God would be like a man, and such a human conception of God must be rejected. This is most probably again aimed at the Manicheans. The "right hand" symbolizes the state of blessedness and Christ's power as a Judge, both now and at the last judgement.

Text, Translation and Commentary:

(**7,14**) Credimus etiam, quod sedet ad dexteram Patris. nec ideo tamen quasi humana forma circumscriptum esse Deum Patrem arbitrandum est, ut de illo cogitantibus dextrum aut sinistrum latus animo occurrat; aut idipsum, quod sedere Pater dicitur, flexis poplitibus fieri putandum est, ne in illud incidamus sacrilegium, in quo exsecratur apostolus eos, qui *commutaverunt gloriam incorruptibilis Dei in similitudinem corruptibilis hominis.*

"We also believe that He sits at the right hand of God. But one should not therefore think that God the Father is described as having a human form, so that to those who think about Him there occurs to the mind a right or left hand side, neither should the fact that it says of the Father that He sits be thought of as happening with bended knees, lest we fall into that sacrilege in which the Apostle curses those who have changed the glory of the incorruptible God into the likeness of a corruptible man (Rom. 1,23)."

It seems that Augustine here answers a charge made by the Manicheans against the Creed, for in *De agone christ.* 26,28 (a text which is largely directed against the Manicheans) he says that one should not listen to those who deny that Christ is at the right hand of God by saying that this implies that God has, as bodies have, a left hand and a right hand side: Nec eos audiamus, qui negant ad dexteram Patris sedere Filium. Dicunt enim: Numquid Deus Pater habet dextrum aut sinistrum sicut corpora? This is an old problem for Augustine. In the *Confessions* he tells us that ever since the time he began to hear about philosophy he avoided the idea that God should have a human form, and he was glad to discover that the Catholic faith did not imply this either, see 7,1: non te cogitabam, deus, in figura corporis humani, ex quo audire aliquid de sapientia coepi; semper hoc fugi et gaudebam me hoc repperisse in fide spiritalis matris nostrae, catholicae tuae. The Manicheans claim that because of *Gen.* 1,26 the Catholic Christians believe that God does have a human figure, but when Augustine heard Ambrose's sermons he found that this was not true, see *Conf.* 6,3,4: et eum (sc. Ambrosium) quidem in populo verbum veritatis tractantem omni die dominico audiebam, et magis magisque mihi confirmabatur omnes versutarum calumniarum nodos, quos illi deceptores nostri adversus divinos libros innectebant, posse dissolvi. ubi vero etiam conperi ad imaginem tuam hominem a te factum ab spiritalibus filiis tuis quos de matre catholica per gratiam regenerasti, non sic intelligi ut humani corporis forma determinatum crederent atque cogitarent ... gaudens erubui non me tot annos adversus catholicam fidem, sed contra carnalium cogitationum figmenta latrasse. (On the comparison between heretics and barking dogs see also Irenaeus, *Adv. Haer.* 2,11,1, Athanasius, *Contra Arianos* 2,1, Tertullian, *Adv. Marc.* 1,5, cf. *Th.W.N.T.* III, pp 1100ff and V. Pöschl/H. Gärtner/W. Heyke, *Bibliographie zur antiken Bildsprache,* Heidelberg 1964, s.v. "Hund".) As *Gen.* 1,26 could give simple believers the impression that God has a human figure, so the notion of the "sitting at the right hand of God" could do the same, but in both cases a spiritual understanding makes it clear that this is not so. (This spiritual interpretation is given by Ambrose, *Hexaem.* 3,7,32; 6,7,40ff, see P. Courcelle, *Recherches sur les Confessions de Saint Augustin,* pp 97ff, Ambrose refers the image of God not to the human body but to the human soul,- the traditional interpretation given by most early Christian writers, which is already found in Philo, *De opif. mundi* 69 (**XXX**)). Christians always denied (*e.g.* by explaining *Is.* 66,1) that the sitting of God on the throne takes place in a human way (with bended knees); such a human figure would also imply that God is confined in space, see *e.g.* Irenaeus, *Adv. Haer.* 4,4,3: primo quidem nesciunt quid sit coelum thronus et terra suppedaneum. nec enim sciunt quid sit Deus, sed putant eum more hominis sedere, et contineri, non autem continere, Tertullian, *Adv. Marc.* 2,25,2, Hilary of Poitiers, *De Trin.* 1,6, Augustine, *Epist.* 120,3,14, *Sermo* 53,12,13ff.- God a human figure would be a finite and corruptible being and therefore an idol,- this is the traditional objection against anthropomorphism, see *e.g.* Athanasius, *Contra Gentes* 22 (**XXXI**), cf. Aristides, *Apol.* 3,2, see further J. Geffcken, *Zwei griechische Apologeten*, p. 50.

tale enim simulacrum Deo nefas est christiano in templo collocare; multo magis in corde nefarium est, ubi vere est templum Dei, si a terrena cupiditate atque errore mundetur.

"For it is not permissible to place such an image to God in a Christian temple; much less permissible still is it to place it in the heart, where the temple of God truly is, if the heart is cleansed from earthly desire and error."

The Biblical background to this statement is *I Cor.* 3,16: Nescitis quia templum Dei estis, et Spiritus Dei habitat in vobis? and *II Cor.* 6,16: Qui autem consensus templo Dei cum idolis? Vos enim estis templum dei vivi, (texts to which Augustine refers *e.g.* in *Sermo* 23,7,7). In *De div. quaest.*

LXXXIII 20 Augustine stresses that if the temple is called the place of God, this is an incorrect use of the word,- God is not contained by the temple but is present in it. The best thing that can be thought of as such a temple is a clean heart: Et omnia igitur in ipso sunt, et locus non est. Locus tamen Dei abusive dicitur templum dei, non quod eo contineatur sed quod ei praesens est. Id autem nihil melius quam anima munda intelligitur, cf. *De Trin.* 7,3,6: Deus autem habitat in templo suo. Non enim tamquam minister habitat Spiritus Dei in templo Dei ... (see further the explanatory note given by G. Bardy in *Oeuvres de Saint Augustin,* 10, pp 709f). If man wants God to dwell in his heart, he should cleanse his heart, *Sermo* 261,5,5: Si ergo promitterem venturum me in domum tuam mundares eam: Deus in cor tuum venire vult, et piger es ei domum mundare? If somebody holds views about God which make God into an idol, his heart is not clean and is not a temple of God, for idols pollute temples. He accuses the Manicheans (who claim that the Catholic Christians believe in a god with a human figure) of polluting their hearts with such idols, see *Conf.* 7,2,3 where he says after quoting and refuting the Manichean doctrine of salvation (see the quotation given *supra,* 67f): sat erat ergo istuc adversus eos omni modo evomendos a pressura pectoris, quia non habebant qua exirent sine horribili sacrilegio cordis et linguae sentiendo de te ista et loquendo.

ad dexteram ergo intellegendum est sic dictum esse "in summa beatitudine", ubi iustitia, pax et gaudium est, sicut ad sinistram haedi constituuntur, id est in miseria, propter iniquitatis labores atque cruciatus.

"At the right hand" should therefore be taken to mean: "in highest blessedness", where there are justice, peace and joy: as the goats are placed at the left hand (Matth. 25,33) which is in misery because of the travail and torture of their iniquity."

The same explanation is given in *De agone christiano* 26,28, *Epist.* 120,15, *Sermo* 213,4,4; 214,8. So the right hand has no spatial meaning. If it had this would lead to the absurd consequence that the Father is at the left hand of Christ, see *Epist.* 120,3,15: non tamen ita putandum est sedere ad dexteram Patris ut ei Pater ad sinistram sedere videatur, (cf. Athanasius, *Contra Arianos* 1,61 (**XXXII**), this would mean that whilst Christ is in blessedness, the Father is in misery) and Ambrose, *De fide* 2,12,105: Ad dexteram quoque sedere nulla praelatio est, neque ad sinistram iniuria; divinitas enim gradus nescit, nec loco aliquo circumscribitur, nec temporibus definitur.

sedere ergo quod dicitur Deus, non membrorum positionem, sed iudiciariam significat potestatem, qua illa maiestas numquam caret, semper dignis digna tribuendo, quamvis in extremo iudicio multo manifestius inter homines unigeniti Filii Dei iudicis vivorum atque mortuorum claritas indubitata fulsura sit.

"So what is called the sitting of God does not indicate the position of limbs, but His judicial power, which that Majesty never lacks, by always giving worthy things to those who deserve them, although at the final judgement the splendour of the only- begotten Son of God who judges the living and the dead will shine, undoubted, much more clearly among men."

The same explanation of Christ's sitting is given by Ambrose, see *De fide* 3,13,106: illi (sc. angeli) stant, hic (sc. filius) sedet, ut verbo tamen usus utamur humani, hic iudicat, hi ministrant, cf. 5,14,174.- From His ascension until His second coming Christ is the Judge who lets evil happen to those who deserve it; the righteousness of this is not yet as apparent as it will be on the day of judgement. On this obscurity of God's judgement during this life see e.g. *Conf.* 7,6,10: tu enim, domine, iustissime moderator universitatis, consulentibus consultisque nescientibus occulto instinctu agis, ut, dum quisque consulit, hoc audiat, quod eum oportet audire occultis meritis animarum ex abysso iusti iudicii tui. cui non dicat homo: 'quid est hoc', 'ut quid hoc', non dicat, non dicat, homo est enim. (This is said in connection with the fact that sometimes predictions made by astrologers can prove to be correct: this shows God's distributive power, not the correctness of astrology.)

Chapter 8

Introduction: A brief discussion of the second coming of Jesus as the Judge of the living and the dead. The time of the second coming is called "most convenient", but this is not further explained. The second coming is part of the dispensation in time.

Text, Translation and Commentary:

(**8,15**) Credimus etiam inde venturum convenientissimo tempore et iudicaturum vivos et mortuos. sive istis nominibus iusti et peccatores significentur, sive quos tunc ante mortem in terris inventurus est, appellati sunt vivi, mortui vero, qui in eius adventu resurrecturi sunt,

"We also believe that He will come from there at the most convenient time and will judge the living and the dead. Whether these words refer to both the righteous and the sinners or whether those whom He will find on earth before their death are called the living, and the dead those who will rise at His coming,"

Here it is merely said that Christ's second coming will be at the most convenient time,- in a long discussion in *Epistula* 199 Augustine reveals his thoughts on this matter. Regarding the question of whether this moment will be sooner or later, Augustine says that he who believes the second coming to be near speaks desirably, but if he proves to be wrong, it can be a dangerous error, for it is hard to bear if it is not true. He who says that the Lord's coming is still far away, but nevertheless believes in, hopes for and loves His coming, if he is wrong regarding the fact that it is far away, errs happily: he will have a greater patience if it is true, and he will have a greater joy if it is not true. But it is better to say that one does not know when that moment will be, but to confess that the second coming will take place and to hope it to be soon and to be able to endure if it is late,- then one will not err, since (regarding the moment of the second coming) one neither affirms nor denies anything; see *Epist.* 199,13,53 where firstly three possibilities are listed: Unus dicit, Vigilemus et oremus, quia citius venturus est Dominus; alter dicit, Vigilemus et oremus quia brevis et incerta est ista vita, quamvis tardius venturus sit Dominus: tertius dicit, Vigilemus et oremus, quia et brevis et incerta est ista vita, et nescimus tempus quando venturus est Dominus. Then he says of these three attitudes, *Epist.* 199,13,54: Quapropter qui dicit Dominum citius esse venturum, optabilius loquitur, sed periculosius fallitur. Utinam ergo sit verum, quia erit molestum, si non erit verum! Qui autem dicit dominum tardius esse venturum, et tamen credit, sperat, amat eius adventum, profecto de tarditate eius etiamsi fallitur, feliciter fallitur, habebit enim maiorem patientiam, si hoc ita erit, maiorem laetitiam si non erat ... qui autem quid horum sit verum ignorare se confitetur, illud optat, hoc tolerat, in nullo eorum errat, quia nihil eorum aut affirmat aut negat.- The two explanations of "the living and the dead" are given in passing without further explanations, they are also given in *Ench.* 55. In *Sermo* 212,1 he explains this expression in the light of the two natures of Christ: He will come in the form of the servant in order to judge the living and the dead, in the form He wanted to share with the dead whilst being the Life of the living: In hac forma servi, venturus est iudicare vivos et mortuos: in qua particeps esse voluit mortuorum cum sit vita vivorum.

haec dispensatio temporalis non tantum est sicut illa generatio secundum Deum, sed etiam fuit et erit. nam fuit Dominus noster in terris et nunc est in caelo et erit in claritate iudex vivorum atque mortuorum. ita enim veniet, sicut ascendit, secundum auctoritatem, quae Apostolorum Actibus continetur. ex hac itaque temporali dispensatione loquitur in Apocalypsi, ubi scriptum est: *haec dicit qui est et qui fuit et qui venturus est.*

"this dispensation in time is not only like that generation from God, but also was and shall be. For our Lord was on earth, is now in Heaven, and shall be, in glory, the Judge of the living and the dead. For He shall come as He ascended, according to the (authority of) the Acts of the Apostles (1:11). With reference to the dispensation in time He says in the Book of Revelations (where it is written): This says He who is and who was and who shall be.(1:8)"

On the difference between the eternal generation which only knows the (eternal) now and the dispensation in time which is characterized by past, present and future see *supra,* 62f. The dispensation in time was firstly referred to in connection with the incarnation (which now belongs to the past); at the end of the expositions about the the Son, where the future is discussed, it is referred to again. It is important to Augustine that the second coming of Christ is an event in time and not in eternity, since as such it is one of the temporal actions committed by the eternal Son on behalf of temporal man in order to give eternity to man. The fact that Christ will come back as He ascended to heaven implies several things: It is an indication of the resurrection of the body, see *De civ.* 22,29,6: Et videbit omnis homo Christum Dei: qui utique in corpore visus est, et in corpore videbitur, quando vivos et mortuos iudicabit, 22,29,6: ... Deus nobis erit notus atque conspicuus ut ... videatur et per corpora in omni corpore quocumque fuerint spiritualis corporis oculi acie perveniente directi.- Christ will come back as He ascended and as such will be the Judge: He will come in the form of a man, which means He will judge in the form in which He was judged. The good will see Him in the form of that man in whom they believed, and the evil will see Him in the form of that man whom they held in contempt. But the evil will not see Him in the form of God, for only the clean of heart are blessed, because they will see God (*Matth.* 5,8), see *Sermo* 214,9: In ea forma iudicabit Christus, in qua iudicatus est ... Illa forma erit conspicua vivis et mortuis, bonis et malis ... Et illi videbunt in forma hominis in quem crediderunt, et illi quem contempserunt. Formam vero Dei ... impii non videbunt, sicut dicit ... Beati mundo corde, quoniam ipsi Deum videbunt. So man's reaction to the incarnation will be the criterium of his judgement on the Latter Day.- The fact that Christ will come back in the way He ascended is also interpreted in the sense that in heaven Christ is not subjected to time and does not grow older, see *In Ioann.* 21,13: Est quidem illud iam corpus dignum caelesti habitatione, non subiacens morti, non mutabile per aetates. Non enim sicut ad illam aetatem ab infantia creverat, sic ab aetate quae iuventus erat vergit ad senectutem: manet sicut ascendit, venturus ad eos quibus antequam veniat verbum suum voluit praedicari, see further *Oeuvres de Saint Augustin,* 72, pp 302f, note 100.-There is also a relation between the Latter Day and the last day of the life of the individual believer: Man's own last day of this life is the day on which he goes out of this life, as such he has to be judged on the Latter Day. In this sense the Latter Day comes to individual men at various times on the last day of their lives. If one has to wake lest one is unprepared for the Latter Day this means that one wakes lest one is unprepared for the last day of one's life, see *Epist.* 199,1,3: Tunc enim unicuique veniet dies ille, cum venerit ei dies ut talis hinc exeat qualis iudicandus est illo die. Ac per hoc vigilare debet omnis christianus, ne imparatum inveniat eum Domini adventus. Imparatum autem inveniet ille dies, quem imparatum invenerit suae vitae huius ultimus dies. For this reason man should regard every day of his life as his last day, *Sermo* 309,3,5: Ita sibi consulit, qui ex fide vivens et satagens ne ab extremo praeoccupetur die, extremum computat omnem diem, et sic deo placitos mores perducit usque ad extremum diem.- The authority of what is said about the second coming of Christ in the book of the Acts of the Apostles is elsewhere specified as an angelic testimony, see *Sermo* 214,9: ... secundum evidentissimum angelicum testimonium quod scriptum est in Actibus Apostolorum. The reason why an angelic testimony has special authority is that the angels see the "principales causae" of the world and therefore know all times for sure and cannot err, see *De civ.* 9,22: Et ideo certius etiam temporalia et mutabilia ista noverunt (sc. angeli), quia eorum principales causas in Verbo Dei conspiciunt, per quas factus est mundus ... numquam illi omnino falluntur, cf. *De civ.* 11,4,1, *De Trin.* 4,17,22, *De consensu evang.* 1,24,37.

IV

PART III
(9,16 - 9,20)

FAITH IN GOD THE HOLY SPIRIT AND EXPOSITIONS ON THE TRINITY

Chapter 9

Introduction: The Christian faith in God as Father, Son and Holy Spirit is clearly expressed. Father, Son and Spirit are neither (as the Sabellians teach) identical nor are they three separate gods. Each divine person is fully and essentially God. When Scripture speaks about "gods" in a positive way it means the believers who have become divine through participation in God (9,16). Two examples from the realm of creation are produced for the faith in the triune God: the well, river and water, and the root, trunk and branches. These are traditional images, and Augustine twists them for his own purpose, underlining that all images taken from the visible realm are in fact inadequate to express the Divine; the first image can be misunderstood in a Sabellian way, the second one in an Arian way. These images must show that it is not absurd to believe in the Father, Son and Holy Spirit as each being God without regarding them as three gods (9,17). The ecclesiastical tradition of the doctrine of the Trinity distinguishes between the Father who generates and the Son who is generated. There are in Scripture three groups of texts about the Son: the first group expresses the ontological equality of the Son with the Father, the second one stresses the inferiority of the Son to the Father in the state of the incarnation, the third one signifies that the eternal Son stems from the eternal Father and owes all He is to the Father (whilst the Father owes nothing He is to anybody). This must be understood in order to resist the heretics who try to show by means of texts from the second and the third group that the Son is ontologically inferior to the Father (9,18). Ecclesiastical writers before Augustine have written relatively little about the Holy Spirit, simply stating that the Son is generated whilst the Holy Spirit proceeds. This excludes the possibility that the Holy Spirit is the son of the Son, i.e. the grandson of the Father (which would in the view of orthodox theologians imply a kind of Pagan theogony). Some of them have said in addition to this that the Holy Spirit is the bond or the love between the

Father and the Son, and that He is the deity of Father and Son. This is an interpretation of the Trinity which Augustine, when seeking to understand the Creed, cautiously approves of and provides Scriptural confirmation for (9,19). The objection made that love is not a substance, but that it should be a substance if it is to be the Holy Spirit (thus producing three different substances in the Divine) is countered by the answer that the objectors think about God in corporeal terms and therefore cannot understand that love is a substance. In the divine substance there are no changeable *accidentia.* The argument reproduced about the Holy Spirit, *viz.,* that it is the deity, love, bond of Father and Son is not in itself faith, but an attempt to understand faith. Faith is faith in the triune God, it excludes tritheism, Arianism and Sabellianism. In order to have a vision of God's being the believer needs a pure heart (9,20).

Text, Translation and Commentary:

(9,16) Digesta itaque fideique commendata et divina generatione Domini nostri et humana dispensatione adiungitur confessioni nostrae ad perficiendam fidem, quae nobis de Deo est, Spiritus sanctus non minore natura quam Pater et Filius, sed, ut ita dicam, consubstantialis et coaeternus, quia ista trinitas unus est Deus:

"So having dealt with and committed to our faith both the divine generation of our Lord and His dispensation as man, the Holy Spirit is added to our confession in order to make perfect our faith about God, the Holy Spirit who is not of a minor nature than the Father and the Son, but as it were of the same substance and eternity, because that Trinity is one God:"

In the Introduction to the Symbol it was denied (see *supra,* 22) that the treatment of the Symbol was committed to the memory of the believers, now it says that the divine generation (which is more or less: the divine nature) and the human dispensation (which is more or less: the human nature) is committed to the faith. But not the expositions about these natures are committed to the faith, only the fact that Christ is both God and man,- this knowledge is indispensable in fighting off the heretics', especially the Manicheans', attack on the orthodox faith.- Since Christian faith is faith in Father, Son and Holy Spirit, faith is not perfect unless the Holy Spirit is mentioned. So the article about the Holy Spirit makes it possible to discuss the Holy Trinity (cf. J.Rivière, *op. cit.,* p 46, note 2). Augustine here expresses some hesitation about the word consubstantialis(*homooysios*),hence the words "ut ita dicam", this hesitation seems to be expressed because of the fact that the word consubstantialis is unusual

Latin. It appears that Augustine has no objections against the word *homooysios* which he usually translates with "unius et eiusdem substantiae". The Arians used to point out that this is an unbiblical term, see e.g. Athanasius, *De Syn.* 39, Augustine, *Contra sermonem Arianorum* 36,34: ... qui nos quasi macula novi nominis vocant Homousianos. Augustine obviously is not impressed by this objection. His hesitations about this word only concern the language used here, not the matter which is indicated by these words. In a similar way he expresses hesitations about using the word "deitas", see 9,19 (*infra*, 121) and about the word "essendi", see *De div. quaest. LXXXIII* 21: ... quia ut ita dicam essendi causa est (cf. what he says about the word "essentia", *De civ.* 12,2: ab eo quod est esse vocatur essentia: novo quidem nomine, quo usi veteres non sunt latini sermonis auctores, sed iam nostris temporibus usitato, ne deesset etiam linguae nostrae quod Graeci appellant oysian . Hoc enim verbum e verbo expressum est, ut diceretur essentia. Augustine gives the impression that with "essentia" he uses a fairly new word, but this is not the case, see the explanatory note given by G. Bardy in *Oeuvres de Saint Augustin, 37, La Cité de Dieu. Livres XI-XIV,* Paris 1959, pp 494-496) and *De div. quaest. LXXXIII* 23: ipsa est enim species prima, qua sunt, ut ita dicam, speciata. In defending the word *homooysios* Augustine points out that the Apostle (in *II Tim.* 2,16-17: Profanas verborum novitates evita: Multum enim proficiunt ad impietatem, et sermo eorum sicut cancer serpit), does not prohibit any new words, but only new words which have a Pagan meaning,- new words are allowed when they are in accordance with the Christian doctrine, the word *homooysios* is an example of such a word: it is a new word, but the matter it signifies is not new, see e.g. *In Ioann.* 97,4: non ait, verborum novitates, sed addidit, profanas. Sunt enim et doctrinae religionis congruentes novitates ... Adversus impietatem quoque Arianorum haereticorum novum nomen Patres homousion condiderunt: sed non rem novam tali nomine signaverunt. The word *homooysios* indicates the meaning of *John* 10,30: "I and the Father are one", cf. *Sermo* 139, *Epist.* 238,5, 29, *Contra Max.* 2,14,2ff. (Athanasius defends the use of this word with similar arguments, *De Syn.* 39).- Regarding the word co-eternal, Augustine concedes that in the human realm sons are not of the same age as their fathers, but then he produces the example of the fire which always generates splendour, in a similar way the Father generates the eternal Son, see *Sermo* 118,2: Non invenis in hominibus nisi minores filios, maiores patres, non invenis coaevos: sed do tibi ... splendorem coaevum igni patri suo. Generat enim ignis splendorem, sed numquam sine splendore. Cum ergo videas splendorem igni esse coaevum, permitte deum generare coaeternum. (Athanasius uses for the same reason the similar image of the sun and its light, see *Contra Arianos* 2,17; 3,32, *De Decr.* 12, whilst he is very cautious about images from human life, cf. E.P. Meijering, *God Being History. Studies in Patristic Philosophy,* Amsterdam/ Oxford/New York 1975, pp 81f.)

non ut idem sit Pater qui est Filius et Spiritus sanctus,

" not in the sense that the Father is the same as He who is the Son and the Holy Spirit,"

The Sabellian interpretation of the Trinity is here excluded, see 4,5, *supra,* 53.

sed ut Pater sit Pater, et Filius sit Filius, et Spiritus sanctus Spiritus sanctus, sed haec Trinitas unus Deus, sicut scriptum est: *audi, Israhel: Dominus Deus tuus, Deus unus est.* tamen si interrogemur de singulis et dicatur nobis, Deus est Pater? respondebimus: Deus. si quaeratur, utrum Deus sit Filius, hoc respondebimus. nec si fuerit de Spiritu sancto talis interrogatio, aliud eum esse debemus respondere quam deum,

"but in the sense that the Father is the Father, the Son is the Son and the Holy Spirit is the Holy Spirit, but this Trinity is one God, as it is written, Hear Israel, the Lord your God, the Lord is one (Deut. 6,4). Nevertheless if we were asked about the separate persons, and it is said to us:"Is the Father God?" we shall answer:"Yes, He is." If it is asked whether the Son is God we shall give this answer. Nor if such question is asked about the Holy Spirit, ought we to answer that He is anything else than God;"

What has been rejected so far is that there is no distinction between Father, Son and Holy Spirit at all, and the idea that the Son and the Holy Spirit are not fully God, i.e. both the Sabellian and the Arian position has been rejected. This is done with a reference to *Deut.* 6,4 (on Augustine's use of this text see A.M. la Bonnardière, *Biblia Augustiniana, A.T. Deuteronome,* Paris 1967, p 21 and pp 41f. We do not agree with la Bonnardière's view that this verse was not used by Augustine against the Arians before 418 A.D. and that in writings before that date it was only used against the Manicheans. Since in the *De fide et symbolo* the Arians are clearly attacked (see *supra,* 53ff) the verse seems to be used in the present context against the Arians as well.) But Augustine still wants to avoid the misunderstanding that faith in God the Father, Son and Holy Spirit means belief in three gods:

vehementer caventes sic accipere, quomodo de hominibus dictum est: *dii estis.* non enim sunt naturaliter dii, quicumque sunt facti atque conditi ex Patre per Filium dono Spiritus sancti. ipsa enim significatur Trinitas, cum apostolus dicit: *quoniam ex ipso et per ipsum et in ipso sunt omnia.*

"hereby we take the greatest care not to understand it in this way in which it is said about men, You are gods (Psalm 81,6). For not all those are by nature gods who have been made and created such by the Father through the Son through the gift of the Holy Spirit. For the Trinity itself is meant when the Apostle says, For from Him, through Him and in Him are all things (Rom. 11,36)."

There can be no plurality of gods and *Psalm* 81,6 (Dii estis) does not indicate such a plurality. Augustine interprets this text in the traditional way, in the sense that the "gods" are the believers who have received from God the gift of immortality, see e.g. Irenaeus, *Adv. Haer.* 3,6,1: His scilicet (dicit) qui adoptionis gratiam adepti sunt, per quam clamamus: Abba Pater, Tertullian, *Adv. Herm.* 5,2: nam et dei erimus, si meruerimus illi esse, de quibus praedicavit: Ego dixi, vos dii estis . . . sed ex gratia ipsius, non ex nostra proprietate, quia ipse est solus, qui deos faciat. On the difference between those who were made gods and God who is God by nature see also *De civ.* 14,13,2: Dii enim creati, non sua veritate, sed Dei veri participatione sunt dii, 22,30,3: Aliud est enim esse Deum aliud participem Dei (on *Rom.* 11,36 see further *infra,* 130f, cf. 157).

quamquam ergo de singulis interrogati respondeamus Deum esse, de quo quaeritur, sive Patrem sive Filium sive Spiritum sanctum, non tamen tres deos a nobis coli quisquam existimaverit.

"Although, when we are asked about each one separately, we reply that he who is referred to is God, whether Father, Son or Holy Spirit, let no one think that three gods are being worshipped by us."

All that has been said in this paragraph is an expression of faith and not yet an attempt to understand the contents of faith in a spiritual way; it is a rejection of the Sabellian heresy and of tritheism, and the affirmation of the belief in the Father, Son and Holy Spirit who are one God. This is the Christian faith, see 9,20, *infra,* 133. Elsewhere, in *De Trin.* 1,4,7 Augustine explicitly states that this is the Catholic faith which is expressed by all those ecclesiastical writers before him whose works he had read: Omnes quos legere potui, qui ante me scripserunt de Trinitate quae Deus est, divinorum librorum veterum et novorum catholici tractatores, hoc intenderunt secundum Scripturas docere, quod Pater et Filius et Spiritus sanctus unius eiusdemque substantiae inseparabili aequalitate divinam insinuent unitatem; ideoque non sint tres dii, sed unus Deus, quamvis Pater Filium genuerit, et ideo Filius non sit qui Pater est, Filiusque a Patre sit genitus, et ideo Pater non sit qui Filius est; Spiritusque sanctus nec Pater sit nec Filius, sed tantum Patris et Filii Spiritus, Patri et Filio etiam ipse coaequalis, et ad Trinitatem pertinens unitatem . . . Haec et mea fides est, quando haec est catholica fides (see further M. Mellet's and P.Th. Camelot's explanatory note in *Oeuvres de Saint Augustin, 15, La Trinité, Livres I-VIII,* Paris 1955, pp 566-568.)- In the now following paragraphs an attempt will be made to understand this faith.

(9,17) Nec mirum, quod haec de ineffabili natura dicuntur, cum in his etiam rebus, quas corporeis oculis cernimus et corporeo sensu diiudicamus, tale aliquid accidat.

"And it is not surprising that these things are said about the ineffable Nature, for also in these things which we see with our bodily eyes and about which we pass judgement with our bodily sense, something like that happens."

It seems strange to say that Father, Son and Holy Spirit are not three gods but one God (each person being fully divine), but this becomes somewhat less strange when we realize that even on the level of the physical realm which is clearly inferior to the Divine, something similar can happen. If it can be perceived in the realm of sense-perception it is not surprising if the human mind, illuminated by God, can say this about God's being. It is the argument *a minori ad maius:* if extraordinary things can be observed in the sensible world they certainly can be believed and be tried to be understood in the divine world with the help of God's revelation.

nam cum de fonte interrogati non possumus dicere, quod ipse sit fluvius, nec de fluvio interrogati possumus eum fontem vocare, rursus potionem, quae de fonte vel fluvio est, nec fluvium possumus appellare nec fontem, tamen in hac trinitate aquam nominamus et cum de singulis quaeritur, singillatim aquam respondemus. nam si quaero utrum aqua in fonte sit, respondetur aqua; et si quaeram utrum aqua sit in fluvio, nihil aliud respondetur, et in illa potione non poterit esse alia responsio; nec tamen eas tres aquas, sed unam dicimus.

"For when we are asked about a well we cannot say that it is the river itself, neither can we, when asked about the river, call it the well, and again a draught from the well or river we can call neither river nor well. Nevertheless in this trinity we use the word water, and when we are asked about them separately, we

answer that each of them is water. For if I ask whether water is in the well, the answer is affirmative, and if I asked whether water is in the river, the same answer is given, and with that draught the answer cannot be different: nevertheless we do not call them three waters but one water."

So well, river and draught correspond with Father, Son and Holy Spirit, the water corresponds with the one God these three are. This is a traditional image, see e.g. Tertullian, *Adv. Prax.* 8,5, Athanasius, *De sententia Dionysii* 24 (where Dionysius of Alexandria is quoted), Marius Victorinus, *Adversus Arium* 1,47,20ff, 4,31,31-53, *Hymnus* 3,30-32 (cf. J. Rivière, *op. cit.*, p 50 note 1, G.C. Stead, *Divine Substance,* pp 262ff). In Tertullian and Dionysius the image has an anti-Sabellian intention: as the well is the origin of the river, so the Father is the Origin of the Son. As such, the image has a subordinationist implication which Athanasius already explains away and which is absent from the present context of Augustine as well. The draught is added by Augustine, it can be compared with the Holy Spirit, i.e. God's gift which men can enjoy. The anti-Sabellian element expressed in subordinationist terms is absent here, in fact Augustine feels obliged to warn against a Sabellian interpretation of this image (which also means that he has some fears about Marius Victorinus' use of this image).

sane cavendum est, ne quisquam ineffabilem illius maiestatis substantiam sicut fontem istum visibilem atque corporeum vel fluvium vel potionem cogitet. In his enim aqua illa, quae nunc in fonte est, exit in fluvium nec in se manet; et cum de fluvio vel de fonte in potionem transit, non ibi permanet, unde sumitur. itaque fieri potest, ut eadem aqua nunc ad fontis appellationem pertineat, nunc ad fluvii, nunc ad potionis, cum in illa Trinitate dixerimus non posse fieri, ut Pater ipse aliquando sit Filius, aliquando Spiritus sanctus.

"We certainly have to take care lest anyone should think that the ineffable substance of that Majesty is like that of a visible and bodily well, river or draught. For in these, that water which is now in the well goes out into the river and does not remain in itself. And when it changes from river or well into a draught, it does not remain there from where it is taken. So it can happen that the same water refers at one moment to the name of well, at another moment to that of river, and again at another moment to that of draught, whilst in the Trinity we say that it cannot be that the Father himself is at one moment the Son and at another moment the Holy Spirit."

Augustine had said that in the act of the generation the Father remains unchangeably what He is (see *supra,* 47). But this is not the case in the image used here. The way in which this image is used here by Augustine can be applied to the Sabellian doctrine of the Trinity (at least as it is presented by the orthodox): the Father extends Himself into the Son, see e.g. Hilary of Poitiers, *De Trin.* 1,16; 2,4, *De Syn.* 45. For this reason Hilary in fact rejects the image of the well and the river (and the next image given by Augustine: the tree and the branches), see *De Trin.* 9,37; see also the reservations expressed by Gregoy Nazianzen, *Oratio* 31,15 (cf. F.C. Baur, *Die christliche Lehre von der Dreieinigkeit I,* pp 447f, J. Rivière, *op. cit.,* pp 50f, note 2).

sicut in arbore radix non est nisi radix nec robur est aliud quam robur nec ramos nisi ramos possumus dicere; non enim quod dicitur radix, potest dici et robur et rami; nec lignum, quod pertinet ad radicem, potest aliquo transitu nunc in radice esse, nunc in robore, nunc in ramis, sed tantummodo in radice, cum illa regula nominis maneat, ut radix lignum sit et robur lignum et rami lignum, nec tamen tria ligna dicantur, sed unum.

"As in a tree the root is only a root, the trunk is nothing but the trunk, and we can call the branches only branches, for what is called root cannot be called trunk and branches, neither can the wood which belongs to the root by some transition be at one moment in the root, at another in the trunk and again at another in the branches, but only in the root, although there remains this rule of language that the root is wood and the trunk is wood and the branches are wood, and that they are nevertheless not called three woods but one."

Again this is traditional language, see Tertullian, *Adv. Prax.* 8,5, Athanasius, *De sententia Dionysii* 10, and in this image the root equals the Father who is the Origin of the Son. (The ancients knew that branches are nourished by their roots, but they did not understand how the leaves themselves by photosynthesis help to maintain the whole plant, see G.C. Stead, *Divine Substance,* p 264).

aut si haec habent aliquam dissimilitudinem, ut possint non absurde tria ligna nominari, ut etiam tria ligna dici possunt propter firmitatis diversitatem,

"Or if there is some dissimilarity between these, so that it is not absurd to speak of three woods as one can also speak of three woods because of a difference in solidity,-"

In this case the image would suggest belief in three gods who each have their own being, and since the difference in the three types of wood is a difference in solidity this could also imply that there is a difference in the quality of the wood, which in the present context would come dangerously close to the Arian position about the Son who is inferior to the Father.- There seems to be no generally known theory about types of wood (*Th.l.l. VII* 2, p 1385 quotes the present sentence but provides no parallels),- Ambrose, *Hexaem.* 3,13,54 comes fairly close: ... quemadmodum in arboribus ipsis aetas aut senilis aut novella deprehenditur: iunioribus enim exiliores rami, antiquioribus validiora et nodosa sunt bracchia, illis folia levigata atque diffusa, istis contractiora et aspera. Here there is a reference to the difference of wood in the various periods of the life of a tree, a difference which shows similarity with the one Augustine detects in the various parts of the tree.

illud certe omnes concedunt, si ex uno fonte tria pocula inpleantur, posse dici tria pocula, tres autem aquas non posse dici, sed omnino unam aquam; quamquam de singulis poculis interrogatus in quolibet horum aquam esse respondeas, quamvis nullus hic transitus fiat, sicut de fonte in fluvium dicebamus.

"certainly all concede this that if three cups are filled from one well they can be called three cups but not three waters, but certainly one water. Although, if you were asked about each of these cups, you would answer that in each of these there is water, although here there can be no transition as we said happened from well into river."

The image of the well and the river could imply the Sabellian heresy, the image of the tree with root, trunk and branches could imply the Arian heresy (because that speaks of three different beings, although not of three gods); therefore both images ought to be viewed with the necessary caution. (But Augustine will make it clear in the next sentence that not even the image of the three cups of water is adequate.) In *De Trin.* 9,4,7 he produces an image which at first sight might seem very suitable: in one drink which is a mixture of wine, water and honey, these three substances together form one substance, they are three and each is in the whole, but they are each of a different substance (and this latter fact leaves the door open to Arianism): Num ergo sicut ex vino et aqua et melle una fit potio, et singula per totum sunt ... tale aliquid arbitrandum est esse simul haec tria, mentem, amorem, notitiam? Sed non unius substantiae sunt, aqua, vinum, et mel, quamvis ex eorum commixtione fiat una substantia potionis. Augustine prefers the well-known analogies taken from the realm of the human mind, but even these are inadequate: It is Augustine's view that all images taken from the realm of creation are inadequate to express the Creator's being, see e.g. *Sermo* 117,10,15: Ante omnia tamen servate hoc, quidquid de creatura potuimus colligere, aut sensu corporis, aut cogitatione animi, inenarribiliter transcendere Creatorem, cf. Tertullian, *Adv. Marc.* 1,4,2: De deo agitur, cuius hoc principaliter proprium est, nullius exempli capere comparationem, Hilary of Poitiers, *De Trin.* 1,19: Si qua vero nos de natura Dei et nativitate tractantes comparationum exempla adferemus, nemo ea esistimet absolutae in se rationis perfectionem continere. Comparatio enim terrenorum ad Deum nulla est, Athanasius, *De Decr.* 12 (**XXXIII**), cf. *Contra Arianos* 2,17 (on the word "*amydros*" as a technical term in Middle Platonism for "inadequate" see C. Andresen, *Logos und Nomos. Die Polemik des Kelsos wider das Christentum,* Berlin 1955, pp 338f, J. Daniélou. *Message évangélique et culture hellénistique aux IIe et IIIe siècles,* Tournai 1961, p 50, J.H. Waszink, Bemerkungen zu Justins Lehre vom Logos spermatikos, *Mullus, Festschrift für Theodor Klauser* (Jahrbuch für Antike und Christentum, Ergänzungsband 1, Münster i.W. 1964, p 386; on Plotinus as an acute critic of his own images see A.H. Armstrong, Plotinus, *The Cambridge History etc.,* pp 220,240).

sed haec non propter illius divinae naturae similitudinem, sed propter visibilium etiam unitatem corporalia exempla data sunt, ut intellegeretur fieri posse, ut aliqua tria non tantum singillatim, sed etiam simul singulare nomen obtineant, ne quisquam miretur et absurdum putet, quod Deum dicimus Patrem, Deum Filium, Deum Spiritum sanctum nec tamen tres deos in ista Trinitate, sed unum Deum unamque substantiam.

"However, these bodily images were not given on account of any resemblance to the divine nature, but because they express also a unity of visible things, in order that it might be understood that it is possible for a certain trinity to obtain, not only each separately, but also together, one single name, lest anybody be surprised and believe it to be absurd that we call the Father God, the Son God and the Holy Spirit God, and nevertheless do not speak of three gods in this Trinity, but of one God and one substance."

The implication of this is that although the mystery of the Trinity transcends human understanding, it does not contradict human understanding since human understanding can perceive a feeble image of it in the realm of sense-perception. So the attempt to understand this mystery is not absurd, or in other words: revelation is not confirmed by reason (and does not need such a confirmation), but it is not in conflict with reason either.

(9,18) Et de Patre quidem ac Filio multis libris disseruerunt docti et spiritales viri, quibus, quantum homines hominibus poterant, et quemadmodum non unus esset Pater et Filius, sed unum essent, et quid proprie Pater esset et quid Filius, insinuare conati sunt: quod ille genitor, ille genitus; ille non de Filio, ille de Patre; ille huius principium, unde et *caput Christi* dicitur, quamvis et Christus *principium,* sed non Patris; hic vero illius *imago,* quamvis nulla ex parte dissimilis et omnino indifferenter aequalis.

"Now with the Father and the Son, learned and spiritual men have dealt in many books in which they have tried to make us know -in so far as they could do this as men to men- how the Father and the Son are not one person but are a unity, and what are the properties of the Father and what of the Son, that the Father generates and the Son is generated, that the Father is not from the Son, but the Son from the Father, that the Father is the Beginning of the Son, wherefore He is also called the head of Christ (I Cor. 11,3), although Christ, too, is a Beginning (John 8,25), but not of the Father; but the Son is the Image of the Father, although He is in no respect dissimilar and is totally, without difference, equal."

As was usual amongst both early Christian and Pagan authors, Augustine is rather vague in naming his sources, cf. B. Altaner, Augustins Methode der Quellenforschung. Sein Studium der Väterliteratur, *Kleine Patristische Schriften* (TU 83), Berlin 1967, p 165. Since what follows is fairly generally taught, no definite conclusions regarding his sources can be drawn from what follows.- The reason why those ecclesiastical writers can, as human beings, only partly explain the Trinity to other men was given in the previous paragraph: in the end it transcends human understanding.- On the unity of the Father and the Son (quemadmodum non unus esset Pater et Filius sed unum essent) see e.g. *De Trin.* 7,6,12: Et unum dixit, et sumus: unum secundum essentiam quod idem Deus; sumus secundum relativum, quod ille Pater, hic Filius, see further Tertullian, *Adv. Prax.* 22,11: Si enim dixisset: "unus sumus" potuisset adiuvare sententiam illorum, unus enim singularis numeri significatio videtur . . . Unum sumus, dicens, ego et Pater, ostendit duos esse quos aequat et iungit, Hilary of Poitiers, *De Trin.* 1,17: . . . hanc evangelici ac profetici praeconii rationem in confessione Dei Patris et Dei Filii adferemus, ut unum in fide nostra sint uterque non unus . . ., 2,23, Ambrose, *De Spiritu sancto* 3, 16, 117: . . . haereticam iugulat saevitatem Sabellianorum, quia unum dixit sumus, non unus sumus: Arianorum, quia, ego et Pater, non, Pater et ego, dixit.- On the "proprietas" of the Father to be the "genitor" and of the Son to be "genitus", see e.g. Ambrose, *De fide* 1,2,16: Non enim Pater ipse qui Filius: sed inter Patrem et Filium generationis expressa distinctio est, Hilary of Poitiers, *De Trin.* 4,33: Est ergo unus ab uno. Neque praeter innascibilem Deum innascibilis Deus alius est, neque praeter unigenitum Deum unigenitus Deus quisquam est. Uterque itaque unus et solus est, proprietate videlicet in unoquoque innascibilitatis et originis.- Augustine also calls the Father "ingenitus" which is a translation of "*agennètos*" and not of "*agenètos*"). The Arians call the Father "*agenètos*", the orthodox called Him (as the Father of the Son) "*agennètos*". As the Arians objected to the orthodox doctrine that the word "*homooysios*" is unbiblical, the orthodox objected to the Arians that the word "*agenètos*" is unbiblical, see e.g. Athanasius, *Contra Arianos* 1, 30ff, *De Decr.* 28ff (cf. G.-L. Prestige, *Dieu dans la pensée patristique,* Paris 1955 (transl.), pp 54ff). This explains why Augustine concedes that "ingenitus" (to which, although it is a translation of *agennètos* and not of *agenètos* can be made the same objection as to *homooysios* and *agennètos*, that it is not a Biblical term, but insists that it has become a common term to those who deal with such a great thing as the Trinity, see *De Trin.* 15,26,47: Pater enim solus non est de alio, ideo solus appellatur ingenitus non quidem in Scripturis, sed in consuetudine disputantium, et de re tanta sermonem qualem valuerint proferentium.- The Father is the Origin of the Son: This is an important tenet in both Greek and Latin fathers. It can be said to express the clear subordination of the Son to the Father, in this sense it is used by Origen. Origen calls the Father the origin and the well of the Son and the Holy Spirit, see *De Princ.* 2,2,1. This implies *inter alia* that the Son is not "*aytotheos*" and "*aytoagathos*", but that the Son's divinity and goodness are derived from the Father, in this sense He is "*agathos*" and not "*aytoagathos*", "*theos*" and not "*aytotheos*", see *In Ioann.* 2,2, *De Princ.* 1,2,13, *In Matth.* 15,10. A consequence is that, according to Origen, prayer should be directed to the Father and not to the Son, see *De orat.* 15,4.- Tertullian stresses the subordination of the Son to the Father in fighting Sabellianism, see e.g. *Adv. Prax.* 8,5: omnis origo parens est et omne quod ex origine profertur progenies est . . ., 9,2: Pater enim tota substantia est, Filius vero derivatio totius et portio sicut ipse profitetur: Quia Pater maior me est . . . Sic et Pater alius a Filio dum Filio maior, dum alius qui generat, alius qui generatur. Judged by later criteria Tertullian's views cannot, of course, be called orthodox, since he stresses in his opposition against Sabellianism the subordination of the Son too much. (Augustine, however, does not criticize him in this respect.) But this tenet can also be used in a mildly subordinationist context, when it is said (in line with Nicene orthodoxy) that the Father and the Son are of the same substance, but also that the Father is as the well and as the cause of the Son more than the Son. This doctrine appears in the Cappadocians and in Hilary of Poitiers, see e.g. Gregory Nazianzen, *Oratio theologica* 3,15; 3,3; 4,7, *Oratio* 20,7; 20,10; 25,25; 40,43 (see further A. von Harnack, *Lehrbuch der Dogmengeschichte II,* pp 266ff), Hilary of Poitiers, *De Trin.* 9,56: Maior itaque Pater est dum Pater est, sed Filius dum Filius est, minor non est. Nativitas Filii Patrem constituit maiorem. Minorem vero Filium esse nativitatis natura non patitur, cf. 3,12; 3,15. Augustine incorporates this latter doctrine into his own exegesis of Biblical texts (see *infra,* 117).- In Athanasius the doctrine of the Father as the origin of the Son functions in a different way: he wants to refute with this idea the possibility that there is any divine being which is not the eternal Father of the eternal Son, so here an originally philosophical tenet, *viz.,* that a cause is more than what is caused (see *supra,* 44) functions in an anti-philosophical way (for details see E.P. Meijering, *God Being History,* pp 89ff).- On the Son as the Image of the Father which does not allow any difference between them (a distinction is allowed, but not a difference which makes the Son inferior to the Father), cf. Hilary of Poitiers, *De Trin.* 7,37: Filius autem Patri non secundum haec (sc. inanima picta vel sculpta) imago est, quia viventis vivens imago est; et ex eo natus non habet naturae diversitatem, et in nullo diversus tenet naturae eius ex qua non diversus est potestatem.- The Son is Himself the Beginning, though not of the Father, but of creation: this is a reference to *John* 8,25 (Principium quod et loquor vobis) and to *Gen.* 1,1, see e.g. *De Trin.* 1,12,24: Secundum formam enim Dei, principium est quod et loquitur nobis, in quo principio fecit Deus caelum et terram, and *De Gen. a.l.* 1,5,10, it was fairly common Patristic exegesis to interpret *John* 8,25 and *Gen.* 1,1 in this way, see e.g. Ambrose, *De fide* 3,7,49, *Hexaem.* 1,4,15. (Jerome opposes this interpretation "ad litteram" but approves of it "ad sensum" and says that a majority adhere to it, see *Liber Hebraicarum quaestionum in Genesin,* PL 23, 937: Plerique existimant . . . in Hebraeo haberi: "In Filio fecit caelum et terram", quod falsum esse ipsius rei veritas comprobat.)

tractantur haec latius ab eis, qui non tam breviter quam nos totius christianae fidei professionem volunt explicare.

"These things are treated more broadly by those who want to explain the profession of the whole Christian faith not so briefly as we do."

Again it is not clear whom exactly Augustine has in mind, one may think of Ambrose's *De fide* and Hilary's *De Trinitate.*

itaque, in quantum Filius est, de Patre accepit, ut sit, cum ille de Filio id non acceperit; et in quantum hominem mutabilem, scilicet creaturam in melius commutandam, ineffabili misericordia temporali dispensatione suscepit, multa de illo in Scripturis inveniuntur ita dicta, ut inpias haereticorum mentes prius volentes docere quam nosse in errorem miserint, ut putarent eum non aequalem Patri, nec eiusdem esse substantiae, qualia sunt illa: quoniam *Pater maior me est,* et: *caput mulieris vir, caput viri Christus, caput autem Christi Deus,* et: *tunc ipse subiectus erit ei, qui illi subiecit omnia*, et: *vado ad Deum meum et Deum vestrum*, et nonnulla huiusmodi:

"Therefore, in so far as He is the Son, He received His being from the Father, whilst the Father did not receive His from the Son, and in so far as He assumed manhood, viz., a changeable creature which had to be changed for the better, with ineffable mercy in the dispensation of time, many things are found to have been said in Scripture in such a way that they have led the impious minds of the heretics, who want to teach before they know, into error, so that they believe that He is not equal to the Father nor of the same substance, e.g. those words, Because the Father is more than I (John 14,28), Man is the head of woman, Christ is the head of man, but the head of Christ is God (I Cor. 11,3), Then He will Himself be subjected to Him who subjected all things to Him (I Cor. 15,28), I go to My God and your God (John 20,17), and several words of this kind."

Therefore texts which must either be explained by the fact that the Son finds His (eternal) origin in the Father or by the fact that they refer to Christ's state in the incarnation are taken by the heretics as a proof that the Son is not fully God and not of the same substance as the Father.- The heretics want to teach before they know. This is one of Augustine's major objections against the Manicheans: whilst they promise reason they in fact just make claims which they cannot prove. But there is also another thought behind this: Since one receives one's knowledge and understanding from God (see *supra,* 19ff), this means that the heretics give explanations of these texts on their own authority instead of following the ecclesiastical writers, cf. *En. in Psalmos* 118, *Sermo* 17,3: . . . Deus quando vult docere prius dat intellectum, sine quo ea quae ad divinam doctrinam pertinent, homo non potest discere, cf. what Hilary of Poitiers says of the Arians, *De Trin.* 10,2: . . . neque doceri se desiderantes, sed doctores ad id quod desiderant congregantes . . . Qui enim doctrinae profectus est placita magis quam docenda conquirere. Aut quae doctrinae religio est, non docenda desiderare, sed desideratis coacervare doctrinam?- On *John* 14,28 and the Arian use of it see *Contra Max.* 2,25; 1,5. Augustine relates this text to the state of incarnation, see *Ench.* 35: Quocirca in quantum deus eset, ipse et Pater unum sunt, in quantum autem homo est, Pater maior est illo, cf. *De Trin.* 1,8,15; 1,11,22. (Hilary of Poitiers explains the text in the first one of the two ways suggested by Augustine in connection with such texts, *viz.,* as a reference to the Son who finds His origin in the Father, see *De Trin.* 9,54ff and the quotation given *supra,* 113).- On the Arians' use of *I Cor.* 11,3 see *Coll. cum Max.* 1,10 (cf. Ambrose, *De fide* 4,3,27ff). Augustine's reply to this Arian interpretation is: the human mind is, so to speak, the head of human substance, since man with his mind is man, therefore it can be said with greater justification that the Word which is God with the Father is the head of Christ (as man and mediator), although Christ cannot be understood without the Word which became flesh, see *De Trin.* 6,9,10: Si mentem recte dicimus principale hominis, id est, tamquam caput humanae substantiae, cum ipse homo cum mente sit homo; cur non multo congruentius verbum cum Patre quod simul Deus est, caput est Christi, quamvis Christus homo nisi cum Verbo quod caro factum est intelligi non possit. So in His divinity and as the second Person of the Trinity, Christ is the head of Christ as man and in this respect the Father, too, is the head of Christ as man, see *ibid.:* Sed rursus si Deus non nisi omnia simul tria, quomodo caput Christi Deus, id est, caput Christi Trinitas, cum in Trinitate sit Christus ut sit Trinitas? Ambrose provides a similar interpretation, see *De fide* 4,3,32: Est ergo caput Christi Deus, ubi servi, hoc est hominis, non Dei forma tractatur.- On the Arian use of *I Cor.* 15,28 see *Contra Max.* 1,8. Augustine relates this text to the state of the incarnation and not to the Son as the eternal Son of the eternal Father, see *De div. quaest. LXXXIII* 69,2, cf.. *De Trin.* 1,8,15ff and Hilary of Poitiers, *De Trin.* 11,40ff, Ambrose, *De fide* 5,13,164ff, especially 5,14,175: Ergo sicut in illa cruce non divinitatis plenitudo, sed nostra fragilitas erat subiecta: ita etiam postea subiectus erit Filius Patri, in nostrae utique participatione naturae. On the Arian use of *John* 20,17 see *Coll. cum Max.* 16. Augustine relates the text to the state of incarnation, see *Contra Maximin.* 2,16,1, cf. Hilary of Poitiers, *De Trin.* 11,8ff, especially 11,14: Manens igitur in forma servi qui manebat ante in Dei forma, homo Jesus Christus locutus est: Ascendo . . .- On further texts which the Arians use see A. von Harnack, *Lehrbuch der Dogmengeschichte II,* p 203.

quae omnia posita sunt, non ut naturae atque substantiae inaequalitatem significent, ne falsa sint illa: *ego et Pater unum sumus,* et: *qui me vidit, vidit et Patrem meum,* et: *Deus erat Verbum*- non enim factus deus, cum omnia per ipsum facta sint- et: *non rapinam arbitratus est esse aequalis Deo,* et cetera talia:

"All these have been written down, not in order to indicate an inequality of nature and substance, in case these words are fallacious, I and the Father are one (John 10,30), Who has seen Me has also seen My Father (John 14,9), The Word was God (John 1,3), for He has not been made God, since all things have been made through Him, and, He did not regard being equal to God as a robbery (Phil. 2,6)), and other words of this kind;"

The texts produced here have belonged to the stock quotations in the defence of the divinity of the Son ever since Alexander of Alexandria, see A. von Harnack, *Lehrbuch der Dogmengeschichte II,* p 205. We give a few characteristic quotations from Augustine in connection with these texts; 1) *John* 10,30: The Jews had a better understanding of this text than the Arians, since because of these words they wanted to stone the Son, see *In Ioann.* 48,8: Ecce Iudaei intellexerunt quod non intelligunt Ariani. Ideo enim irati sunt, quoniam senserunt non posse dici, Ego et Pater unum sumus, nisi ubi aequalitas est Patris et Filii, cf. *In Ioann.* 36,9 and Hilary of Poitiers, *De Trin.* 7,22f. The Arians interpret the unity of Father and Son as a unity of will, not of essence, see e.g. Athanasius, *Contra Arianos* 3,17, Ambrose, *De fide* 4,3,33, they seek support for this view from *John* 17,22: Ut omnes unum sint, sicut tu, Pater in me, et ego in te, ut et ipsi in nobis unum sint, this is the reason why Augustine stresses that Father and Son are in each other in a way which differs from the way in which we are in them, see *In Ioann.* 110,1: Ac per hoc et cum in nobis sunt Pater et Filius, vel etiam Spiritus sanctus, non debemus eos putare naturae unius esse nobiscum. Sic itaque sunt in nobis, vel nos in illis ut illa unum sint in natura sua, nos unum in nostra. Sunt quippe ipsi in nobis, tamquam Deus in templo suo: sumus autem nos in illis, tamquam creatura in Creatore suo. 2) *John* 14,9: (The addition of "meum" after "Patrem" can either have been caused by *John* 14,7 (Si cognovistis me et Patrem meum cognovistis) or by *John* 20,17 quoted earlier in the present chapter.) Philippus wanted to be shown the Father, whom he believed to be better than the Son, and in believing this he did not know the Son. Christ's answer is meant as a correction which must show that the Father and the Son are similar and cannot be separated, see *In Ioann.* 70,3: Tamquam enim melior esset Pater quam Filius, ita Philippus Patrem nosse cupiebat: et ideo nec Filium sciebat quo melius esse aliquid credebat. Ad hunc sensum corrigendum dictum est, Qui vidit . . . Video quomodo tu dicas: non alterum quaeris videre similem, sed illum putas esse meliorem . . . Cur in similibus distantiam cupis cernere? cur inseparabiles separatim desideras nosse?, cf.

Hilary of Poitiers who says after quoting this text, *De Trin.* 9,52: Quae utique differentiam non habent ex aequalitate naturae. 3) *John* 1,3: This text proves that the Arian doctrine about Christ is false, see the quotation given *supra,* 51. 4) On Phil. 2,6 see *supra,* 58.

sed illa posita sunt partim propter administrationem suscepti hominis, qua dicitur: *semet ipsum exinanivit-* non quia mutata est illa Sapientia, cum sit omnino incommutabilis, sed quia tam humiliter hominibus innotescere voluit-

"but these words have been written down partly because of the dispensation of assumed manhood, of which it says, He has emptied Himself, (Phil. 2,8), not because Wisdom was changed, since It is completely unchangeable, but because He wanted to become known to men in such humility,"

On the Wisdom which remains unchanged in the act of the incarnation and the anti-Manichean implication of this tenet in Augustine see *supra,* 42, on the revelation in humility see *supra*, 58f.

partim ergo propter hanc administrationem illa ita scripta sunt, de quibus haeretici calumniantur, partim propterea, quia Filius Patri debet, quod est, hoc etiam debens utique Patri, quod eidem Patri aequalis aut par est; Pater autem nulli debet quidquid est.

"therefore, these things on which the heretics base their slander were written in this manner partly because of this dispensation, partly because the Son is indebted for what He is to the Father, being particularly indebted to the Father for being equal to or of equal rank as the Father. But the Father is not indebted for whatever He is to anyone."

This means that there are in fact three groups of texts about the Son (cf. the explanatory notes given by M. Mellet and Th. Camelot, *Oeuvres de Saint Augustin,* 15, pp 574f and p 577): In the first one the equality of the Father and the Son is expressed, in the second one the Son is, as man, inferior to the Father, in the third one the Son is neither completely equal to the Father nor inferior to Him, but in this group of texts it is indicated that the Son stems from the Father (the position held by the Cappadocians and Hilary of Poitiers), see e.g. *De Trin.* 2,1,3: Quaedam itaque ita ponuntur in Scripturis de Patre et Filio, ut indicent unitatem aequalitatemque substantiae sicuti est (*John* 10,30 and *Phil.* 2,6 are quoted) . . . Quaedam vero ita, ut minorem ostendant Filium propter formam servi, id est propter assumptam creaturam mutabilis humanaeque substantiae, sicuti est

(*John* 14,28 and 5,21,27 are quoted). Quaedam porro ita ut nec minor nec aequalis tunc ostendatur, sed tantum quod de Patre sit intimetur, ut est illud (*John* 5,26 and 19 are quoted), cf. *Contra Max.* 2,14,8, *De Trin.* 1,12,23ff, *De div. quaest. LXXXIII* 69,1. Hilary of Poitiers recommends an exegesis on the basis of the first two groups mentioned by Augustine, see *De Trin.* 9,15ff, but the third group functions, as we have seen (*supra,* 113), in his exegesis as well. It must have been a difficulty to Augustine in this context that his sources sometimes varied in ascribing texts to the distinctive groups. Ambrose e.g. explains both *I Cor.* 15,28 and 11,3 not only in the light of the state of the incarnation (see *supra*), but also in the light of the eternal generation, see *Comm. in Epist. ad Cor. I* 11,3: Dignum est ut Filii caput Pater dicatur quasi genitor eius . . . Deus autem ideo caput Christi est, quia de eo vel ab ipso genitus est, and 15,26: Nemo ergo dubitet Filium semper regnaturum cum Patre. Traditio autem haec regni est, ut cum omnia Filio fuerint subiecta, et adoraverint illum ut Deum, destructa morte, tunc Filius ostendet illis non se esse ex quo sunt omnia, sed per quem sunt omnia: et hoc erit tradere regnum Deo et Patri, ostendere ipsum esse, ex quo omnis paternitas in coelis in terra nominatur: et tunc erit finis.

(9,19) De Spiritu sancto autem nondum tam copiose ac diligenter disputatum est a doctis et magnis divinarum scripturarum tractatoribus, ut intellegi facile possit et eius proprium, quo proprio fit, ut eum neque Filium neque Patrem dicere possimus, sed tantum Spiritum sanctum, nisi quod eum donum Dei esse praedicant, ut Deum credamus non se ipso inferius donum dare.

"But the learned and great commentators of divine Scriptures have not yet dealt so extensively and diligently with the Holy Spirit that Its distinctive character, too, could easily be understood, a distinctive character through which it happens that we can call Him neither Son nor Father, but only Holy Spirit, except that they declare Him to be the gift of God, in order that we may believe that God does not give a gift inferior to Himself."

(Cf. for the following chapter: J.J. Verhees, *God in beweging. Een onderzoek naar de pneumatologie van Augustinus,* Wageningen 1968, pp 289ff). The "autem" at the beginning of this paragraph corresponds with the "quidem" at the beginning of the previous paragraph: Whilst previous ecclesiastical writers have dealt extensively with the Father and the Son, they have not yet done so with the Holy Spirit. The distinctive characters of Father and Son are that the Father generates and that the Son is generated; the only distinctive character given to the Holy Spirit is "gift of God". Augustine claims that there are not many expositions about the Holy Spirit's distinctive character; he cannot mean in general that little has been written about the Holy Spirit, he will certainly have known Ambrose's *De Spiritu sancto* and will certainly have heard of Basil's piece of writing with the same title.- When he refers to the distinctive character which is given to the Holy Spirit, *viz.,* "gift of God", he could have in mind statements made by Hilary of Poitiers, see *De Trin.* 2,1 where the Spirit is called a gift (munus): Nec deesse quicquam consummationi tantae repperietur, intra quam sit in Patre et Filio et Spiritu sancto infinitas in aeterno, species in imagine, usus in munere (Augustine quotes this sentence and tries to explain it in *De Trin.* 6,10,11), see also 2,29: . . . Spiritus est Dei donum fidelium, cf. 2,33 and the explanatory note given by M. Mellet and Th. Camelot in *Oeuvres de Saint Augustin, 15,* pp 588f. The statement that God does not give less than Himself could be a conclusion drawn by Augustine himself. He will prove this in the present chapter by pointing out that the gift of the Spirit is love and that God is love. So the Spirit is, just like the Father and the Son, fully and essentially God.

servant tamen ut non genitum Spiritum sanctum tamquam filium de Patre praedicent- unicus enim est Christus- nec de Filio tamquam nepotem summi Patris

"Nevertheless they take care not to preach the Holy Spirit as generated as if He were a son generated from the Father, for Christ is the only one, nor as generated from the Son as if He were the grandson of the Highest Father,'

The Arians in fact ask why the Holy Spirit was not called Son from the substance of the Father, just as the Son, who is from the substance of the Father, is called Son, and why only the Son and nobody else is called son, see *Coll. cum Max.* 14: Cum enim et Spiritum sanctum de substantia Patris esse dicatis, si Filius ex substantia Dei Patris est, de substantia Patris et Spiritus sanctus, cur unus Filius est, et alius non est filius? Athanasius, *Ad Ser.* 1,15 quotes the same argument produced by the Arians and also their critical question whether the Father is the grandfather of the Spirit who is the son of the Son **(XXXIV)**, *Ad Ser.* 4,5 and Gregory Nazianzen, *Oratio* 31,7, cf. F.C. Baur, *Die christliche Lehre von der Dreieinigkeit I,* pp 516f. Athanasius rejects this argument as typically Greek or Pagan, since it presupposes a kind of theogony. In refuting this Arian argument Augustine says that the Son is *generated* whilst the Holy

Spirit *proceeds,* but he admits to be unable to make further distinctions between these two, see *Contra Max.* 2,14,1: De Patre est Filius, de Patre est Spiritus sanctus: sed ille genitus, iste procedens: ideo ille Filius est Patris, de quo est genitus, iste autem Spiritus utriusque, quoniam de utroque procedit . . . Non omne quod procedit nascitur, quamvis omne procedat quod nascitur . . . Haec scio: distinguere autem inter illam generationem et hanc processionem nescio, non valeo, non sufficio, cf. *In Ioann.* 99,9, *De Trin.* 9,12,17-18; 15,25,44ff, in this latter passage Augustine says that this will not be known before the coming of eternal blessedness, so he obviously did not want to make definite statements on this matter.

nec tamen id quod est nulli debere, sed Patri, ex quo omnia,

"but that He nevertheless does not owe to anyone what He is, except to the Father from whom are all things,"

Just like the Son, the Spirit finds His origin only in the Father.- On the Father who has no beginning Himself, but is the beginning of the Son, see *supra*, 111, and *In Ioann.* 39,1 where the following argument *a minori ad maius* is given: Si enim Filius principium est qui habet Patrem quanto facilius intelligendus est Deus Pater esse principium, qui habet quidem Filium cui Pater sit, sed non habet de quo sit?

ne duo constituamus principia sine principio, quod falsissimum et absurdissimum est et non catholicae fidei, sed quorundam haereticorum errori proprium.

"lest we set up two principles without a beginning, which is completely false and absurd and which is not characteristic of the Catholic faith but of the error of certain heretics."

There is one Beginning without a beginning, *viz.,* the Father, and there is a Beginning with a Beginning, *viz.,* the Son (He is called the Beginning because of *Gen.* 1,1 and *John* 8,25, see *supra*, 113), see e.g. *De Gen. a. l. lib. imp.* 3,6: Est enim Principium sine principio et est Principium cum alio principio. Principium sine principio solus Pater est, ideo ex uno principio esse omnia credimus: Filius autem ita Principium est, ut de Patre sit, cf. *De Trin.* 5,13,14. The heretics who are attacked here for establishing two Principles without a beginning are, of course, in the first place the Manicheans who teach that God and evil matter are the two Principles, see *supra,* 26, and *In Ioann.* 39, *De mor. eccl. cath.* 1,10,16-17, and, of course, the Marcionites who teach the evil god of the Old Testament and the good God revealed by Christ.

ausi sunt tamen quidam ipsam communionem Patris et Filii atque, ut ita dicam, deitatem, quam Graeci "*theotèta*" appellant, Spiritum sanctum credere, ut, quoniam Pater Deus et Filius Deus, ipsa deitas, qua sibi copulantur et ille gignendo Filium et ille Patri cohaerendo, ei a quo est genitus aequetur.

"Nevertheless some have dared to believe that the actual communion of Father and Son, and, so to speak the deity, which the Greeks call "theotèta", are the Holy Spirit so that, since the Father is God and the Son is God, the deity itself, through which they are bound together, the Father by generating the Son and the Son by cohering to the Father, is declared equal to Him by whom He (the Son) is generated."

The word "nevertheless" (tamen) refers to the fact that Augustine firstly had said that the ecclesiastical writers had said of the Holy Spirit only that He is the gift and that they had only distinguished Him from the Son by saying that the Spirit proceeds whilst the Son is generated. Now another statement is quoted which will be developed in the present chapter: The Spirit is the communion, the deity of God the Father and God the Son. Some writers "dared to believe this" (ausi sunt credere), this at first sight might suggest that Augustine disapproves of this as a heretical statement, since the heretics used to be attacked by the orthodox for their "audacia" with which they proclaim new and faulty doctrines, see e.g. Augustine, *In Ioann.* 97,2-3, Irenaeus, *Adv. Haer.* 1,25,2; 3,1,1, Tertullian, *Adv. Marc.* 1,19,5; 2,17,1. One may also think of the fact that Augustine defines "audacia" as a vice. He who has "audacia" has no fear just like the blessed ones and the corpses, but for different reasons: the blessed because of their tranquillity of mind, the audacious because of temerity, the corpses because of senselessness, so not every kind of lack of fear should be striven after, see *De div. quaest. LXXXIII* 34: Audacia vitium est. Non ergo quisquis non metuit, audax est, quamquam omnis qui audet, not metuat. Item cadaver omne non metuit. Quapropter cum commune sit non metuere beatissimo et audaci et cadaveri, sed beatissimus id habeat per tranquillitatem animi, audax per temeritatem, cadaver quia omni sensu caret, neque non amandum est non metuere, quoniam beati esse volumus, neque solum amandum, quoniam audaces et inanimes esse nolumus. But it appears in this chapter that Augustine appoves of this sentence. The "audere" cannot refer to the unusual Latin which is used here, *viz.*, the word "deitas" which is an unusual and literal translation of the Greek "*theotès*" whilst "divinitas" would be the more appropriate Latin, see *De civ.* 7,1: Hanc divinitatem, vel, ut sic dixerim, deitatem, nam et hoc verbo uti iam nostros non piget, ut de Graeco expressius transferant id quod illi *theotèta* appellant. Augustine's reservations about this term are expressed by the words "ut sic dixerim". (The word "deitas" was used by Christian Latin writers, sometimes with an explicit reference to the Greek "*theotès*", see *Th. l.l. V*[1], p 413; "divinitas" is the usual Latin word, see *Th. l.l. V*[1], p 1614, and J. Doignon, *Hilaire de Poitiers avant l'exil. Recherches sur la naissance, l'enseignement et l'épreuve d'une foi épiscopale en Gaule au milieu du IVe siècle,* Paris 1971, pp 174f. So if it does not trouble the ecclesiastical writers to use this word, one could also say that they have the courage to use it. But we believe the mild criticism voiced in the words "ausi sunt credere" to refer to something else: these writers declare the statement that the Holy Spirit is the deity of Father and Son to belong to the level of faith. Augustine will say in 9,20 that it belongs to the level of understanding (see *infra,* 133f. He obviously approves of this statement provided it is not made more important than it is. He also quotes his sources as saying that this deity should be understood as love and charity of Father and Son (see the next sentence). So what his sources indicate to be on the level of understanding should not be made by them the object of faith.- It is not necessary to look for a number of writers who say this (in accordance with the "quidam"), since Augustine in such instances uses rhetorically, so as to lend authority to what he is saying, the plural where only one person is meant, see B. Altaner, *Kleine Patristische Schriften,* p 166. It is possible that Augustine, when referring to those who say that the Holy Spirit is the communion of the Father and the Son, is thinking of Marius Victorinus (cf. B. de Margerie, La doctrine de Saint Augustin sur l'Esprit Saint comme communion et source de communion, *Augustinianum* (12) 1972, pp 108ff), see *Hymnus* 1,4: adesto, sancte Spiritus, Patris et Filii copula, cf. 3,242. But since neither the word "communio" nor the word "deitas" is used this cannot be stated with absolute certainty. But it is significant that Augustine uses the word "copulari" in the present section and later will use the word "copulatio". (P. Hadot points out that there are only very few parallels to the statement made by Marius Victorinus, see *Marius Victorinus, traités théologiques sur la Trinité II, Commentaire,* Paris 1960, pp 1059f.) When the Spirit is the communion between God the Father who generates and God the Son who is generated, then God the Spirit is equal to the Father, i.e. of the same substance, as was said in 9,16, see *supra,* 102. For similar statements by Augustine on the Spirit as the bond of love see e.g. *De Trin.* 15,19,37: Et si charitas qua Pater diligit Filium, et Patrem diligit Filius, ineffabiliter communionem demonstrat amborum, quid convenientius quam ut ille dicatur charitas proprie, qui Spiritus est communis amborum, cf. 15,17,30; 7,3,6; 5,11,12, *De agone christ.* 16,18. Augustine is obviously aware of the Porphyrian background, for in *De civ.* 10,23 he says that Porphyry speaks about God the Father and the Son, whom he calls in Greek the paternal intellect or mind, but that he says nothing about the Holy Spirit, or if he does, he does not do so clearly, although, according to Augustine, he must mean the Holy Spirit when he speaks of the Principle between the Father and the Son: Dicit enim Deum Patrem et Deum Filium quem graece appellat paternum intellectum, vel paternam mentem: de Spiritu autem sancto, aut nihil, aut non aperte aliquid dicit: quamvis quem alium dicat horum medium, non intelligo, cf. P.Hadot, La Métaphysique de Porphyre, *Porphyre (Entretiens sur l'Antiquité classique, t. XII),* Geneva 1966, p 138 who points out that this medium is called the "Power" by Porphyry.- Regarding the statement that the Spirit is the deity (deitas) of the Father and the Son one can refer to Marius Victorinus who comes fairly close when he says that the Spirit is the substance of the Father and of Christ, see *Adv. Arium* 4,4, cf. 1,30f, 1,55; 3,6. On the surface, Hilary of Poitiers and Ambrose seem to say something similar. Hilary stresses that both the Father and the Son are Spirit, see *De Trin.* 2,31f and 3,4, but he does not mean by this that the Spirit is the deity of Father and Son, let alone that He is the bond between them.- Ambrose argues strongly in *De spiritu sancto* 1,12,126-131 that the peace, grace, love and communion of Father, Son and Holy Spirit are one, but this refers to the peace, grace, charity and communion which the believers receive from the one God, Father, Son and Holy Spirit.- He also expresses his belief in the divinity (deitas, *theotès*) of the Spirit, see *De Spiritu sancto* 3,10,59: Nec solum hoc loco (sc. *Act.* 5,3f) evidenter sancti Spiritus *theotèta*, hoc est, deitatem, Scriptura testatur, sed etiam ipse Dominus dixit in evangelio, Quoniam Deus Spiritus est.- So when Augustine says that according to some ecclesiastical writers the Holy Spirit is the bond and the deity (*theotès*) of the Father and the Son, this could be a combination of Marius Victorinus' doctrine that He is the bond of the Father and the Son, of Hilary's view that Father and Son are Spirit, and of Ambrose's insistence on the deity, *theotès* of the Holy Spirit. (See on this matter also the learned expositions given by O. du Roy, *L'intelligence de la foi en la trinité selon Saint Augustin, Genèse de sa théologie trinitaire jusqu' en 391,* Paris 1966, pp 486f).

hanc ergo deitatem, quam etiam dilectionem in se invicem amborum caritatemque volunt intellegi, Spiritum sanctum appellatum dicunt multisque scripturarum documentis adsunt huic opinioni suae: sive illo quod dictum est: *quoniam caritas Dei diffusa est in cordibus nostris per Spiritum sanctum qui datus est nobis,* sive aliis multis talibus testimoniis,

"They say therefore that this deity, which they want to be understood as being the mutual love and charity of both, is called Holy Spirit, and they produce ma-

ny Scriptural proofs for this view of theirs, either with the text, Because the love of God has been poured into our hearts through the Holy Spirit which has been given to us, (Rom. 5,5) or with many other proofs;"

It is likely that when Augustine refers in this paragraph to ecclesiastical writers he has in mind, amongst others, Marius Victorinus. But since the text *Rom.* 5,5 seems not to have been quoted by Marius Victorinus (see P. Hadot, *Marius Victorinus, Traités* etc, II, p 1107) we have to look for other authors as the background to this statement. Ambrose comes fairly near, *De Spiritu sancto* 1,8,94: Effundit ergo Deus de Spiritu, effunditur etiam charitas Dei per Spiritum . . . Sicut enim de Spiritu sancto Deus effundit, ita etiam, charitas Dei effusa est in cordibus nostris per Spiritum sanctum, ut intelligamus non esse opus sanctum Spiritum qui divinae arbiter et fons profluus charitatis est. The words "love" and "charity" are synonymous, according to Augustine, see *De Trin.* 15,18,32: . . . dilectio sive charitas (nam unius rei est utrumque nomen).

et eo ipso quod per Spiritum sanctum reconciliamur Deo: unde etiam cum donum Dei dicitur, satis significari volunt caritatem Dei esse Spiritum sanctum.

"they consider the fact that we are reconciled to God through the Holy Spirit (which is why He is also called a gift from God) as a sufficient indication that the Holy Spirit is the love of God."

It had already been stated that God gives nothing inferior to Himself (see *supra,* 118, so we are reconciled to God through God's gift, i.e. God's Spirit, and since reconciliation is an act of God's love, God's love is God's Spirit. God's love is unchangeable and did not begin at the moment of reconciliation, it existed before the creation (which can only mean that love belongs to God's being and is fully divine), cf. *In Ioann.* 110,6: Quapropter incomprehensibilis est dilectio qua diligit Deus, neque mutabilis. Non enim ex quo ei reconciliati sumus per sanguinem Filii eius, non coepit diligere, sed ante mundi constitutionem dilexit nos, ut cum eius Unigenito etiam nos filii eius essemus, priusquam omnino aliquid essemes, cf. Athanasius, *Contra Arianos* 2,75ff, see also *infra,* 131f.

non enim reconciliamur illi nisi per dilectionem, qua etiam *filii dei* appellamur, non iam sub timore tamquam servi, quia *consummata dilectio foras mittit timorem,* et Spiritum libertatis accepimus, *in quo clamamus, Abba Pater.*

"For we are only reconciled to Him through love, because of which we are also called sons of God, (I John 3,1): no longer as slaves under fear, because perfect love drives out fear (I John 4,18), and we have received the Spirit of freedom, in which we cry, Abba, Father. (Rom. 8,15)."

On being adopted as sons of God see *supra,* 87.- The difference between slaves who obey out of fear and sons who obey out of love is the difference between the Old and the New Testament. The Lord gave smaller precepts through the prophets and servants to the people whom He still had to bind to Himself with fear and greater ones through His Son to the people whom it suited to be liberated through love, see *De sermone domini in monte* 1,1,2: Unus tamen Deus per sanctos Prophetas et famulos suos, secundum ordinatissimam distributionem temporum, dedit minora praecepta populo quem adhuc timore alligari oportebat; et per Filium suum maiora populo quem charitate iam liberari convenerat (cf. *De spir. et litt.* 17,29, *De div. quaest. LXXXIII* 66,1, *Contra Adim.* 17,2 ff, *Sermo* 156,13,14.) There is a diference between the Old and the New Testament, but not a contrast (this would be the Manichean position), therefore Augustine can also say positive things about the fear of the people in the Old Testament, see *De doct. christ.* 2,7,9f (cf. *Sermo* 347,2,2): it is the first step towards knowledge of God. This is a traditional way of speaking about the two covenants, see e.g. Irenaeus, *Adv. Haer.* 4,19,1: Maior est igitur legisdatio quae in libertatem quam quae data est in servitutem, 4,24,2: Etenim Lex quippe servis posita, per ea quae foris erant corporalia animam erudiebat, velut per vinculum attrahens eam ad obedientiam praeceptorum ubi disceret homo servire Deo: Verbum autem liberans animam, et per ipsam corpus voluntarie emundari docuit. Quo facto, necesse fuit auferri quidem vincula servitutis quibus iam homo assueverat, et sine vinculis sequi Deum, superextendi per decreta libertatis. This fearlessness of the Christians is sharply separated by Augustine from the fearlessness of the Epicureans (who boast to have no fear, because they do not believe in Providence and life after death) and of the Stoics (who boast to have no fear because of the virtue of their mind and who in their pride regard not being afraid as a good in itself), see *Sermo* 348,2,3: Quapropter irridendi sunt huius mundi philosophi, non solum Epicurei qui . . . fortissimos se iactant, et nihil omnino timere se dicunt: quia nec quidquam Deum res humanas curare arbitrantur, et consumpta ista vita nullam postea credunt futuram . . . sed etiam ipsi Stoici . . . Nam et Stoici se fortissimos praeferunt, et non propter corporis voluptatem, sed propter animi virtutem, idipsum non timere propter non timere custodientes, typho turgidi, et non sapientia sanati, sed errore durati. For the Epicurean denial of Providence see e.g. Cicero, *De nat. deor.*

1,17,45, Lactance, *De ira dei* 17,1-2, the Epicureans' denial of fear refers especially to the fear of death, see Lucrece, *De rer. nat.* 3, 830f, see further the quotations given by C.J. de Vogel, *Greek Philosophy III,* Leiden 1959, pp 34f. For the Stoics' contempt of fear (fear is one of the four "*pathè*" which must be eradicated) see the quotations given by C.J. de Vogel, *op. cit.,* pp 172f. Augustine states that the Stoics reckon fear to be together with "cupiditas" and grief "perturbationes mentis" which a wise man should not have, this fear is the negative opposite of the positive notion of caution, see *De civ.* 14,8: Stoici tres esse voluerunt, pro tribus perturbationibus in animo sapientis, pro cupiditate voluntatem, pro laetitia gaudium, pro metu cautionem. Augustine emphasizes himself that in eternal life there will be no fear, but in this life such *apatheia* should be shunned by those who live "secundum Deum" (and not as the Stoics "secundum animam"), see *De civ.* 14,9,4 (cf. *infra,* 146): Si autem apatheia illa est ubi nec metus ullus exterret, nec angit dolor, aversanda est in hac vita, si recte, hoc est secundum Deum, vivere volumus: in illa vero beata, quae sempiterna plane speranda est, cf. *In Ioann.* 60,3. Some sorts of fear are during this life also in the believers, see *De civ.* 14,9,5 and *In Ioann.* 85,3: est timor quem perfecta charitas foras mittit, et est alius timor castus permanens in saeculum saeculi, this latter fear is explained with *Rom.* 11,20 (Noli autem sapere, sed time). (On Augustine's evaluation of the Stoic doctrine of *apatheia* see also G. Bardy's explanatory note in *Oeuvres de Saint Augustin,* 35, pp 533f and M.L. Colish, *op. cit.*, pp 221ff.)

et quia reconciliati et in amicitiam revocati per caritatem poterimus omnia Dei secreta cognoscere, popterea de Spiritu sancto dicitur: *ipse vos inducet in omnem veritatem;*

"And because we have been reconciled and recalled to friendship through love and as such shall be able to know all God's secrets , for this reason it is said about the Holy Spirit: He will lead you into all truth, (John 16,13)."

The gift of love takes place through the Holy Spirit, so does the revelation of truth. That men can become friends of God is elsewhere described by Augustine as God's justification, the only matter in which man should glory, see *In Ioann.* 85,3: Nos autem, charissimi, ut amici Domini esse possimus, quid noster Dominus faciat sciamus. Non solum enim homines, verum etiam iustos ipse facti nos, et non ipsi nos . . . Ab ipso quidquid boni est donatur. Ergo quia et hoc bonum est, ab ipso utique donatur ut sciatur a quo bonum omne donetur, ut omnino de omnibus bonis qui gloriatur, in Domino glorietur. (On man's restitution to the state of friend of God see also Irenaeus, *Adv. Haer.* 3,19,6). What Augustine says about the revelation given to the friends of God sometimes is anti-Manichean in character: when the Manicheans ask why God created the world at the moment He did (hereby suggesting that the Creator acted arbitrarily) Augustine retorts that when one wants to know the will of God, one should become the friend of God by cleansing one's conduct by that aim of the law which is love out of a clean heart,- if the heretics (Manicheans) had done this, they would not be heretics, see *De Gen. c. Man.* 1,2,4: Et si voluntatem Dei nosse quisquam desiderat, fiat amicus Deo . . . Non autem quisquam efficitur amicus Dei, nisi purgatissimis moribus, et illo fine praecepti de quo Apostolus dicit, finis autem praecepti est charitas de corde puro et conscientia bona et fides non ficta (*I Tim.* 1,5),- quod si haberent, non essent haeretici. In explaining *John* 16,13 he stresses against the heretics that no new doctrines are promised here, but a deeper understanding of the Scriptural revelation (again a statement with an anti-Manichean aim), see *In Ioann.* 96ff.

propterea et confidentia praedicandae veritatis, qua inpleti sunt in adventu eius apostoli, recte caritati tribuitur, quia et diffidentia timori datur, quem consummatio caritatis excludit.

"Therefore also the confidence to preach the truth with which the Apostles were filled at His coming, (Acts 2,4)) is rightly attributed to love, because diffidence, too, is attributed to fear which the perfection of love excludes. (I John 4, 18)."

The gathering together of the Apostles on Whitsun Day is elsewhere contrasted with the lawgiving to Moses: then the people were prevented by horrible fear to come to that place where the law was given, see *De spir. et litt.* 17,29: . . . ubi populus accedere ad locum, ubi lex datur, horrendo terrore prohibetur, hic autem in eos supervenit Spiritus sanctus, qui eum promissum exspectantes in unum fuerant congregati.- Love is given in Christ's miraculous birth, fear is excluded through His death and resurrection, see *De ut. cred.* 15,33: ille nascendo mirabiliter et operando conciliavit charitatem, moriendo autem et resurgendo exclusit timorem.

et ideo donum Dei dicitur, quia eo quod quisque novit non fruitur, nisi id diligat. frui autem sapientia Dei nihil est aliud quam ei dilectione cohaerere, neque quisquam in eo quod percipit permanet nisi dilectione;

" And therefore it is called a gift of God because everybody enjoys what he knows only if he loves it. Now to enjoy the wisdom of God is nothing else but to

adhere to it in love. And one remains in what one perceives only if it is with love."

This must show again that the gift of God, the Holy Spirit, is fully God. Augustine shows this by working with the well-known concept of "frui" (to enjoy) which he clearly distinguishes from "uti" (to use): to enjoy something means to adhere to it in love because of itself, to use something means to use it in order to receive what one loves, see *De doctr. christ.* 1,4,4: Frui autem est amore alicui rei inhaerere propter se ipsam. Uti autem quod in usum venerit ad id quod amas obtinendum referre, in this sense one should enjoy God, see 1,5,5, cf. *De Trin.* 10,10,13, *De civ.* 11,25. One should use creation in order to love the Creator, if one loves creation because of itself, this is "cupiditas", see e.g. *De Trin.* 9,8,13: Quod verbum amore concipitur, sive creaturae, sive Creatoris, id est, aut naturae mutabilis aut incommutabilis veritatis. Ergo aut cupiditate, aut charitate: non quo non sit amanda creatura, sed si ad Creatorem refertur ille amor, non iam cupiditas, sed charitas erit. Tunc enim est cupiditas, cum propter se amatur creatura. Tunc non utentem adiuvat, sed corrumpit fruentem, (cf. on this subject R.M. Markus, Augustine: Human Action: Will and Virtue, *The Cambridge History etc.,* pp 390f, 414ff). The love of the Wisdom of God is permanent love, because the object of love is eternal. Temporal things are loved more before they are obtained, eternal things are loved even more once they have been obtained, cf. *De doct. christ.* 1,38,42: Inter temporalia quippe atque aeterna hoc interest quod temporale aliquid plus diligitur antequam habeatur, vilescit autem cum advenerit . . . aeternum autem ardentius diligitur adeptum quam desideratum. This is the reason why true love drives out fear, for fear is to be afraid to lose what one loves, see *De div. quaest. LXXXIII* 33: Nulli dubium est non aliam metuendi esse causam nisi ne id quod amamus aut adeptum amittamus aut non adipiscamur speratum, cf. *De beata vita* 11, Hilary of Poitiers, *De Trin.* 1,1, Athanasius, *Contra Gentes* 3.

et ideo Spiritus sanctus dicitur, quoniam ad permanendum sanciuntur quaecumque sanciuntur nec dubium est a sanciendo sanctitatem vocari.

"And therefore it is called Holy Spirit, because all things that are sanctified are sanctified in order to last, and there is no doubt that the word "sanctity" stems from the word "to sanctify"."

Sanctification means inter alia the gift of immortality, see *infra*, 146ff. For the etymology of "sanctitas" from "sancire" see Marius Victorinus, *Adver-*

sus Arium 3,15: Ipse vero Spiritus sanctus dictus quod sanciat sanctos, id est sanctos faciat.

maxime autem illo testimonio utuntur assertores huius sententiae, quod scriptum est: *quod natum est de carne, caro est; et quod natum est de Spiritu, spiritus est: quoniam Deus Spiritus est.* hic enim regenerationem nostram dicit, quae non secundum Adam de carne est, sed secundum Christum de Spiritu sancto. quapropter si Spiritus sancti hoc loco facta est commemoratio, cum dictum est, *quoniam Deus Spiritus est,* animadvertendum dicunt, non dictum esse "quoniam Spiritus Deus est" sed, *quoniam Deus Spiritus est,* ut ipsa deitas Patris et Filii hoc loco dicta sit Deus, quod est Spiritus sanctus.

"Those who hold this view make most use of that testimony which is written, What is born from flesh is flesh, what is born from the Spirit is spirit, (John 3,6), because God is Spirit, (John 4,24). For here he means our regeneration which is not in accordance with Adam from the flesh but in accordance with Christ from the Holy Spirit. Therefore, if the Holy Spirit is mentioned here, when it is said, Because God is Spirit, they say that one should pay attention to the fact that it has not been said, Because the Spirit is God, but, God is Spirit, so that the deity itself of Father and Son is called God in this place, and that is the Holy Spirit."

Augustine claims that ecclesiastical writers with the help of *John* 3,6 (in an amplified way, since under the influence of *John* 4,24 "quoniam Deus Spiritus est" is added) want to say that the deity of the Father and the Son is the Spirit, and that, as the deity of Father and Son, the Spirit is God. If it were said in the Bible "the Spirit is God", then the deity of the Holy Spirit would have been referred to, but since it says "God is Spirit" this means, according to Augustine and the ecclesiastical writers he is following here (or at least pretends to be following), that the deity of God (Father and Son) is Spirit, i.e. the Holy Spirit. Here Augustine seems to be twisting his sources: Marius Victorinus draws from *John* 3,6 the conclusion that Christ is Spirit like the Father, see *Adv. Arium* 4,6, and that the Father, Son and Holy Spirit are Spirit, see *Adv. Arium* 4,9: Sit igitur nobis fixa sententia quod deus spiritus sit et spiritus de quo et filius spiritus, et spiritus sanctus spiritus. De spiritu enim quod nascitur, spiritus est. This comes fairly close, but, unlike what Augustine says *John* 3,6, it is interpreted in the context of eternal generation. This is not the interpretation quoted by Augustine which is in the context of regeneration. In this latter context it appears in Ambrose, *De Spiritu sancto* 3,10,63ff, but Ambrose says what Augustine does not say: The text indicates the divinity of the Holy Spirit, and Ambrose denies that the text refers to the Father as Spirit. Augustine makes his source say that the deity of Father and Son is the Holy Spirit, whilst Marius Victorinus says that Father, Son and Holy Spirit are Spirit (explaining *John* 3,6 in the context of eternal generation), whilst Ambrose says that the Holy Spirit is God.

huc accedit aliud testimonium quod dicit Iohannes apostolus, *quoniam Deus dilectio est.* etiam hic enim non ait "Dilectio Deus est", sed: *Deus dilectio est,* ut ipsa deitas dilectio intellegatur.

"To this is added another testimony given by the Apostle John , Because God is love, (I John 4,16). For here, too, he does not say, Love is God, but, God is love, in order that the deity itself may be understood as love."

The Holy Spirit had already been called the love of the Father and the Son (see *supra*), and this view is now confirmed with *I John* 4,16 which is interpreted *per analogiam* as "God is Spirit". There seems to be no source of this exegesis of *I John* 4,16, cf. D. Dideberg, *Saint Augustin et la première èpître de Saint Jean. Une theologie de l'agapè,* Paris 1975, pp 142f.

et quod in illa enumeratione conexarum sibi rerum, ubi dicitur: *omnia vestra sunt, vos autem Christi, Christus autem Dei,* et, *caput mulieris vir, caput viri Christus, caput autem Christi Deus,* nulla fit commemoratio Spiritus sancti, ad hoc pertinere dicunt, quia non fere in his, quae sibi conexa sunt, numerari solet ipsa conexio.

"And of the fact that in that enumeration of things connected with each other, where it says, All things are yours, but you are Christ's and Christ is God's, (I Cor. 3,22-23), and, The head of the woman is man, the head of man is Christ, but the head of Christ is God, (I Cor. 11,3), there is no mention of the Holy Spirit, (of this fact) they say that it is part of this that usually when counting things connected one does not mention the connection itself."

We are unable to produce examples of this explanation.

unde in illo etiam loco Trinitatem ipsam videntur agnoscere, qui legunt adtentius, cum dicitur: *quoniam ex ipso et per ipsum et in ipso sunt omnia: ex ipso,* tamquam ex eo, qui nulli debet quod est; *per ipsum,* tamquam per mediatorem; *in ipso,* tamquam in eo, qui continet, id est copulatione coniungit.

"Hence also in that place those who read more attentively seem to recognize the Trinity when it says, Because from Him and through Him and in Him are all

things, (Rom. 11,36). "From Him" as from Him who owes to nobody what He is, "through Him" as through the Mediator, "in Him" as in Him who contains, i.e. binds together."

Such a Trinitarian explanation is given by Marius Victorinus, *Adv. Arium* 1,18: Ex ipso, ut dicitur de patre, per ipsum ut de Christo, in ipso ut de sancto spiritu. But Marius Victorinus also follows the reading "ex ipso et per ipsum et in ipsum omnia", *Adv. Arium* 1,37 (on his anti-Anhomoean interpretation of this text see P. Hadot, *Marius Victorinus, Traités* etc. II, pp 813ff). See also Ambrose, *De Spiritu sancto* 2,9,88ff, who also stresses the prepositions ex, per and in, which are used in *Rom.* 11,36 for respectively Father, Son and Holy Spirit: all apply also to each of the three Persons, see 100: non est dubium quin per quem omnia, ex eo omnia: et ex quo omnia, per eum omnia: et in quo omnia, per eum vel ex eo omnia esse intelligere debeamus, cf. Basil, *Liber de spiritu sancto* 2,4ff (this is opposition against the doctrine that the various prepositions refer to different beings).- On the Father who owes His being to nobody see *supra*, 114, on the Son through whom are all things see *supra*, 38ff, on the Holy Spirit as the bond between Father and Son see *supra*, 121ff.

(9,20) Huic sententiae contradicunt, qui arbitrantur istam communionem, quam sive deitatem sive dilectionem caritatemve appellamus, non esse substantiam; quaerunt autem secundum substantiam sibi exponi Spiritum sanctum, nec intellegunt non aliter potuisse dici: *Deus dilectio est,* nisi substantia esset dilectio.

"This interpretation is objected to by those who think that this communion, which we call either deity or love or charity, is not a substance, for they want the Holy Spirit to be explained to them as a substance, and they do not understand that the words "God is love" could only have been said if love were a substance;"

Perhaps orthodox theologians could have objected to this interpretation that it is close to Sabellianism. But it seems more likely that these objectors are radical Arians, the Anhomoeans, who want Father, Son and Holy Spirit to be different substances, who may be of one mind as men can be, see *Coll. cum Max.* 12. But "being of one mind or love" cannot be a substance as the Father, Son and Holy Spirit are, see also *De agone christ.* 16,18: Nec eos audiamus qui Patrem solum verum Deum et sempiternum esse dicunt, Filium autem non de ipso genitum, sed ab ipso factum de nihilo, et fuisse tempus quando non erat, sed tamen primum locum tenere in omni creatura, et Spiritum sanctum minoris maiestatis esse quam

Filium, et ipsum factum esse post Filium, et horum trium diversas esse substantias, tamquam aurum et argentum et aeramentum (although the Arians are not named they are obviously meant), cf. *Contra serm. Arian.* 5,5. In *Sermo* 34,2,3 Augustine puts God who is love in contrast with idols which man forms for himself, God who is love is not corporeal, nevertheless He is a reality which must be loved: Quid lineamenta disponis? quid membra componis? quid staturam placitam formas? quid pulchritudinem corporis imaginaris? Deus charitas est. Quis color in charitate? quae lineamenta? quae forma? Nihil horum videmus et tamen amamus. See also *De Trin.* 15,17,29: Ut scilicet in illa simplici summaque natura, non sit aliud substantia et aliud charitas, sed substantia ipsa sit charitas, et charitas sit substantia . . .

ducuntur quippe consuetudine rerum corporalium, quoniam, si duo sibi corpora copulentur, ita ut iuxta invicem conlocentur, ipsa copulatio non est corpus, quandoquidem separatis illis corporibus, quae copulata fuerant, nulla invenitur; nec tamen quasi discessisse et migrasse intellegitur, sicut illa corpora.

"because they are led by what usually happens with corporeal things, for if two bodies are bound together in such a way that they are placed closely besides each other, the binding itself is not a body, for when these bodies which had been bound together have been separated, no binding is found, nevertheless it is not understood to have, so to speak, gone away and moved like such bodies."

So the Arians are accused of speaking about God in a corporeal way (cf. *supra,* 27, and 93, where the same charge is made against the Manicheans). A bodily being is changeable, as is the case here with the bodies which can be put together and separated. Augustine is completely opposed to the idea that God should have such a being, see e.g. *De Trin.* 1,1; 8,2,3, *In Ioann.* 99,3. This is the traditional accusation made against the Arians, e.g. in connection with their claim that when the Father is more (greater) than the Son, the Father cannot be in the Son, see Athanasius, *Contra Arianos* 3,1, Hilary of Poitiers, *De Trin.* 8,24. In the present context the bodily interpretation means (this is the clear implication of Augustine's reply to the Arian objection) that as bodies can be bound together and separated, the Father and the Son can love each other and stop loving each other. The orthodox are, of course, opposed to this idea, see e.g. Athanasius, *Contra Arianos* 3,62ff, Ambrose, *De fide* 4,9,102ff. Augustine was obviously aware of the fact that his opposition against a bodily interpretation of the Trinity was shared by ecclesiastical writers before him see *Epist.* 147,6,18ff (in explaining a long quotation from Ambrose, *In Lucam* 1,1,11) and *Epist.* 148,2,10 where he gives the names of Athanasius, Gregory Nazianzen, Ambrose.

sed hi tales cor mundum faciant, quantum possunt, ut videre valeant in dei substantia non esse aliquid tale, quasi aliud ibi sit substantia, aliud quod accidat substantiae, et non sit substantia; sed quidquid ibi intellegi potest, substantia est.

"But let these people with such ideas make their hearts clean, as far as they can, so that they can see that something of this kind is not in the substance of God, as if there were a difference between the substance and the "accidens" of a substance which is no substance. But all that can be understood there is substance."

On the cleansing of the heart in this context see *infra*, 134f.- Augustine rejects the idea that God is a substance with "accidentia". The reason is that "accidentia" are changeable: a substance can have them at one moment and not have them at another moment, see e.g. *De Trin.* 5,4,5: Accidens autem non solet dici, nisi quod aliqua mutatione eius rei cui accidit amitti potest. This is again a traditional argument against the Arians, see e.g. Athanasius, *Contra Arianos* 1,20 **(XXXV)**, 1,36; 3,65 (cf. Origen, *De Princ.* 1,2,10; 1,5,5; 1,6,2; 1,8,3, see also G.C. Stead, *Divine Substance*, p 187, for rejection of "accidentia" in God see also Albinus, *Epitome* 10,4, Plotinus, *Enneads* 6,8,9,36f). Therefore the unchangeable God is only substance and has no "accidentia".

verum haec dici possunt facile et credi; videri autem nisi corde puro quomodo se habeant, omnino non possunt. quapropter sive ista vera sit sententia, sive aliud aliquid sit, fides inconcussa tenenda est, ut Deum dicamus Patrem, Deum Filium, Deum Spiritum sanctum, neque tres deos, sed istam Trinitatem unum Deum, neque diversas naturas, sed eiusdem substantiae, neque ut Pater aliquando sit Filius, aliquando Spiritus sanctus, sed Pater semper Pater et Filius semper Filius et Spiritus sanctus semper Spiritus sanctus.

"But these things can easily be said and believed, but it certainly can only be seen how they are by a clean mind. Therefore whether this interpretation is true or whether there is any other interpretation, the faith has to be maintained unshaken that we call the Father God, the Son God, the Holy Spirit God,- neither three gods, but this Trinity as one God, nor different natures, but of the same

substance, nor that the Father is at one time the Son and at another time the Holy Spirit, but that the Father is always the Father, the Son always the Son, the Holy Spirit always the Holy Spirit."

The words "whether this interpretation is true or whether there is any other interpretation" do not mean that Augustine refrains from passing a negative or positive judgement on the tenet quoted in the previous paragraph: the Holy Spirit is the deity, love, bond of the Father and the Son (as P.C. Eichenseer, *op. cit.,* p 354 suggests: "Abschliessend entscheidet sich Augustin in seinem Frühwerk für keine der eben aufgezählten Meinungen, trägt aber auch keine eigene Erklärung vor." The Benedictines went even further and described the tenet quoted by Augustine as a heretical one, see PL 42, 612. By providing Scriptural support for this doctrine as he does in the previous paragraph and by saying that he himself calls the Holy Spirit such (see the first sentence of this paragraph) he expresses approval of it (cf. J. Rivière, *op. cit.,* p 57 note 5). But what he is saying here is that such speculations may be true but are not the object of faith or the expression of faith, they are an attempt to understand this faith. Faith is faith in one God, *viz.,* the Father, the Son and the Holy Spirit, this faith rejects the notion of three gods of different being (the Arian position), it rejects the Sabellian idea that for a while the Father becomes the Son or the Holy Spirit (cf. *supra,* 104f, 9,16).

nec temere de invisibilibus aliquid adfirmemus tamquam scientes, sed tamquam credentes, quoniam videri nisi mundato corde non possunt.

"And let us not rashly affirm things about what is invisible, as if we knew about them,- but as believing, because they can only be seen by a heart which has been cleansed."

Such rashness which should be avoided is detected by Augustine in the Manicheans (who promise reason, see *supra,* 21, but do the opposite: make irrational claims), see e.g. *De Gen. contra Man.* 1,2,3: temere volunt reprehendere quod diligenter quaerere debuerunt, *De Gen. a.l. lib. imp.* 1,1, *De Gen. a.l.* 1,19,38-39; 1,20,40; 7,1,1; 12,1,1. Such temerity is not based on the Apostolic truth, cf. *Sermo* 52,2,1 where he says in connection with faith in the Trinity: Fides enim nostra, id est, fides recta, fides catholica, non opinione praesumptionis, sed testimonio lectionis collecta, nec haeretica temeritate incerta, sed apostolica veritate fundata, hoc insinuat.

et si quis ea videt in hac vita *ex parte*, ut dictum est, atque *in aenigmate*, non potest efficere, ut et ille videat, cui loquitur, si cordis sordibus inpeditur. *Beati* autem *mundi corde, quoniam ipsi Deum videbunt.*

"And if somebody sees these things in this life partly, as it is said, and in a riddle, (I Cor. 13,12), he cannot make him to whom he speaks see it as well, if he is hindered by the dirt of his heart. But blessed are those with a clean heart, because they will see God, (Matth. 5,8)."

Augustine had invited his opponents to cleanse their hearts in order to obtain the right view of God,- if they refuse to do so he cannot communicate his own view to them, cf. Ambrose, *In Lucam* 1,27 (quoted by Augustine in *Epist.* 147,6,18 and 147,11,25: neque is qui Deum videre noluerit, potest Deum videre. According to Augustine *Matth.* 5,8 wants to say that stupid are those who want to see God with bodily eyes, since He can only be seen with a clean heart, as the visible light can only be seen with clean eyes, see *De serm. Domini in monte* 1,2,8: Quam ergo stulti sunt qui Deum istis exterioribus oculis quaerunt cum corde videatur . . . Hoc est mundum cor quod est simplex cor: et quemadmodum lumen hoc videri non potest, nisi oculis mundis, ita nec Deus videtur, nisi mundum sit illud quo videri potest, cf. *Sermo* 4,4; 88,4,4; 117,10,15; 261,4,4f, *Epist.* 147,14,37, *De Trin.* 8,4,6. *Matth.* 5,8 used to be interpreted in this way, see e.g. Athanasius, *Contra Gentes* 1, Origen, *De Princ.* 1,1,9. The general idea is this: God is not corporeal, so the body cannot see God, since like can only be known by like, therefore God must be known by the human mind which has been created in God's image, and therefore the mind must cleanse itself from bodily affections if it wants to see God (cf. on this matter further E.P. Meijering, *Athanasius: Contra Gentes,* pp 111f and the literature quoted there.)- The seeing "in aenigmate" is interpreted by Augustine as knowledge of God with the help of (inadequate) similarities found in the realm of creation, see *De Trin.* 15,9,16: Proinde . . . sicut nomine speculi imaginem voluit intelligi, ita nomine aenigmatis quamvis similitudinem, tamen obscuram, et ad perspiciendam difficilem. Cum igitur speculi et aenigmatis nomine quaecumque similitudines ab Apostolo significatae intelligi possint, quae accomodatae sunt ad intelligendum Deum, eo modo quo potest; nihil tamen est accomodatius quam id quod imago eius non frustra dicitur, cf. J. Moignt's explanatory note in *Oeuvres de Saint Augustin,* 16, pp 646f.

haec fides est de Deo conditore et renovatore nostro.

"This is the faith about God our Creator and Renovator."

This sentence is meant as a summary of what has so far been said about the Christian faith in God: God is the Creator through the Son and God is the Redeemer through the Son and the Spirit, which means that in the act of creation and recreation the one God, Father, Son and Holy Spirit is at work. Similarly in the beginning of the expositions about the Son, He was already in the context of creation referred to as the "liberator" and "rector" (see *supra,* 38).

V

PART IV
(9,21 - 10,24)

BELIEF IN THE HOLY CHURCH, FORGIVENESS OF SINS AND THE RESURRECTION OF THE FLESH

Chapter 9,21-10,21

Introduction: The commandment of love of God and love of the neighbour is the background to the faith in the one Catholic church. Heretics do not love God, because they hold the wrong views about God, schismatics do not love their neighbours, therefore both do not belong to the Catholic church (9,21-10,21). The schismatics do not want to forgive their neighbours, therefore there can be no forgiveness of sins for them in which the Christians believe (10,21).

Text, Translation and Commentary:

(9,21) Sed quoniam dilectio non tantum in Deum nobis imperata est, cum dictum est: *diliges dominum Deum tuum ex toto corde tuo, et ex tota anima tua, et ex tota mente tua;* sed etiam in proximum: *nam, diliges,* inquit, *proximum tuum tamquam te ipsum-* nisi autem ista fides congregationem societatemque hominum teneat, in qua fraterna caritas operetur, minus fructuosa est-,**(10,21)** credimus et sanctam ecclesiam, utique catholicam.

"But since not only love of God has been commanded to us when it was said, You shall love the Lord your God with all your heart, all your soul and all your mind, but also love of the neighbour, for He says, Thou shalt love your neighbour as yourself (Mark 10,30-31), but if this faith does not maintain the congregation and fellowship of men, in which love of the brethren can be at work, it is less fruitful, (therefore) we also believe in the Holy Church, of course, the Catholic one."

In *De div. quaest. LXXXIII* 81,1 Augustine gives the reason why God has to be loved in a triple way (with heart, soul and mind): He is the triune God, cf. *Sermo* 9,6,7 where he says that the first three commandments refer to love of the triune God, the seven others to the love of the neighbour.- Love of God and love of the neighbour belong together and therefore also love and faith. This insight is the necessary background for the understanding of the meaning of the faith in the Holy Church, for both heretics and schismatics fail to see that these two kinds of love belong together and that love and faith belong together:

nam et haeretici et schismatici congregationes suas ecclesias vocant. sed haeretici de Deo falsa sentiendo ipsam fidem violant; schismatici autem discissionibus iniquis a fraterna caritate dissiliunt, quamvis ea credant quae credimus. quapropter nec haeretici pertinent ad ecclesiam catholicam, quoniam diligit Deum; nec schismatici, quoniam diligit proximum.

"For the heretics and the schismatics, too, call their congregations churches. But the heretics violate faith by holding false views about God, the schismatics jump out of fraternal love through unjust divisions, although they believe the things we believe. Therefore neither the heretics belong to the catholic Church, because it loves God, nor the schismatics, because it loves its neighbour."

On the definition of a heretic see *supra,* 20f. On the difference between heretics, schismatics and bad Catholics see *Quaestiones XVII in evang. sec. Matth.* 11,1f: Inter haereticos et malos catholicos hoc interest, quod haeretici falsa credunt, illi autem vera credentes non vivunt ita ut credunt. Solet autem quaeri, schismatici quid ab haereticis distent, et hoc inveniri quod schismaticos non fides diversa faciat, sed communionis disrupta societas, cf. *Epist.* 185,1 where he says of the Arians that they hold the wrong views about the Trinity, whilst the Donatists have the right views on this but are in opposition to the unity of the Catholic Church. The schismatics, i.e. the Donatists, lack love since they do not want to belong to the unity of the church, cf. *Sermo* 269,3 and *Contra litt. Petiliani* 2,77, 172: vobis solemus ostendere quomodo non prosit hominibus quamvis in eis sint vel sacramenta vel fides, ubi charitas non est; ut cum ad unitatem catholicam venitis intelligatis quid vobis conferatur, et quantum sit quod minus habebatis: charitas enim christiana nisi in unitate ecclesiae non potest custodiri, cf. *Sermo* 88,18,21 where he accuses the Donatists of acting in a way contrary to love and unity and *De Trin.* 12,7,11 where he says: opera vero misericordiae nihil prosunt ... quibuscumque haereticis vel schismaticis ubi fides et dilectio et sobria sanctificatio non invenitur (cf. W.H.C. Frend, art. Donatismus, *R.A.C. 4,* p 143). The heretics have no love of God, since they hold the wrong views about God, but love of God needs the right instruction about God, see *De mendacio* 19,40.-The love of the neighbour is also part of the purification of the heart which leads to the vision of God (so the schismatics, despite their correct views about faith cannot reach this vision), see *In Ioann.* 17,8: Tu autem quia Deum nondum vides, diligendo proximum promereris quem videas; diligendo proximum purgas oculum ad videndum Deum (see also M.-F. Berrouard's explanatory note in *Oeuvres de Saint Augustin,* 72, pp 725f).

et ideo peccatis proximi facile ignoscit, quia sibi precatur ignosci ab illo, qui nos reconciliavit sibi, delens omnia praeterita et ad vitam novam nos vocans: quam vitam donec perfectam capiamus, sine peccatis esse non possumus; interest tamen qualia sint.

"And therefore it easily forgives the sins of the neighbour, because it prays that forgiveness may be given to itself by Him who reconciled us to Him, by deleting all past sins and by calling us to a new life; and until we receive that life in its perfection we cannot be without sins; it nevertheless makes a difference of what kind they are."

With their view on a pure church the Donatists in fact show that they do not want to forgive their neighbours, whilst the Catholics forgive because in the Lord's Prayer they themselves ask for forgiveness. The new life will not be received completely before the consummation, this well-known Augustinian tenet is here expressed briefly.- On the difference between sins see *De div. quaest. LXXXIII* 26: there are sins caused by weakness, by lack of knowledge and by malice, weakness is the opposite of strength, lack of knowledge is the opposite of wisdom, malice is the opposite of goodness. The first two categories can be forgiven, the third one deserves punishment in this life and in the life to come: Alia sunt peccata infirmitatis, alia imperitiae, alia malitiae. Infirmitas contraria est virtuti, imperitia contraria est sapientiae, malitia contraria est bonitati. Quisquis igitur novit quid sit virtus et sapientia Dei potest existimare quae sint peccata venialia. Et quisquis novit quid sit bonitas Dei, potest existimare quibus peccatis certa poena debeatur et hic et in futuro saeculo. (On the anti-Stoic background to this insistence on the inequality of sins -the Stoics regarded all sins as equal in seriousness- see G. Bardy's explanatory note in *Oeuvres de Saint Augustin, 10,* p 713.) Presumably under the influence of the Pelagian controversy Augustine modified his position in this respect and said that only God can determine the difference between light and grave sins, see *Ench.* 78: Quae sint autem levia, quae gravia peccata, non humano, sed divino sunt pensanda iudicio. There are sins which are believed to be light, but are proved by Scripture to be grave, see *Ench.* 79: Sunt autem quaedam quae levissima putarentur, nisi in Scripturis demonstrarentur opinione graviora. He still maintains that ignorance and weakness are the causes of sin, but stresses that one can only fight sin successfully with God's help, see *Ench.* 81: Duabus ex causis peccamus, aut nondum videndo quid facere debeamus, aut non faciendo quod debere fieri iam videmus, quorum duorum illud ignorantiae malum est, hoc infirmitatis. Contra quae quidem pugnare nos convenit: sed profecto vincimur nisi divinitate adiuvemur.

(10,22) Nec de peccatorum differentia modo tractandum est, sed credendum omnino nullo modo nobis ignosci ea, quae peccamus, si nos inexorabiles ad ignoscenda peccata fuerimus. itaqe credimus et remissionem peccatorum.

"But it is not now our task to deal with the difference between sins, but we should certainly believe that our sins are in no way forgiven, if we cannot be moved to forgive sins. So we also believe in the forgiveness of sins."

Again the implication is that the schismatics, Donatists, do not want to forgive and therefore do not receive forgiveness themselves. In *Ench.* 64 Augustine says that the church stands with the remission of sins which is mentioned in the Symbol: Ideo post commemorationem sanctae Ecclesiae in ordine Confessionis ponitur remissio peccatorum. Per hanc enim stat Ecclesia quae in terris est . . . In *Sermo* 213,8 he closely connects the remission of sins with the hope of eternal life: Haec in ecclesia si non esset ... nulla futurae vitae et liberationis aeternae spes esset. In this life it has, since the Fall, become inevitable for man to sin, the forgiveness of sins is a great miracle, the final abolition of sin (and death) in eternal life is an even greater miracle, but this latter miracle is the perfection of the first one.

Chapter 10,23-24

Introduction: The traditional doctrine of man's tripartition into spirit, soul and body functions as an argument in favour of the resurrection of the body. Firstly man's spirit is subjected to God, then man's soul to man's spirit and finally man's body to man's soul (and so to the spirit and to God). The latter takes part in the resurrection, which is later than the subjection of the spirit and the soul. The implication is that if man's body were not raised, man would not be saved in his totality, and the Manicheans would be justified in their depreciation of the body.- "The corruptible" of which Paul speaks in *I Cor.* 15,52 is the body and not the soul (which can also be called corruptible and mortal despite its immortality), since Paul points his finger towards it, and only a body can be pointed at, Augustine claims, following a traditional interpretation of this text (23). Those who regard the resurrection of the body as impossible can be refuted with plausible arguments: Philosophers admit that in the series of the four elements (earth, water, air, fire) one element can be transformed into another, then it is not impossible that through God's will such a transformation takes place quickly. This argument could be interpreted as saying that the human body is transformed into a fiery, i.e. ethereal or heavenly one. (In the *Retractationes* Augustine will criticize this view.) The will of God in connection with the resurrection also has a root in Platonic philosophy: when, according to Plato, God's will can preserve the world from destruction, then the will of God can also preserve the body from death, Augustine argues, again following a traditional way of reasoning in connection with the gift of eternal life.- Eternal life after the resurrection is a life in complete fruition of God's love (10,24).

Text, Translation and Commentary:

(**10,23**) Et quoniam tria sunt, quibus homo constat: spiritus, anima et corpus, quae rursus duo dicuntur, quia saepe anima simul cum spiritu nominatur- pars enim quaedam eiusdem rationalis, qua carent bestiae, spiritus dicitur- principale nostrum spiritus est; deinde vita, qua coniungimur corpori, anima dicitur; postremo ipsum corpus, quoniam visibile est, ultimum nostrum est.

"And since there are three parts of which man consists: spirit, soul and body, which are also called two, because often the soul is named together with the spirit- for a certain rational part of it, which the animals lack, is called spirit-, our main part is the spirit; then the life with which we are bound to the body is called soul; finally the body itself, since it is visible, is our lowest part."

In 4,8 Augustine works with the two parts of which man consists, see *supra,*70ff., cf. also *De div. quaest. LXXXIII* 7: Anima aliquando ita dicitur, ut cum mente intelligatur, veluti cum dicimus hominem ex anima et corpore constare: aliquando ita, ut excepta mente dicatur (cf. G. Bardy's explanatory note in *Oeuvres de Saint Augustin, 10,* pp 705f which deals with the use of anima, animus and mens, and with the Stoic background). The tripartition which distinguishes in the soul between the mind in which man differs from the animals and life which man has in common with the animals, suits Augustine better in the present context: the spirit can be subjected to God, the soul to the spirit, albeit more slowly, so in the end the body, too, can be subjected to the spirit,- this way of arguing must make the resurrection of the body more plausible.- Here he says that the soul is the life with which we are bound to the body, elsewhere he calls the soul the life of the body, see e.g. *Sermo* 273,1: est ipsa anima sui corporis vita, *De div. quaest. LXXXIII* 67,5, *Conf.* 10,6,10; 10,20,29, *De lib. arb.* 2,16,41. This is, of course, traditional material, usually the tenet that the soul is the life of the body is specified in the sense that the soul moves the body, see Plato, *Phaedrus* 245C ff, Albinus, *Epitome* 5,5, Numenius, *fragm.* 47 (ed. Des Places), Plutarch, *De an. procr.* 1013C, 1016A, Cicero, *De nat. deor.* 2,32, Calcidius, *Commentarius* 57, Ps.- Justin, *Coh.* 6, Tertullian, *De anima* 6,1 (cf. J.H. Waszink's edition, pp 120f), Athanasius, *Contra Gentes* 33.

haec autem *omnis creatura ingemiscit et parturit usque nunc;* dedit tamen primitias spiritus, quia credidit Deo et bonae iam voluntatis est.

"Now this whole creation has been sighing and has been in travail until now (Rom. 8,22), but it has given its first fruits of the spirit, because it has believed God and is already of good will."

What is described here is the third stage in the four stages of men (see *infra*, 146, *viz.*, when in this life the spirit is through faith subjected to God, see *De div. quaest. LXXXIII* 66,3: tertia actio est, quando iam plenissime credimus Liberatori nostro, nec meritis nostris aliquid tribuimus, sed eius misericordiam diligendo, iam non vincimur delectatione consuetudinis malae, cum ad peccatum nos ducere nititur, sed tamen adhuc eam interpellantem patimur quamvis ei non tradamur.- "This whole creation" is not creation in its totality, but man in his spirit, soul and body,-the angels who live in a spiritual life and the animals do not take part in this "sighing" see *De div. quaest. LXXXIII* 67,5: in homine omnis creatura est, quia et intelligit et vivit et corpus habet; sed non tota creatura in ipso est, quia sunt praeter ipsum et angeli, qui intelligant et vivant et sint, et pecora quae vivant et sint, et corpora quae tantummodo sint. The "until now" does not apply to those who are already in eternal blessedness, but to those who have not yet been liberated, *ibid.:* Usque adhuc autem recte dixit: quia etiam si sint aliqui iam in sinu Abrahae; et latro ille cum Domino in paradiso constitutus, illo die quo credidit, dolere destiterit, tamen usque adhuc omnis creatura congemiscit et dolet, quia in iis qui nondum liberati sunt, omnis est, propter spiritum et animam et corpus. According to Augustine, the first fruits are the spirit, because the truth first takes possession of the spirit in order to take hold of the rest through the spirit, see *De div. quaest. LXXXIII* 67,6: Et bene dixit, primitias habentes spiritus: id est, quorum iam spiritus tamquam sacrificium oblati sunt Deo, et divino charitatis igne comprehensi sunt. Hae sunt primitiae hominis, quia veritas primum spiritum nostrum obtinet, ut per hunc caetera comprehendantur. (In the sentence under discussion we take "omnis creatura" to be the subject of "dedit", and we take "spiritus" as a genetive, so we do not agree with J. Rivière's translation: Pourtant l'esprit a donné ses prémices.)

hic enim spiritus etiam mens vocatur, de quo dicit apostolus: *mente servio legi Dei,* qui item alio loco dicit: *testis est enim mihi Deus, cui servio in spiritu meo.*

"For this spirit is also called mind, about which the Apostle says, In my mind I serve the law of God, (Rom. 7,25), who speaks in the same way in another place, God is my witness, whom I serve with my spirit, (Rom. 1,9)."

The same texts are quoted in the same context in *De div. quaest. LXXXIII* 67,6. The combination of these texts must prove that "spiritus" and "mens" are identical.

anima vero, cum carnalia bona adhuc adpetit, caro nominatur et resistit spiritui non natura, sed consuetudine peccatorum.

"But when the soul still strives after fleshly goods, it is called flesh and resists the spirit, not by nature, but by the habit of sins."

This is the period after the Fall and before the law was given (see *infra,* 146), see *De div. quaest. LXXXIII* 66,3: Ante legem actio est, cum peccatum ignoramus, et sequimur carnales concupiscentias. It is, of course, very important to Augustine that the soul is evil not by nature, but by habit, this is stressed by him against Manichean determinism, see e.g. *De duab. animabus* 13,19ff, cf. J. Rivière, *op. cit.,* p 67 note 4.

unde dicitur, *Mente servio legi Dei, carne autem legi peccati.* quae consuetudo in naturam versa est secundum generationem mortalem peccato primi hominis.

"Hence it says, With my mind I serve the law of God, but with my flesh the law of sin, (Rom. 7,25). This habit is transformed into nature according to the generation which has become mortal through the sin of the first man."

This is the well-known doctrine that men became mortal sinners through the sin of Adam who was immortal before the Fall, see e.g. *De div. quaest. LXXXIII* 66,3: Quia enim oportebat atque id iustum erat ut posteaquam natura nostra peccavit, amissa beatitudine spirituali ... animales carnalesque nasceremur. Man is unable to free himself without faith from this habit which has become his nature, this is already stressed by Augustine before the Pelagian controversy, see *Conf.* 8,5,10,12; 10,40,65.- It is anti-Manichean to stress that the original nature of the soul was good, and that the evil of the soul is caused by habit. But it goes already beyond traditional Christian moralism to say that after Adam's Fall this habit became nature (so that man not only became mortal by nature but also a sinner by nature). The presupposition of this is, of course, that Adam could have used his freedom in a different way, and this means that Augustine speaks about Adam before the Fall in a Pelagian way, and in this respect he never changed his mind (cf. A. von Harnack, *Lehrbuch der Dogmengeschichte III,* Tübingen 1910^4, p 216).

ideoque scriptum est: *et nos aliquando fuimus natura filii irae,* id est vindictae, per quam factum est, ut serviamus legi peccati.

"And therefore it has been written, We, too, were once by nature sons of wrath, (Eph. 2,3), which is: of punishment through which it has come about that we serve the law of sin."

Again it is important that the present state of sin is a punishment, if it were man's natural state the Manicheans would be right. The punishment shows that man could have been different, cf. *De civ.* 12,3: Non enim quisquam de vitiis naturalibus, sed de voluntariis poenas luit. Nam etiam quod vitium consuetudine nimiove progressu roboratum velut naturaliter inolevit, a voluntate sumpsit exordium.

est autem animae natura perfecta, cum spiritui suo subditur et cum sequitur sequentem Deum. ideo *animalis homo non percipit quae sunt Spiritus Dei.*

"But the nature of the soul is perfect when it subjects itself to its spirit and when it follows the spirit which follows God. Therefore the animate man does not perceive the things which are of the Spirit of God."(I Cor. 2,14)

In *De mor. eccl. cath.* 1,3,5 Augustine gives as a general rule that every man should follow what is best: Oportet autem omnem hominem id quod optimum est sequi. In man the soul is better than the body, therefore the body should follow the soul and the soul should follow God, 1,4,6ff. J. Rivière, *op. cit.*, p 68 note 1 refers as background to the Stoic axiom "sequi Deum", see on this M. Pohlenz, *Die Stoa. Geschichte einer geistigen Bewegung I*, Göttingen 1970[4], p 186 and *II*, Göttingen 1972[4], pp 61f. But the question of free will and determinism which is closely connected with this Stoic axiom is not explicitly discussed here by Augustine. (On Augustine and Stoicism see *supra*, 41, and further G. Verbeke, Augustin et le Stoicisme, *Recherches augustiniennes (1)* 1958, pp 67ff, and M. Spanneut, Le Stoicisme et Saint Augustin, *Forma Futuri. Studi in onore del cardinale Michele Pellegrino*, Turino 1975, pp 896ff.) But Plato's famous and often quoted statement in Theaetetus 176A/B, that the goal of life is the "*homoioosis theoo kata to dynaton*" seems a more important background, see on this E.P. Meijering, *Athanasius: Contra Gentes*, p 17, and the literature quoted there.

sed non tam cito anima subiugatur spiritui ad bonam operationem, quam cito spiritus Deo ad veram fidem et bonam voluntatem, sed aliquando tardius eius inpetus, quo in carnalia et temporalia diffluit, refrenatur.

"But the soul is not so quickly subjected to the spirit towards doing good as the spirit is subjected to God in order to have the true faith and the good will, but its striving by which it disperses into fleshly and temporal things is sometimes restrained more slowly."

When the soul is subjected to the spirit it means that its fleshly desires are restrained and are led towards doing good, when the spirit is subjected to God this leads to faith and a good will. This implies that the subjection of the soul is the second stage, *viz.*, the stage under the law, see *De div. quaest. LXXXIII* 66,3 where it says of the soul which still refuses to obey: Sub lege est actio cum iam prohibemur a peccato, et tamen consuetudine eius victi peccamus, quoniam nos nondum adiuvat fides.

sed quoniam et ipsa mundatur, recipiens stabilitatem naturae suae dominante spiritu, quod sibi caput est, cuius capitis caput est Christus, non est desperandum etiam corpus restitui naturae propriae; sed utique non tam cito quam anima, sicut neque anima tam cito quam spiritus, sed tempore opportuno *in novissima tuba, cum mortui resurgent incorrupti, et nos inmutabimur.*

"Because it, too, is cleansed, receiving the stability of its nature through the dominance of the spirit, because it is its head,- of which head Christ is the head,-

there is no reason to despair that the body, too, is restituted to its proper nature, but certainly not so quickly as the soul, as also the soul is not restituted so quickly as the spirit, but at the right moment, at the last trumpet, when the dead will rise incorruptible and we shall be changed, (I Cor. 15,52)."

In itself the human soul (although immortal, see *infra,* 149) is changeable, God's life is unchangeable, see e.g. *In Ioann.* 19,11: Vivit Deus, vivit et anima: sed vita Dei incommutablis est, vita animae mutabilis est. So when the soul is entirely subjected to the spirit (and the spirit to God), then the soul receives unchangeable life, i.e. stability. Augustine argues *per analogiam* that also the body must receive eternal life, i.e. rise again, and be restituted to its proper nature, i.e. the nature God wanted it to have if man had not fallen, see *De cat. rud.* 18,29, *De Gen. a.l.* 6,25,36. As we have seen, Augustine distinguishes in *De div. quaest. LXXXIII* 66,3ff between four stages of men after the Fall: 1. Before the law, this is the life of the "homo carnalis" who is governed by the body without knowing it. 2. The "homo animalis" who is governed by bodily desires but who can through the law know better. 3. The "homo spiritalis" who through faith has subjected his spirit to God. 4. The "homo liberatus" in eternal life. The "homo spiritalis" is the nearest to the state of the resurrection, the "homo carnalis" is at the greatest distance by far, but since the whole man will be saved, there is no reason not to believe that what is now at the greatest distance will take part in the salvation just the same as what is nearest. The flesh is moved more slowly towards obedience, therefore the "homo carnalis" is at the greatest distance from salvation. These stages in history also appear in human lives. When men are now in the first or second stage this implies criticism: they are still in stages which they should have overcome by following God's revelation.- A similar partition of men into "homines carnales", "homines animales" and "homines spiritales" is made by Hilary of Poitiers, cf. E.P. Meijering, *Hilary of Poitiers on the Trinity,* pp 15ff. Just like Hilary who portrays the "homo carnalis" as an Epicurean and the "homo animalis" as a Stoic Augustine declares that the Epicureans live "secundum carnem", the Stoics "secundum animam", but Paul and the Christians "secundum Deum", see *Sermo* 156,7,7: contulerunt cum illo quidam philosophorum Epicureorum et Stoicorum (*Act.* 17,18): contulerunt cum illo secundum carnem viventes, contulerunt cum illo secundum animam viventes, contulit cum illis secundum Deum vivens. Dicebat Epicurus: Mihi frui carne, bonum est. Dicebat Stoicus: Mihi frui mea mente, bonum est. Dicebat Apostolus: Mihi autem adhaerere Deo, bonum est, cf. *De civ.* 14,2,1 and *supra*, 126.- The resurrection of the body will take place at the right moment, at the last trumpet. The "last trumpet" is interpreted by Augustine as the last sign which will be given that these things will be fulfilled, see *Epist.* 205,14: in novissima tuba, hoc est, in novissimo signo quod dabitur, ut ista compleantur. (Such a last sign should certainly be given at the right moment.)

et ideo credimus et carnis resurrectionem, non tantum quia reparatur anima, quae nunc propter carnales affectiones caro nominatur, sed haec etiam visibilis caro, quae naturaliter est caro, cuius nomen anima non propter naturam, sed propter affectiones carnales accepit, haec ergo visibilis quae proprie dicitur caro sine dubitatione credenda est resurgere.

"And therefore we believe in the resurrection also of the flesh, not only because the soul is repaired which is now called flesh, because of the fleshly inclinations, but also this visible flesh which is flesh by nature, whose name the soul did receive not because of its nature, but because of its fleshly inclinations. So this visible flesh in the proper sense ought without any doubt to be believed to rise."

The body obviously has an influence on the soul, and such a great one at that, that the soul can be called "flesh" because of its fleshly behaviour. If there were no resurrection of this flesh, then the Manicheans and Platonists like Porphyry would be right, since part of God's creation would not be worthy of redemption (cf. *supra*, 79f, and *infra*, 152). Furthermore, if the effects of flesh, *viz.,* the fleshly inclinations of the soul are repaired, then the cause, *viz.,* flesh ought to be repaired as well. The argument can be brought in connection with what was said in 4,8: only if Christ assumed total Man, Man in his totality could be saved, the assumption of total Man implies the resurrection of total Man with spirit, soul and body.

videtur enim Paulus apostolus eam tamquam digito ostendere, cum dicit: *oportet corruptibile hoc induere incorruptionem.* cum enim dicit, "hoc", in eam quasi digitum intendit.

"For the Apostle Paul seems, so to speak, to point towards it his finger when he says, This coruptibility must put on incorruption, (I Cor. 15,52). For when he says "this" he, so to speak, directs his finger towards it."

This must exclude the possibility that Paul has the corruptible soul in mind. The same explanation is given by Origen, *De Princ.* 2,3,3: Quod enim ait, corruptibile hoc, et, mortale hoc, velut tangentis et ostendentis affectu, cui alii convenit nisi materiae corporali?, and by Tertullian, *De res.* 51,9: Ac ne putes aliud sentire apostolum, providentem sibi et, ut de carne dictum intellegas laborantem: cum dicit istud corruptivum et istud mortale, cutem ipsam tenens dicit, see als *Adv. Marc.* 5,10,14.- Augustine is well aware that what can be pointed at with the finger can much more easily be perceived than what must be understood with the mind, see *De doct. christ., Prol.* 3: . . . illis qui haec quae scribimus non intelligunt, hoc dico: me ita non esse reprehendendum, quia haec non intelligunt, tamquam si lunam veterem vel novam, sidusve aliquod minime clarum vellent videre quod ego intento digito demonstrarem. This suits the present context well: It is the lowest material part of man which must share in redemption.

quod autem visibile est, id potest digito ostendi,

"Now, what is visible can be pointed at with the finger,"

What can be touched is bodily, this Platonic and Epicurean tenet which is, of course, a truism (see Plato, *Timaeus* 28B (**XXXVI**); Lucrece, *De rer. nat.* 1,304: tangere enim et tangi nisi corpus nulla potest res) was adopted by Tertullian, see *De anima* 5,1 and *Adv. Marc.* 4,8,3 (cf. J.H. Waszink's edition p 130). Augustine gives as a general rule that what can be touched or seen or perceived in another bodily way is inferior to what can be thought, since the senses are inferior to thinking, see *De duab. animabus* 2,2: . . . illud consequi ut cuncta quae tactu et visu, vel quolibet alio modo corporaliter sentiretur tanto essent inferiora his quae intelligendo asequeremur, quanto ipso sensus intelligentiae cedere videremus. This is also the implication of what is said here: the body is inferior to the soul and the spirit, but in the end will rise and be saved as well.

quoniam potest etiam anima corruptibilis dici; nam vitiis morum ipsa corrumpitur.

"for also the soul can be called corruptible, for it is itself corrupted by the sins of its behaviour."

The corruptible soul is not seen and is not bodily, therefore Paul cannot have it in mind when he points his finger to the corruptibility which must put on incorruptibility.

et mortale hoc induere inmortalitatem cum legitur, eadem significatur visibilis caro, quia in eam identidem velut digitus intenditur. potest enim et anima sicut corruptibilis propter morum vitia, ita etiam mortalis dici.

"When we read, And this mortality (must) put on immortality, (I Cor. 15,53), this same visible flesh is indicated for towards it he similarly points so to speak with his finger. For the soul, too, as it can be called corruptible because of its behaviour, can in the same way also be called mortal."

The qualification of "corruptible" and "mortal" can both be applied to the body and the soul, therefore the pointing of the finger is necessary in order to make sure that in both cases the body and not the soul is meant.- According to Augustine, the soul is both mortal and immortal, see *De Gen. a.l.* 7,28,43: ... de anima ... nihil confirmo nisi ... quod sit immortalis secundum quendam vitae modum, quem nullo modo potest amittere; secundum quandam vero mutabilitatem, qua potest vel deterior vel melior fieri, non immerito etiam mortalis possit intelligi.

mors quippe animae est apostatare a Deo: quod primum eius peccatum in paradiso sacris Litteris continetur.

"For the death of the soul is to forsake God, this is contained in the Holy Scripture as its first sin in Paradise."

On the death of the soul through sin cf. *De duab. animab.* 8,10: Etenim anima quamvis sit immortalis, tamen ... mors eius recte dicitur a Dei cognitione aversio, cf. *Sermo* 65,6,7: scitote certumque tenete, corpus mortuum esse sine anima: animam mortuam esse sine Deo. Omnis homo sine Deo mortuam habet animam. The cause of man's defection from God is man's "superbia", see *supra*, 58. In the present context this is hinted at, for the words "Mors quippe animae apostatare a Deo, quod primum eius peccatum in paradiso sacris in Litteris continetur" are an allusion to *Sap. Sir.* 10,14: Initium superbiae hominis apostatare a Deo.

(10,24) Resurget igitur corpus secundum christianam fidem, qae fallere non potest.

"So the body will rise according to the Christian faith which cannot deceive."

The Christian doctrine cannot make the believers err (falli),- "to make err" (fallere) is the same as "to lie" (when used for persons), since when one lies one knows that one does not speak the truth, whilst when one errs one does not know, see e.g. *Sermo* 133,4: Fallitur qui putat verum esse quod dicit et quia verum putat, ideo dicit ... mentitur autem qui falsum esse aliquid putat, et pro vero dicit ... fallere affectat. This the Christian doctrine, as it is expressed in the Symbol, cannot do, since it is based on God's revelation and God does not and cannot lie (see *supra*, 29, 43), cf. what Augustine says in the introduction to a sermon on the resurrection, *Sermo* 362,5,5: Non vos fallo, audite quod credidi. Non vobis vilescat, quia quod credidi auditis: auditis enim veracem confessionem . . . Si ergo, fratres, omnes nos, et, ut credimus sanctorum litteris, omnes etiam qui ante nos in carne vixerunt, et per quos loquens Spiritus Dei distribuit hominibus tantum quantum satis esset significari peregrinantibus, omnes quod credimus loquimur: Dominus autem ipse, quae noverat.

quod cui videtur incredibile, qualis nunc sit caro adtendit, qualis autem futura sit non considerat: quia illo tempore inmutationis angelicae non iam caro erit et sanguis, sed tantum corpus.

"He to whom this seems incredible only pays attention to how the flesh now is, but does not consider how it will be, because at that time of angelical transformation there will no longer be flesh and blood, but only body."

Augustine always adhered to the tenet (which goes back to *Matth.* 23,30, cf. on this matter G. Bardy's explanatory note in *Oeuvres de Saint Augustin, 10,* p 728) that in eternal life men will be like angels, see e.g. *De agone christ.* 32,34, *De div. quaest. LXXXIII* 47, *De Gen. a.l.* 4,24,41; 6,19,30; 6,24,35; 12,35,68, *De civ.* 22,17. But to a certain degree he changed his mind on the implications of this doctrine: in *De agone christ.* and *De div. quaest. LXXXIII* he seems to believe that the substance of the flesh will be changed into heavenly or ethereal substance, see *De agone christ.* 32,34: Cum enim hoc factum fuerit, iam non erit caro et sanguis, sed caeleste corpus, and *De div. quaest. LXXXIII* 47: . . . angelica corpora, qualia nos habituros speramus, lucidissima atque aetherea esse credendum est. In the *Retractationes* he criticizes these statements, because they could be understood as meaning that the risen flesh has no substance (2,3: non sic accipiendum est quasi carnis non sit futura substantia, 1,26: si hoc sine membris quae nunc habemus, et sine substantia, quamvis incorruptibilis, tamen carnis accipiatur, erratur). In *De civ.* 22,17 he makes it clear that in the resurrection men will be like angels in respect of immortality and felicity, not of flesh, as the equality is not in respect of the resurrection which the angels did not need, since they could not die: Aequales utique angelis immortalitate ac felicitate, non carne: sicut nec resurrectione, qua non indiguerunt angeli, quoniam nec mori potuerunt. The argument in the present paragraph will be criticized by Augustine in the *Retractationes* for the same reason for which he criticizes the statements made on this subject in the *De agone christiano* and the *De div. quaest. LXXXIII.* So at the time of the *Retractationes* he feared that what was said here in the *De fide et symbolo* about the angelic body could be understood as applying to an ethereal body.- Augustine gives the following reasonable argument for man's transformation into angelic substance: if God can make man from sordid dust, He can certainly make an angel from man, see *Sermo* 45,10: Si de sordibus fecit hominem, de homine non faciet angelum? . . . De istis sordibus fecit hominem et praefecit aliis animalibus; de homine non faciet angelum? Faciet prorsus. The dust from which man was created by God was also created by God (see *supra,* 30). So this argument is in fact the same one as the traditional argument which Augustine reproduces elsewhere: if God can make man from nothing, He can raise man as well, see *Sermo* 264,6: Qui potuit te facere cum non esses, non potest reparare quod fueras, et non potest dare honorem claritiatis fidei tuae ...? Cf. for this argument also Irenaeus, *Adv. Haer.* 5,3,2 **(XXXVII)**. Here the resurrection is made plausible with the belief in the creation from nothing: Augustine also makes it plausible with belief in the incarnation: the Lord showed that sin and not the substance of flesh is evil, the flesh could, together with the soul, be assumed by Him and could also be raised by Him, see *De civ.* 10,24: Bonus itaque verusque Mediator ostendit peccatum esse malum, non carnis substantiam vel naturam; quae cum anima hominis et suscipi sine peccato potuit, et haberi, et morte deponi, et in melius resurrectione mutari. Again this is a traditional argument, see e.g. Irenaeus, *Adv. Haer.* 5,14,1: Si enim non haberet caro salvari, nequaquam Verbum Dei caro factum esset, Tertullian, *De res. mort.* 2,6: obducti dehinc de deo carnis auctore et de Christo carnis redemptore, iam et de resurrectione carnis revincentur, congruenter scilicet de deo carnis auctori et Christo carnis redemptori.

cum enim de carne apostolus loqueretur, *alia,* inquit, *caro pecorum, alia volucrum, alia piscium, alia serpentum. et corpora caelestia, et corpora terrestria.* non enim dixit, et caro caelestis, dixit autem: *et caelestia et terrestria corpora.* omnis enim caro etiam corpus est, non autem omne corpus etiam caro est: primo in istis terrestribus, quoniam lignum corpus est, sed non caro; hominis autem vel pecoris et corpus et caro est; in caelestibus vero nulla caro, sed corpora simplicia et lucida, quae appellat apostolus spiritalia, nonnulli autem vocant aetherea. et ideo non carnis resurrectioni contradicit illud quod ait: *caro et sanguis regnum Dei non possidebunt,* sed quale futurum sit, quod nunc caro et sanguis est, praedicat,

"For when the Apostle spoke about flesh he said, There is a difference between the flesh of the animals, of the birds, of the fish, of the snakes, and there are heavenly and earthly bodies, (I Cor. 15,39f). For he did not say: "and heavenly flesh", but he did say: "and heavenly and earthly bodies". For all flesh is also body, but not every body is also flesh. In the first place (this can be seen) in these earthly things, because wood is a body, not flesh; with man and the animals it is both body and flesh; in the heavenly things, however, there is no flesh at all, but simple and shining bodies which the Apostle calls spiritual, but some call ethereal. And therefore that word which he speaks, Flesh and blood will not inherit the Kingdom of God, (I Cor. 15,50) does not contradict the resurrection of the flesh, but it preaches how that which is now flesh and blood will be; "

The only possible interpretation of this argument is that flesh and blood will be transformed into a heavenly and ethereal body which no longer is flesh and blood. Augustine criticizes this in *Retract.* 1,17 and says that this must be corrected because it can be understood as implying that such a body has no limbs and that there will be no substance of flesh (by saying that it can be understood in this way he leaves open the possibility that this need not be the case,- it seems to us that it can only be understood in the way Augustine rejects it): Sed quisquis ea sic accipit, ut existimet ita corpus terrenum quale nunc habemus, in corpus caeleste resurrectione mutari, ut nec membra ista, nec carnis sit futura substantia, procul dubio corrigendus est. It is not easy to explain why Augustine initially spoke about the resurrection in a way which could be thus interpreted . In 6,13 he had given an interpretation which excluded the idea that the human body is transformed into spirit (see *supra,* 90). Furthermore, *I Cor.* 15,52 was traditionally interpreted in a way that did not contradict the resurrection of the flesh and could imply that risen man is not devoid of flesh, since the flesh is transformed from mortal to immortal (and not into a completely different substance), and since "flesh and blood" suggest the fleshly behaviour of sinners, see Irenaeus, *Adv. Haer.* 5,9ff, cf. Tertullian, *Adv. Marc.* 5,10,11ff, De res. 48ff. It could be that Augustine, after his Manichean depreciation of the flesh, at first found the transformation of the human body into an ethereal body a more attractive idea than the transformation of mortal flesh into immortal flesh. This implies that men are transformed into angels, later on this initial position will be qualified by Augustine in the sense that men will be in certain respects like angels. In his initial view the angels could be like the lower gods whom, as Plato says, the Demiurge addresses, see *Timaeus* 41A/B, and whom Augustine calls "dei caelestes" who have "corpora visibilia" or "caelestia", see *Sermo* 242,8,8, *De civ.* 22,26 (on Augustine's use of this passage from the *Timaeus* see also *infra,* in the present paragraph).

in qualem naturam quisquis hanc carnem converti posse non credit, gradibus ducendus est ad fidem. si enim ab eo quaeras, utrum terra in aquam possit converti, propter vicinitatem non ei videtur incredibile. rursus si quaeras utrum aqua possit in aerem, neque hoc absurdum esse respondet; vicina enim sunt sibi. et de aere si quaeras, utrum in aethereum corpus, id est, in caeleste possit mutari, iam ipsa vicinitas persuadet.

"everybody who does not believe that this flesh can be transformed into such nature must be led step by step to such a faith. For if you ask him whether earth can be transformed into water it does not seem unbelievable to him, because they are so near. Again if you ask him, whether water can be transformed into air, he answers that this is not absurd either, because they are near to each other. And if you ask about air whether it can be changed into an ethereal body, which is a heavenly one, the vicinity itself already persuades it to be possible."

These are the four elements, in the sequence mentioned here, from which, according to Plato, the cosmos was made, see *De civ.* 22,11,5 where Augustine quotes Plato's view that fire and earth are the outer elements with water and air between them: si ita est elementorum ordo dispositus, ut secundum Platonem duobus mediis, id est aere et aqua, duo extrema, id est ignis et terra iungantur,- the fourth one is also called ether or heaven, see *Sermo* 242,6,8: rogo te, dic mihi, Terra terra est, Aqua aqua est, Aer aer est, Aether id est caelum, et ignis ille liquidus caelum est. Quatuor nempe ista quasi gradatim construxerunt et aedificaverunt mundum hoc est, ex his quatuor aedificatus est mundus, see Plato, *Timaeus* 32B (**XXXVIII**). In *De civ.* 8,11 Augustine claims that Plato here imitates what he himself had read in *Gen.* 1,1-2: heaven and earth are the elements of earth and fire, the water above which the Spirit was are the elements of water and air: In Timaeo autem Plato, quem librum de mundi constitutione conscripsit, Deum dicit in illo opere terram primo ignemque iunxisse: manifestum est autem quod igni tribuat caeli locum: habet ergo haec sententia quaedam illius similitudinem qua dictum est, In principio fecit Deus caelum et terram. Deinde illa duo media, quibus interpositis sibimet haec extrema copularentur, aquam dicit et aerem: unde putatur sic intellexisse quod sciptum est, Spiritus Dei superferebatur super aquam. On the claim (which was often made by early Christian writers) that Plato (and Greek philosophers in general) had stolen their right ideas from the Bible see e.g. Eusebius, *Praep. Evang.* 11,9,4, Cyril of Alexandria, *Contra Julianum* 1,35, see further H. Chadwick in *The Cambridge History of Later Greek and Early Medieval Philosophy,* p 170.- Here Augustine claims that because the elements are near to each other, they can, according to *the* philosophers, be transformed into each other. In *De Gen. a.l.* 3,3,4 he is much more cautious and says that this is only possible according to *some* philosophers: Alii enim dicunt omnia in omnia posse mutari, atque converti, alii vero esse aliquid omnino proprium singulis perhibent elementis, quod in alterius elementi qualitatem nullo modo vertatur.

quod ergo per hos gradus fieri posse concedit, ut terra in corpus aethereum convertatur, cur non accedente Dei voluntate, qua corpus humanum supra aquas potuit ambulare, celerrime id fieri posse, quemadmodum dictum est: *in ictu oculi,* sine ullis talibus gradibus credit, sicut plerumque fumus in flammam mira cleritate convertitur?

"So what he concedes to be possible through these steps, so that earth is transformed into an ethereal body, why does he not believe that when God's will is added, through which a human body could walk on the water, that this can happen very quickly, as it has been said, in the twinkling of an eye, (I Cor. 15,52), without any such steps, as often smoke is turned into flame with astonishing quickness?"

What happens in nature slowly "through these steps", i.e. through the transformation of one element into the other, can through God's omnipotent will happen quickly as well,- and also in nature such a swift transformation can take place. This must make belief in the resurrection plausible. Augustine produces this argument repeatedly, see e.g. *De civ.* 21,7,1: Sed cum Deus auctor sit naturarum omnium, cur nolunt fortiorem nos reddere rationem, quando aliquid velut impossibile nolunt credere, eisque redditionem rationis poscentibus respondemus, hanc esse voluntatem omnipotentis Dei, cf. 22,25, *Epist.* 102,5, *Sermo* 240,2,2. There is a difference between what happens according to the laws of nature (instituted by God the Creator) and what happens in a swift, miraculous way through God's omnipotence, cf. *De Gen. a.l.* 2,1,2 where he wants to explain the waters above the stars of heaven, not with a reference to God's omnipotence but in accordance with the laws of nature as taught by Scripture: Multi enim asserunt istarum aquarum naturam, super sidereum caelum esse non posse . . . Neque quisquam istos debet ita refellere, ut dicat secundum omnipotentiam Dei, cui cuncta possibilia sunt, oportere nos credere, aquas etiam tam graves quam novimus atque sentimus, caelesti corpori, in quo sunt sidera, superfusas. Nunc enim quemadmodum Deus instituerit naturas rerum secundum Scripturas eius nos convenit quaerere, non quid in eis vel ex eis ad miraculum potentiae suae velit operari. (See on this matter in general also R.M. Grant, *Miracle and*

Natural Law in Graeco-Roman and Early Christian Thought, Amsterdam 1952, especially pp 27f, 215ff, 244f.) As Augustine was obviously well aware, this appeal to God's omnipotent will could be used for apologetic purposes as well, since it seems to find support in the famous passage in Plato's *Timaeus* 41 A/B, where the Demiurge promises the lower gods eternal life through the power of His will (**XXXIX**). In Middle Platonism this text was used as a proof when one argued in favour of both the creation of the world and the duration of the world: what can be created by the will of God can be preserved by the will of God, see Atticus, *fragm.* 4 (ed. Baudry) and Origen, *De Princ.* 2,3,6: dicunt quidam de hoc mundo, quoniam corruptibilis quidem est ex eo quod factus est, nec tamen corrumpitur quia corruptione fortior ac validior est voluntas Dei. Christians applied this tenet to the gift of immortality to the souls of the believers, see e.g. Justin Martyr, *Dial.* 5,1-6,2 (cf. J.C.M. van Winden, *An Early Christian Philosopher. Justin Martyr's Dialogue with Trypho, Chapters 1-9,* Leiden 1971, pp 84ff), Irenaeus, *Adv. Haer.* 2,56 and Athanasius, *Contra Gentes* 33,(cf. E.P. Meijering, *Athanasius: Contra Gentes,* pp 110f). Augustine uses this passage in his defence of the doctrine of the resurrection, see *De civ.* 13,16ff and 22,26, *Sermo* 241,8,8. He quotes this section in Cicero's translation in *De civ.* 22,26: Quoniam estis orti, immortales esse et indissolubiles non potestis: non tamen dissolvemini, neque vos ulla mortis fata periment, nec erunt valentiora quam consilium meum quod maius est vinculum ad perpetuitatem vestram, quam illa quibus estis colligati (with small differences the same quotation in 13,16) and paraphrases it as follows: Vos quidem immortales esse non potestis, sed mea voluntate immortales eritis, and then says that God promises to make them immortal despite the fact that this is impossible, and therefore that God can raise flesh as incorruptible, immortal and spiritual who, according to Plato, promises that He will do the impossible: Qui enim dicit, Vos quidem immortales . . .: quid aliud dicit quam id quod fieri non potest, me faciente tamen eritis? Ille igitur carnem incorruptibilem, immortalem, spiritualem resuscitabit qui iuxta Platonem, id quod impossibile, se facturum esse promisit.- The walking on the water by Christ is, of course, also an argument against the Platonists who say that because of the law of gravity a human body cannot be in heaven (see *supra,* 89): if an earthly body can (against this law) walk on the water it can also be in heaven. For this, too, a natural analogy is produced by Augustine: wood can float on water, see *Sermo* 242,6,8: Terra in fundamento est: ordinem sequere. quid super terram? Aqua. Quare lignum natat super aquam? terrenum est corpus,- si revoces ad illum ordinem ponderum, sub aqua esse debuit, non supra. Augustine does not come forward with this argument in the present paragraph, but he may have had it in mind, hence he may specifically have named wood as an example of what is a body, but not flesh (see *supra*, 152).- The "twinkling of an eye" in which the resurrection takes place must be seen in connection with the angelical state of the risen men: they share in the swiftness of movement (and obedience) of the heavenly bodies, see *Sermo* 277,7,7ff, *De Gen. a.l.* 4,34,55. Interesting in this context is also Augustine's observation that air is more mobile than water and ether more mobile than air, *De Gen. a.l. lib. imp.* 4,14. He ascribes this view to Plato, who defines fire as most mobile, the earth as immobile, with air and water in between, see *De civ.* 8,15,2: Nam et illa ratio Platonis quia elementa quatuor proportione contexit atque ordinat, ita duobus extremis igni mobilissimo et terrae immobili, media duo, aerem et aquam, interserens . . ..- It seems strange that Augustine speaks of the transformation of smoke into fire as a natural phenomenon and not the other way round. The reason seems to be that fire is the highest of the four elements, according to Plato. Augustine argues in favour of a change from the lowest to the highest element, therefore he needs the transformation of smoke (air) to fire. (One *does* sometimes observe fire at the top of smoke above fire). See in this connection also Augustine's observation that fire always tries to transcend air, when one holds a torch upside down, the fire pushes itself upwards, *De Gen. a.l.* 2,3,6: Iam vero ignem ad superna emicantem etiam ipsius aeris naturam velle transcendere, quis non sentiat? quandoquidem si ardentem faculam capite deorsum quisque teneat, nihilominus flammae crinis ad superiora contendit. This also explains the rational argument in favour of the resurrection that as it is a miracle that fire is on earth, so the miracle can happen that a body is in heaven, see *De civ.* 22,11,5.

caro enim nostra utique ex terra est; philosophi autem, quorum argumentis saepius resurrectioni carnis resistitur, quibus asserunt nullum esse posse terrenum corpus in caelo, omne corpus in omne corpus converti et mutari posse concedunt.

"For our flesh certainly stems from the earth, but the philosophers with whose arguments one quite often resists the resurrection of the flesh, arguments with which they assert that no earthly body can be in heaven, concede that any body can be transformed and changed into every body."

On this philosphical argument and Augustine's counterarguments see *supra*, 89, 150ff.

qua corporis resurrectione facta a temporis condicione liberati aeterna vita ineffabili caritate atque stabilitate (sine corruptione) perfruemur.

tunc enim fiet illud, quod scriptum est: *absorta est mors in victoria. ubi est, mors, aculeus tuus? ubi est, mors, contentio tua?*

"When this resurrection of the body has taken place, then we shall, liberated from existence in time, enjoy eternal life, ineffable love and stability (without corruption). For then will come true that word that has been written, Death has been swallowed up in victory, death, where is thy sting, death, where is thy strife? (I Cor. 15,54)?"

The existence in time (temporis condicio) is an obstacle to the enjoyment of eternal life and love, since in time man is torn apart and cannot concentrate on God, see e.g. *Conf.* 11,29,30. This will no longer be the case in eternal life, see *De Gen.* a.l. 4,30,47: ubi semper est dies in contemplatione incommutabilis veritatis, semper vespera in cognitione in seipsa creaturae, semper mane etiam ex hac cognitione in laude Creatoris. In eternal life man remains conscious of his liberation in order not to become ungrateful to his Liberator, see *De civ.* 22,30,3: Erit ergo illius civitatis et una in omnibus, et inseparabilis in singulis voluntas libera, ab omni malo liberata . . . nec tamen ideo suae liberationis oblita, ut liberatori non sit grata. (Here Augustine differs from Plotinus: according to Plotinus, there is no memory of temporal matters in eternity, see *Enneads* 4,3,32 and 4,4,1-4, cf. A. Solignac's explanatory note in *Oeuvres de Saint Augustin,14, Les Confessions, Livres VIII-XIII,* Paris 1963, p 538). Eternal life without sin is not a natural quality of man, but a gift of God, see *De civ.* 22,30,3: hoc autem novissimum eo potentius erit, quo peccare non poterit. Verum hoc quoque Dei munere, non suae possibilitate naturae. Aliud est enim, esse Deum, aliud participem Dei (cf. the reference to Irenaeus and Justin Martyr in which immortality is also described as a gift of God, *supra*, 155). This also explains the clarification Augustine gives in saying that risen men will be like the angels: men will not take part in the angels' nature, but will like the angels take part in the Trinity, see *De civ.* 9,15: Neque enim nos a mortalitate et miseria liberans ad Angelos immortales beatosque ita producit, ut eorum participatione etiam nos immortales et beati simus, sed ad illam Trinitatem cuius angeli participatione beati sunt, cf. *De civ.* 11,12 (on the subject of participation in general see F.Normann, *Teilhabe- Ein Schlüsselwort der Vätertheologie,* Münster 1978, especially pp 278ff).- The ineffable love makes us forget the chaotic existence in time and makes us concentrate on God alone, see *Conf.* 11,29,39: at ego in tempora dissilui, quorum ordinem nescio, et tumultuosis varietatibus dilaniantur cogitationes meae, intima viscera animae meae donec in te confluam purgatus et liquidus igne amoris tui.- On the stability of the body after the resurrection see *supra,* 90.- On Augustines's interpretation of *I*

Cor. 15,54 see *De div. quaest. LXXXIII* 70 where this is interpreted as the victory upon the "vita carnalis": Morte significari arbitror hoc loco carnalem consuetudinem quae resistit bonae voluntati delectatione temporalium fruendorum ... Tunc itaque absorpta erit mors in victoriam, cum per sanctificationem in omni parte hominis perfecta delectatione spiritualium delectatatio carnalis obruetur. In this state of the resurrection men share in the glory of the angels, see *Sermo* 4,4,4: Vivunt autem angeli in gaudio, non creaturae, sed Creatoris. Gaudium enim creaturae est quidquid videtur: gaudium Creatoris est quod non videtur oculis, sed purgata acie mentis.

VI

CONCLUDING STATEMENTS
(10,25)

(**10,25**) Haec est fides, quae paucis verbis tenenda in symbolo novellis christianis datur.

"This is the faith which is given to the newly reborn Christians with few words in the Symbol."

On the necessary brevity of the Symbol as the expression of faith see *supra*, 19ff.

quae pauca verba fidelibus nota sunt, ut credendo subiugentur Deo, subiugati recte vivant, recte vivendo cor mundent, corde mundato quod credunt intellegant.

"These few words are known to the believers, that by believing they subject themselves to God, and having subjected themselves live in the right way and by living in the right way cleanse their heart and having cleansed their heart understand what they believe."

The cleansing of the heart means that one does not think in a bodily way about God and that one is not governed by one's own body - when the believers do this they can reach the spiritual understanding of the contents of the Creed which they need in order to make progress in knowledge, which will reach its goal in eternal life. The same sequence of faith, obedience to God and spiritual understanding of the faith is expressed in *De agone christiano* 13,14: Fides est prima quae subiugat animam Deo, deinde praecepta vivendi, quibus custoditis spes nostra firmatur, et nutritur charitas, et lucere incipit quod antea tantummodo credebatur, cf. 33,35. Behind this lies the typically Platonic doctrine of the ethico-noetic purification, but the specific Christian element is the emphasis on the humility of Christ which sets the example in the act of the incarnation.

CONCLUSIONS AND SOME FINAL OBSERVATIONS

a) Conclusions

Reading the *De fide et symbolo* one sees the still fairly young presbyter before the bishops: it is obviously his intention to show his learned orthodoxy. He has read his sources, the ecclesiastical writers, with great authority, and he can reproduce their arguments in his defence of the Christian faith against the attacks made by the heretics, especially the Manicheans. As such, the *De fide et symbolo* is a traditional piece of writing, not only because the traditional Symbol is explained, but also because it is explained with largely common arguments.

Nevertheless, the Augustinian flavour is apparent everywhere: the whole treatise is presented as an effort to make clear the relation between faith and understanding, a problem with which Augustine struggled during the whole of his life. Faith precedes but also looks for understanding,- understanding does not replace faith but deepens it. Both faith and understanding are a gift of God and lead to a new life, *viz.*, the life of humility which follows the example set in the incarnation of Christ.

Faith in God the Creator means faith in the almighty God who creates from nothing. Creation from nothing is firmly stated against Manichean dualism, and in itself this is traditional material, but Augustine elaborates in his own way the reflections which he found in the ecclesiastical writers about the world which was created formless and then received its forms from God. With this doctrine not only the idea of any weakness on the part of God who is thought to be unable to create unless He creates, just like man, something from something else, but also any anthropomorphous conception of God is avoided, of God who is unable to bring about the world which He sees with the eyes of His mind, but to which matter is an obstacle.

Belief in Christ as the Father's only-begotten Son is firstly explained as faith in God's creative Word through which all things were made. This is traditional material, but Augustine adds his own thoughts by dwelling on the question of in how far words can reliably reveal thoughts. Human words cannot do this, and in stressing this Augustine shows a good deal of scepticism about his own rhetorical education, but God is unlike man and therefore He can reveal Himself truly in His eternal Word.

In transgressing from the doctrine of creation to the doctrine of the incarnation he firstly states what he is expected to state: the difference between the orthodox doctrine of Christ and the Sabellian heresy on the one hand and the Arian heresy on the other hand. The emphasis on the fact that in the act of the incarnation Christ became Man, but remained what He was, i.e. God's eternal Son, is part of the traditional doctrine of the incarnation, but it functions in Augustine also as a specifically anti-Manichean doctrine: according to the Manicheans, redemption is brought about by a war between the realm of light and the realm of darkness, a war in which the Highest God proves to be vulnerable and corruptible. Against this Augustine states that redemption is brought about by the sovereign decision of God to incarnate His Son who in the state of humility remained the unchangeable and incorruptible God. The emphasis on Christ's humility and the example it sets, so that man's sinful pride is overcome, is in itself not absent from the ecclesiastical tradition, but Augustine makes it the core of his doctrine of the incarnation. The reality of the incarnation is defended both against the Manicheans who deny that Christ assumed real flesh and against the Apollinarians who deny that Christ had a rational soul. In both arguments the typically Augustinian doctrine of illumination plays an important part: the Manicheans deny that the incarnation of the true Light is necessary, since the souls of the elected as parts of God are lights in themselves, the implication of the Apollinarian doctrine is that the human mind which distinguishes man from the animals is not assumed and therefore not illuminated. The defence of the reality of the incarnation against the Manicheans is much longer and much more detailed. This is understandable, since Manicheism was the old enemy inside Augustine's own mind; the theories he attacks were once held by himself. This applies also to the ascension of Christ and to His sitting at the right hand of God (Augustine's expositions on Christ's death, burial, resurrection and second coming only provide traditional material): here his old Manichean contempt of earthly bodies and his difficulties with a non-corporeal conception of God become apparent.

The difference between faith and understanding again having been stated, this time in connection with the doctrine of the Trinity (faith acquiring belief in the one God, who as Father, Son and Holy Spirit is fully God), an attempt is made to explain the doctrine of the Trinity, especially of the Son and the Holy Spirit. In a subtle way Augustine shows the inadequacy of images taken from the realm of creation in this context. Two traditional images, *viz.,* the river (with well, stream and draught) and the tree (with roots, trunk and branches) are clearly inadequate, since the

first one can be misinterpreted in a Sabellian way and the second one in an Arian way. This scepticism about such images can be regarded as a prelude to Augustine's later expositions on the Trinity which provide images from the realm of the human mind rather than from the bodily world.- In connection with the doctrine of the Son the ecclesiastical tradition provides all the necessary material which only needs some precise classification: there are Biblical texts which teach the complete equality of the Father and the Son, who is fully God, Christ is inferior to the generating Father, and there are texts which teach that in the state of the incarnation Christ is as man inferior to the Father.- In connection with the doctrine of the Holy Spirit Augustine adopts one tenet which is found in tradition, *viz.*, in Marius Victorinus, that the Holy Spirit is the bond between the Father and the Son. Augustine elaborates this by saying that, as the divinity of the Father and the Son, the Holy Spirit is their bond. This doctrine (which will later play an important part in the *De Trinitate*) enables Him to speak about God as a reality which is spirit and love without conceiving God as a bodily being (as he accuses the Arians of doing).
Faith in the Catholic Church enables Augustine to draw a clear line between the orthodox church on the one hand and the heretics and schismatics on the other hand: the heretics have the wrong views about God and therefore lack love of God, the schismatics do not want to forgive their neighbours and therefore lack love of men. This fight against the heretics and the schismatics will later form Augustine's theology.
The expositions about the resurrection of the flesh are, of course, largely directed against the Manicheans. The traditional doctrine of the tripartition of man, who consists of body, soul and mind, is used in the traditional way as the background to expositions about man as "homo carnalis", "homo animalis" and "homo spiritalis". If man in his totality is to be saved the progress made in this life from "homo carnalis" via "homo animalis" to "homo spiritalis" must be followed by the resurrection of the flesh. This resurrection of the flesh is *inter alia* made plausible with arguments taken from Platonic philosophy: there is a transition from one element to the other, from earth to water, to air, to ether (fire), if this is possible as a gradual natural process, then it must also be believed to happen quickly through the almighty will of God. (Preservation of corruptible things through the almighty will of God which is the cause of these things is a well-known Platonic tenet which was adopted by Christians in connection with the immortality of the souls.) This again implies that Platonic philosophy is to a certain extent suited to provide the arguments against the Manicheans (as Augustine had experienced around the time of his conversion).

b) Some final Observations.

The *De fide et symbolo* is a fairly early work by Augustine. Reading it and analysing its background one is certainly struck by the great continuity in the thought of Augustine. What is said in the *De fide et symbolo* finds confirmation and amplification in the writings dating from all periods of Augustine's life. One may, of course, object that this is only possible because we followed a method in our analysis which, so to speak, "flattens" the thoughts of Augustine: by not allowing for a development in his thought we produced parallels from all his writings. This would be the same criticism as A. von Harnack made of O. Scheel's book on Augustine's anthropology: according to Harnack, Scheel did not distinguish between what was important and what was unimportant during various periods in Augustine's life, and he did not distinguish between those instances where Augustine merely reproduced the ecclesiastical doctrinal positions and those where he revealed his own thoughts (see *Lehrbuch der Dogmengeschichte III,* p 128 note 1, and *supra,* 58).

The Augustine behind the *De fide et symbolo* is the anti-Manichean Augustine. It is obvious that all his major objections against the Manicheans, whether it is in connection with the doctrine of creation, incarnation or resurrection, reappear, often in an amplified way, in other writings in which he attacks the Manicheans. Augustine remained a conscious anti-Manichean throughout his life, also when the Donatists and the Pelagians were his major opponents who largely absorbed his attention. It may seem as if the anti-Pelagian Augustine differs substantially from the anti-Manichean Augustine, since in his anti-Pelagian writings Augustine shows relatively little interest in speculative problems and focuses his attention on grace and redemption. Harnack presents this anti-Pelagian Augustine as the "true Augustine" who, just like the "true Luther", made history, and presents the anti-Manichean Augustine as the "whole Augustine" who largely reproduced traditional material (see *Lehrbuch der Dogmengeschichte III,* pp 220ff, cf. also pp 93ff where Harnack claims that it is most important to trace the development in Augustine's thoughts about the Creed, these being in the *Encheiridion* quite different from in the *De fide et symbolo*).

We should try to let Augustine speak for himself on this matter. The only criticism he himself utters in the *Retractationes* of what he says in the *De fide et symbolo* is about his expositions on the resurrection which could,in his view, be read as a denial of the resurrection of the flesh (see *supra*, 152). This means that the late Augustine has fears that at the time of the *De fide et symbolo* he did not yet disassociate himself enough from the Manichean contempt of flesh. Interestingly he makes no criticism at all about

any statements which could be misinterpreted in a Pelagian way: God reveals Himself to those who deserve it (see *supra,* 43), the believers must cleanse their hearts in so far as possible in order to be able to see God's non-corporeal substance (see *supra,* 133), man must subject his body to his soul, his soul to his mind and his mind to God (see *supra*, 141ff). We do not suggest that these statements were meant in a Pelagian way, but as, according to Augustine, the statements about the resurrection might be misinterpreted in a Manichean way, so one might expect him to have fears that the remarks just referred to might be misunderstood in a Pelagian way. But Augustine obviously harbours no fears about this, which shows that anti-Manicheism preoccupied his thoughts as much as anti-Pelagianism. This is all the more telling, since in the *Retractationes* he is very sensitive about earlier statements in other writings which could be (mis)interpreted in a Pelagian way.
Augustine overcame Manicheism with the authority of the Catholic Church and with the help of Platonic philosophy, he overcame Pelagianism with the help of Paul and to some degree of Platonic philosophy (this latter fact is also acknowledged by Harnack despite the fact that he tries to disassociate the "true Augustine" from Platonism, see *Lehrbuch der Dogmengeschichte III,* p 83,- for a comparison between Plotinus, Pelagius and Augustine see also A.H. Armstrong, *Plotinian and Christian Studies,* XI, pp 27f). The speculative anti-Manichean Augustine has obviously made history in Scholasticism and later Catholic theology, the anti-Pelagian Augustine who focuses his attention on grace and redemption has made history in Potestantism. The anti-Manichean Augustine has as much right to be regarded as the "true Augustine" as has the anti-Pelagian Augustine.

There are good reasons for modern Protestant theology to take the speculative and anti-Manichean aspect of Augustine seriously. Most modern Protestants no longer regard the Creed as the core of their faith, because they regard the statements made in the Creed as supranatural, miraculous and therefore no longer credible. Paul Tillich speaks for many modern Protestants when he defines supranaturalism as the separation of God as a being, the highest being, from all other beings, alongside and above which He has His existence, and as the belief that this highest being brought the universe into being (five thousand or five billion years ago), governs it according to a plan, directs it towards an end, interferes with its ordinary processes in order to overcome resistance and to fulfil His purpose, and bring it to final consummation in a final catastrophe (see *Systematic Theology II*, London 1957, p 6). There can indeed be little doubt that the statements made in the Creed have been interpreted by many Christians in the light of such a conception of God as described by Tillich. According to Tillich, Augustine, Thomas, Luther, Zwingli, Calvin, and Schleiermacher disassociated themselves - albeit in a restricted form-from this kind of supranaturalism. We doubt whether this holds true of the Reformers, but as far as Augustine is concerned it is fairly correct. The *De fide et symbolo* can be read as a serious attempt to explain away crudely and naively anthropomorphous statements about God, and the same tendency is apparent in other writings of Augustine.

In his doctrine of the Trinity Augustine is as uncompromising in his rejection of Sabellianism as he is in his rejection of tritheism. Nevertheless, his doctrine that the Spirit is the divinity of Father and Son and that He is the bond of Father and Son (and later his images for the Trinity taken from the human mind) is closer to Sabellianism than to tritheism,- whilst in popular Christian belief the opposite is probably the case: it is often hardly distinguishable from tritheism.

The first article of the Creed has often meant to Christian believers that God, who was firstly alone, at a certain moment decided to create a world and carried out this plan in six days (or in six thousand years on account of a combination of *Gen.* 1 and *Psalm* 90,4 or even in six billion years if one has capitulated to modern geology). Augustine often goes to great lengths to avoid such ideas by declaring that the creation of formless matter and formed matter coincide and that there was no time before creation. So, according to him, God is not a finite being (albeit: the highest one) in space and time, but as the infinite Being embraces both space and time in a creative activity which itself transcends time but produces a temporal product.

To popular Christian belief, the incarnation of the Son meant the transmutation of a divine being into a human being. Like many other Fathers Augustine qualifies this by saying that Christ assumed manhood whilst remaining what He was, thus healing the breach between God and man, a breach caused by man's pride which is overcome by Christ's humility.- Augustine, of course, expresses no doubts about the miraculous events of the virgin birth, the physical resurrection, the ascension and the second coming of Christ, and the catalogue of miracles he produces in *De civ.* 22,8 showed that he believed to be living in a miraculous world. In this sense there is a supranatural element in the thought of Augustine which seems strange to many people in modern times. But by stressing the meaning and the saving character of these events (the virgin birth must stress the reality of the incarnation against the Manicheans, whilst the resurrection implies the adoption of believers as sons of God, the sitting at the right hand of God and the second coming of Christ also indicate

Christ's judicial power) he makes it clear that these are no arbitrary miracles merely revealing God's omnipotence, but that they are part of God's saving acts, acts which are carried out in a rational way by God. Although Augustine stresses God's omnipotence, he also makes an effort to establish a clear relation between the natural laws instituted by God's will and the miracles wrought by God's will,- thus again taking an element of arbitrariness out of these miracles and at least diminishing the idea of "take it or leave it."

The resurrection of the flesh was firmly believed in by Augustine after some initial hesitations, but he also adds thoughts which go well beyond popular belief. At first sight speculations about the question of whether in the state of the resurrection men can, so to speak, read each other's minds seem futile, but the affirmative answer given to this question allows it to interpret the resurrection as the state in which the human existence becomes completely transparant, and this could be a meaningful statement for anybody who still believes in a life with God after death. Furthermore, the emphasis on the liberation from temporal conditions in eternal life implies that eternal life is not (as it is in the popular imagination of many believers) an endless continuation of an existence in time, but that it is a *finis sine fine* in which man participates in God's "eternal now."

What makes the Creed so unattractive to many modern Protestants (and to more and more modern Catholics) is the idea that the Creed invites people to believe the unbelievable. There is a way out of this difficulty: if P. Ricoeur is right in saying "Le symbole donne à penser" (see *Finitude et Culpabilité II. La Symbolique du Mal,* Paris 1960, pp 323ff), then this general definition should be applied to the Symbol, the Creed, as well. As such, the Symbol gave Augustine much to think about, and his reflections could give us something to think about as well.

GREEK TEXTS

I: *βουληθεὶς γὰρ ὁ θεὸς ἀγαθὰ μὲν πάντα, φλαῦρον δὲ μηδὲν εἶναι κατὰ δύναμιν, οὕτω δὴ πᾶν ὅσον ἦν ὁρατὸν παραλαβὼν οὐχ ἡσυχίαν ἄγον ἀλλὰ κινούμενον πλημμελῶς, εἰς τάξιν αὐτὸ ἤγαγεν ἐκ τῆς ἀταξίας, ἡγησάμενος ἐκεῖνο τούτου πάντως ἄμεινον.*

II: *ἀγαθῷ δὲ οὐδεὶς περὶ οὐδενὸς οὐδέποτ' ἐγγίγνεται φθόνος.*

III: *Δύναται δὲ καθ' ἡμᾶς πάντα ὁ θεὸς ὅπερ δυνάμενος τοῦ θεὸς εἶναι καὶ ἀγαθὸς εἶναι οὐκ ἐξίσταται.*

IV: *ὠδινοῦσα (γῆ ἀόρατος καὶ ἀκατασκεύαστος) μὲν τὴν πάντων γένεσιν διὰ τὴν ἐναποτεθεῖσαν αὐτῇ παρὰ τοῦ δημιουργοῦ δύναμιν, ἀναμένουσα δὲ καθήκοντας χρόνους ἵνα τῷ θείῳ κελεύσματι προαγάγῃ ἑαυτῆς εἰς φανερὸν τὰ κινήματα.*

V: *Λόγον δέ φημι ... οὐδὲ οἷον ἔχει τὸ λογικὸν γένος λόγον τὸν ἐκ συλλαβῶν συγκείμενον, καὶ ἐν ἀέρι σημαινόμενον*

VI: *ὅπερ ἦν μεμένηκε καὶ ὃ οὐκ ἦν προσέλαβε*

VII: *ὁ μὲν τῶν ἀνθρώπων λόγος ... μόνον ἐστὶ σημαντικὸς τῆς τοῦ λαλοῦντος διανοίας.*

VIII: *τοῦτο μὲν τοίνυν τὸ εἶδος οὐκ εἶχεν ἡ ὕλη, ἀλλ' ἦν ἐν τῷ ἐννοήσαντι καὶ πρὶν ἐλθεῖν εἰς τὸν λίθον ... Ἦν ἄρα ἐν τῇ τέχνῃ τὸ κάλλος τοῦτο ἄμεινον πολλῷ· οὐ γὰρ ἐκεῖνο ἦλθεν εἰς τὸν λίθον τὸ ἐν τῇ τέχνῃ, ἀλλ' ἐκεῖνο μὲν μένει, ἄλλο δὲ ἀπ' ἐκείνης ἔλαττον ἐκείνου.*

IX: *Ὄντος δὲ τοῦ προαιρετοῦ βουλευτοῦ ὀρεκτοῦ τῶν ἐφ' ἡμῖν, καὶ ἡ προαίρεσις ἂν εἴη βουλευτικὴ ὄρεξις τῶν ἐφ' ἡμῖν· ἐκ τοῦ βουλεύσασθαι γὰρ κρίναντες ὀρεγόμεθα κατὰ τὴν βούλευσιν*

X: *τῶν δὲ ὀργάνων πρῶτον μὲν φωσφόρα συνετεκτήναντο ὄμματα, τοιᾷδε ἐνδήσαντες αἰτίᾳ, τοῦ πυρὸς ὅσον τὸ* μὲν καίειν οὐκ ἔσχε, τὸ δὲ παρέχειν φῶς ἥμερον, οἰκεῖον ἑκάστης, σῶμα ἐμηχανήσαντο γίγνεσθαι.

XI: οὐκ ἦν (sc. ὁ Υἱὸς) πρὸ τοῦ γεννηθῆναι, ἀλλ' ἀχρόνως πρὸ πάντων γεννηθείς ... οὐδὲ γάρ ἐστιν ἀΐδιος ἢ συναΐδιος ἢ συναγένητος τῷ πατρί.

XII: Ἔγραψαν τοίνυν λέγοντες· Κτίσμα ἐστίν, ἀλλ' οὐχ ὡς ἓν τῶν ποιημάτων.

XIII: Εἰ γὰρ ὅλως καθ' ὑμᾶς κτίσμα ἐστίν, πῶς ὑποκρίνεσθε λέγοντες· Ἀλλ' οὐχ ὡς ἓν τῶν κτισμάτων;

XIV: βουλήσει καὶ θελήσει γεγενῆσθαι τὸν Υἱὸν τοῦ Πατρός

XV: εἰ μέν τις τῶν ὀρθῶς πιστευόντων ἁπλούστερον ἔλεγεν, οὐδὲν ἦν ὑποπτεῦσαι περὶ τοῦ λεγομένου, νικώσης τῆς ὀρθοδόξου διανοίας τὴν ἁπλουστέραν τῶν ῥημάτων προφοράν. Επειδὴ δὲ παρ' αἱρετικῶν ἐστιν ἡ φωνή, ὕποπτα δὲ τῶν αἱρετικῶν τὰ ῥήματα ... φέρε, καὶ τοῦτο τὸ λεγόμενον ἐξετάσωμεν ... Ταὐτὸν γὰρ σημαίνει ὁ λέγων, Βουλήσει γέγονεν ὁ Υἱός, καὶ ὁ λέγων, Ἦν ποτε ὅτε οὐκ ἦν, καὶ, Ἐξ οὐκ ὄντων γέγονεν ὁ Υἱός, καὶ, Κτίσμα ἐστίν.

XVI: ὅτι δὲ ἡ τοῦ, ἔκτισε, μόνη λέξις λεγομένη οὐ πάντως τὴν οὐσίαν καὶ τὴν γένεσιν σημαίνει, ὁ μὲν Δαυὶδ ψαλλει ..., Καρδιάν καθαρὰν κτίσον ἐν ἐμοι, ὁ θεός

XVII: αὐτός ἐστιν πρὸ πάντων καὶ τὰ πάντα ἐν αὐτῷ συνέστηκεν, καὶ αὐτός ἐστιν ἡ κεφαλὴ τοῦ σώματος, τῆς ἐκκλησίας, ὅς ἐστιν ἀρχή ...

XVIII: ὅθεν ὁ τοῦ θεοῦ Λόγος δι' ἑαυτοῦ παρεγένετο, ἵνα ὡς εἰκὼν τοῦ Πατρὸς τὸν κατ' εἰκόνα ἄνθρωπον ἀνακτίσαι δυνηθῇ.

XIX: τὸν Υἱὸν τοῦ θεοῦ γεννηθέντα ἐκ τοῦ Πατρὸς μονογενῆ, τοῦτ' ἐστιν ἐκ τῆς οὐσίας τοῦ Πατρός, θεὸν ἐκ θεοῦ, φῶς ἐκ φωτός.

XX: τό τ' ἦν, τό τ' ἔσται χρόνου γεγηνότα εἴδη, ἃ δὴ φέροντες λανθάνομεν ἐπὶ τὴν ἀΐδιαν οὐσίαν οὐκ ὀρθῶς· λέγομεν γὰρ δὴ ὡς ἦν ἔστιν τε καὶ ἔσται, τῇ δὲ τὸ ἔστιν μόνον κατὰ τὸν ἀληθῆ λόγον προσήκει

XXI: τὸ ὂν οὔτε ποτὲ ἦν οὔτε ποτὲ μὴ γένηται, ἀλλ' ἔστιν ἀεὶ ἐν χρόνῳ ὡρισμένῳ τῷ ἐνεστῶτι μόνῳ. Τοῦτον μὲν οὖν τὸν ἐνεστῶτα εἴ τις ἐθέλει ἀνακαλεῖν αἰῶνα κἀγὼ συμβούλομαι.

XXII: ἔστιν ὁ θεὸς κατ' οὐδένα χρόνον ἀλλὰ κατὰ τὸν αἰῶνα ... οὐ πρότερον οὐδέν ἐστιν οὐδ' ὕστερον ... ἀλλ' εἷς ὢν ἑνὶ τῷ νῦν τὸ ἀεὶ πεπλήρωκε,

XXIII: ἔστι γὰρ ἀεὶ καὶ ὢν ἔστιν ... καὶ αὐτὸς ἔστιν ὁ ὤν,

XXIV: καὶ ὡς ἄνθρωπος ταφεὶς ἀνέστη ἐκ νεκρῶν ὡς θεός, φύσει θεὸς ὢν καὶ ἄνθρωπος,

XXV: ... εἰς τέσσαρας καὶ εἴκοσι ὥρας νυκτὸς καὶ ἡμέρας, ὥς φατε, διῃρημένων· ἑκάστης δὲ ὥρας ἑξήκοντα τμήμασι μεριζομένης. πάλιν δὲ τῶν τμημάτων τούτων ἑκάστου κατὰ τὸν ἰσάριθμον κερματιζομένου).

XXVI: Εἰ δ' ἐβούλετο πνεῦμα ἐξ ἑαυτοῦ καταπέμψαι, τί ἔδειτο εἰς γυναικὸς γαστέρα ἐμπνεῖν; Ἐδύνατο γὰρ ἤδη πλάσσειν ἀνθρώπους εἰδὼς καὶ τούτῳ περιπλάσαι σῶμα καὶ μὴ τὸ ἴδιον πνεῦμα εἰς τοσοῦτον μίασμα ἐμβαλεῖν

XXVII: Ἄνθρωπος γὰρ οὐ κατ' ἰδίαν ἐξουσίαν, ἀλλ' ἀνάγκῃ φύσεως καὶ μὴ θέλων ἀποθνῄσκει.

XXVIII: ἀλλὰ τὸν παρ' ἑτέρων, καὶ μάλιστα τὸν παρὰ τῶν ἐχθρῶν ὃν ἐνόμιζον εἶναι δεινὸν ἐκεῖνοι καὶ ἄτιμον καὶ φευκτόν, τοῦτον αὐτὸς ἐν σταυρῷ δεχόμενος ἠνείχετο· ἵνα καὶ τούτου καταλυθέντος, αὐτὸς μὲν ὢν ἡ ζωὴ πιστευθῇ, τοῦ δὲ θανάτου τὸ κράτος τέλεον καταργηθῇ.

XXIX: ἵν' ὥσπερ ἡ γένεσις αὐτοῦ καθαρωτέρα πάσης γενέσεως ἦν τῷ μὴ ἀπὸ μίξεως ἀλλ' ἀπὸ παρθένου γεννηθῆναι, οὕτως καὶ ἡ ταφὴ ἔχοι τὴν καθαρότητα, διὰ τοῦ συμβολικοῦ δηλουμένην ἐν τῷ ἀποτεθεῖσθαι αὐτοῦ τὸ σῶμα ἐν μνημείῳ καινῷ ὑφεστῶτι.

XXX: τὴν δ' ἐμφέρειαν μηδεὶς εἰκαζέτω σώματος χαρακτῆρι. οὔτε γὰρ ἀνθρωπόμορφος ὁ θεὸς οὔτε θεοειδὲς τὸ ἀνθρωπέριον σῶμα. ἡ δὲ εἰκὼν λέλεκται κατὰ τὸν τῆς ψυχῆς ἡγεμόνα νοῦν.

XXXI: οὓς οὐκ ἀγνοοῦσι δεομένους τῆς αὐτῶν ἐπιμελείας, παρὰ τούτων αὐτοὶ τὰς ἑαυτῶν χρείας ἀξιοῦσιν ἀναπληροῦσθαι. καὶ οὓς ἐν μικροῖς οἰκίσκοις κατακλείουσι, τούτους οὐρανοῦ καὶ γῆς ἁπάσης δεσπότας οὐκ αἰσχύνονται καλοῦντες

XXXII: Ἐκ δεξιῶν γοῦν καθήμενος, ἀριστερὸν οὐ ποιεῖ τὸν Πατέρα. ἀλλ' ὅπερ ἐστὶ δεξιὸν καὶ τίμιον ἐν τῷ Πατρί, τοῦτο καὶ ὁ Υἱὸς ἔχει.

XXXIII: μικρὸν μέν ἐστι τὸ παράδειγμα καὶ λιὰν ἀμυδρὸν πρὸς τὸ ποθούμενον,

XXXIV: οὐκοῦν Υἱός ἐστι καὶ αὐτό, καὶ δύο ἀδελφοί εἰσι αὐτό τε καὶ ὁ Λόγος, καὶ εἰ ἀδελφός ἐστι, πῶς μονογενὴς ὁ Λόγος ... Εἰ δὲ τοῦ Υἱοῦ ἐστι τὸ Πνεῦμα, οὐκοῦν πάππος ἐστιν ὁ Πατηρ τοῦ Πνεύματος.

XXXV: πῶς οὐ τολμηρὸν καὶ δυσσεβὲς εἰπεῖν ... ὅτι ἐπισυμβέβηκε, καὶ δύναται πάλιν μὴ εἶναί ποτε.

XXXVI: ὁρατὸς γὰρ ἁπτός τέ ἐστι καὶ σῶμα ἔχων.

XXXVII: Ὁ γὰρ τὴν ἀρχὴν οὐκ ὄντας (sc. ἀνθρώπους) ποιήσας, ὅποτε ἠθέλησε πολλῷ μᾶλλον τοὺς ἤδη γεγονότας αὖθις ἀποκαταστήσει εἰς τὴν ὑπ' αὐτοῦ διδομένην ζωήν.

XXXVIII: οὕτω δὴ πυρός τε καὶ γῆς ὕδωρ ἀέρα τε ὁ θεὸς ἐν μέσῳ θείς, καὶ πρὸς ἄλληλα καθ' ὅσον ἦν δυνατὸν ἀνὰ τὸν αὐτὸν λόγον ἀπεργασάμενος, ὅτιπερ πῦρ πρὸς ἀέρα, τοῦτο ἀέρα πρὸς ὕδωρ, καὶ ὅτι ἀὴρ πρὸς ὕδωρ, ὕδωρ πρὸς γῆν, συνέδησεν καὶ συνεστήσατο οὐρανὸν ὁρατὸν καὶ ἁπτόν.

XXXIX: θεοὶ θεῶν, ὧν ἐγὼ δημιουργὸς πατήρ τε ἔργων, δι' ἐμοῦ γενόμενα ἄλυτα ἐμοῦ γε μὴ ἐθέλοντος ... δι' ἃ καὶ ἐπείπερ γεγένησθε, ἀθάνατοι μὲν οὐκ ἐστὲ οὐδ' ἄλυτοι τὸ πάμπαν, οὔτι μὲν δὴ λυθήσεσθέ γε οὐδὲ τεύξεσθε θανάτου μοίρας, τῆς ἐμῆς βουλήσεως μείζονος ἔτι δεσμοῦ καὶ κυριωτέρου λαχόντες ἐκείνων οἷς ὅτ' ἐγίγνεσθε συνεδεῖσθε.

LITERATURE

B. Altaner, *Kleine Patristische Schriften,* Berlin 1967

C. Andresen, *Logos und Nomos. Die Polemik des Kelsos wider das Christentum,* Berlin 1955

A.H. Armstrong, Plotinus, in: *The Cambridge History of Later Greek and Early Medieval Philosophy,* Cambridge 1970[2]

A.H. Armstrong, Neoplatonic Valuations of Nature, Body and Intellect, in: *Augustinian Studies* 1972

A.H. Armstrong, *Plotinian and Christian Studies,* London 1979

M. Aubineau, Le Thème du "Bourbier" dans la littérature grecque profane et chrétienne, in: *Recherches de science religieuse* (47) 1959

G. Bardy, *Oeuvres de Saint Augustin (35), La Cité de Dieu, Livres XI-XIV* Paris 1959

F.C. Baur, *Das manichäische Religionssystem nach den Quellen neu untersucht und entwickelt,* Tübingen 1831

F.C. Baur, *Die christliche Lehre von der Dreieinigkeit und Menschwerdung Gottes in ihrer geschichtlichen Entwicklung I,* Tübingen 1841

J.A. Beckaert, *Oeuvres de Saint Augustin,10, Mélanges doctrinaux,* Paris 1952

W. Beierwaltes, *Plotin über Ewigkeit und Zeit. Text. Übersetzung. Kommentar,* Frankfurt/M. 1967

M.-F. Berrouard, *Oeuvres de Saint Augustin (71), Homilies sur l'évangile de Saint Jean I-XVI, Traduction, Introduction et Notes,* Paris 1969

J. Blic, Platonisme et christianisme dans la conception augustinienne du Dieu Creáteur, in: *Recherches de science religieuse* (30) 1940

A.M. la Bonnardière, *Biblia Augustiniana, A.T., Deuteronome,* Paris 1967

A.M. la Bonnardière, *Biblia Augustiniana, A.T. Le Livre de la Sagesse,* Paris 1970

A.M. la Bonnardière, *Biblia Augustiniana, A.T. Le Livre des Proverbes,* Paris 1975

R. Braun, *Deus christianorum. Recherches sur le vocabulaire doctrinal de Tertullien,* Paris 1977[2]

L. Bron, Saint Grégoire de Nazianze et l'antienne "mirabile Mysterium" des landes de la circonsion, in: *Ephemerides Liturgicae* (58) 1944

E. zum Brunn, Le dilemme de l'être et le neánt chez Saint Augustin. Des premiers dialogues aux Confessions, in: *Recherches augustiniennes* (6) 1969

C.F. Burney, Christ as the APXH of Creation, in: *The Journal of Theological Studies* (27) 1926

J.F. Callahan, *Augustine and the Greek Philosophers,* Villanova University Press 1967
H. von Campenhausen, *Urchristliches und Altkirchliches,* Tübingen 1979
F. Cavallera, La doctrine de Saint Augustin sur l'Esprit Saint à propos du "De Trinitate", in: *Recherches de theólogie ancienne et médiévale* (3) 1931
H. Chadwick, *Origen: Contra Celsum, Translated with an Introduction and Notes,* Cambridge 1965[2]
G. Combès, *Oeuvres de Saint Augustin,11, Le Magistère chrétien,* Paris 1949
P. Courcelle, *Recherches sur les Confessions de Saint Augustin,* Paris 1968[2]
P. Courcelle, *Les lettres grecques en occident. De Macrobe à Cassiodore,* Paris 1948
R.E. Cushman, Faith and Reason in the Thought of Augustine, in: *Church History* (19) 1950
J. Daniélou, Message évangélique et culture hellénistique aux IIe et IIIe siècles, Tournai 1961
A. Dihle, *The Theory of Will in Classical Antiquity,* University of California Press, 1982
J. Doignon, *Hilaire de Poitiers avant l' exil. Recherches sur la naissance, l'enseignement et l' épreuve d'une foi épiscopale en Gaule au milieu du IVe siècle,* Paris 1971
H. Dörrie, *Platonica minora,* 1976
U. Duchrow, "Signum" und "superbia" beim jungen Augustin, in: *Révue des études augustiniennes* (7) 1961
P.C. Eichenseer, *Das Symbolum Apostolicum beim heiligen Augustinus mit Berücksichtigung des dogmengeschichtlichen Zusammenhangs,* St. Ottilien 1960
E. Evans, *Tertullian's Treatise against Praxeas,* London 1949
M. Farges, *Oeuvres de Saint Augustin, 11, Le Magistère chrétien,* Paris 1949
K. Flasch, Ars imitatur naturam. Platonischer Naturbegriff und mittelalterliche Philosophie der Kunst, in: *Parusia, Studien zur Philosophie Platons und zur Problemgeschichte des Platonismus, Festgabe für Johannes Hirschberger,* Frankfurt/M. 1965
F.E. van Fleteren, Authority and Reason, Faith and Understanding in the Thought of Saint Augustine, in: *Augustinian Studies* (4) 1973
W.H.C. Frend, Art.: Donatismus, *R.A.C.* 4
J. Gager, Marcion and Philosophy, in: *Vigiliae Christianae* (26) (26) 1972
J. Geffcken, *Zwei griechische Apologeten,* Leipzig/Berlin 1907
E. Gilson, *Introduction à l'étude de Saint Augustin,* Paris 1929
R.M. Grant, *Miracle and Natural Law in Graeco-Roman and Early Christian*

Thought, Amsterdam 1952
P. Hadot, *Marius Victorinus, Traités theólogiques sur la Trinité I-II,* Paris 1960
P. Hadot, La Métaphysique de Porphyre, in: *Porphyre, Entretiens sur l'Antiquité classique,* t. XII, Geneva 1966
A. Hahn, *Bibliothek der Symbole und Glaubensregeln der alten Kirche,* Breslau 1897
A. von Harnack, *Lehrbuch der Dogmengeschichte I-III,* Tübingen 1909/1910[4]
R. Holte, *Sagesse et Beátitude. Saint Augustin et le problème de la fin de l'homme dans la philosophie ancienne,* Paris 1962
Ch. Kannengiesser, *Athanase d'Alexandrie, Sur l'Incarnation du Verbe,* Paris 1973
J.N.D. Kelly, *Early Christian Creeds,* New York 1972[3]
E. König, *Augustinus philosophus. Christlicher Glaube und philosophisches Denken in den Frühschriften Augustins,* München 1970
K. Kremer, Das Warum der Schöpfung: "quia bonus vel/et quia voluit?" Ein Beitrag zum Verhältnis von Neuplatonismus und Christentum an Hand des Prinzips "bonum est diffusum sui", in: *Parusia*
G.F.D. Locher, *Hoop, eeuwigheid en tijd in de prediking van Augustinus,* Wageningen 1961
K.-H. Lütcke, *"Auctoritas bei Augustin. Mit einer Einleitung zur römischen Vorgeschichte des Begriffs,* Stuttgart 1968
G. Madec, Notes sur l'intelligence augustinienne de la foi, in: *Révue des études augustiniennes* (17) 1971
B. de Margerie, La doctrine de Saint Augustin sur l'Esprit Saint comme communion et source de communion, in: *Augustinianum* (12) 1972
R.A. Markus, Alienatio. Philosophy and Eschatology in the Development of an Augustinian Idea, in: *Studia Patristica* (9), Berlin 1966
R.A. Markus, St. Augustine on Signs, in: *Phronesis* (2) 1957
R.A. Markus, Augustine. Reason and Illumination, in: *The Cambridge History of Later Greek and Early Medieval Philosophy,* Cambridge 1970[2]
H.-I. Marrou, Le dogme de la résurrection des corps et la théologie des valeurs humains selon l'enseignement de Saint Augustin, in: *Révue des études augustiniennes* (12) 1966
G. May, *Schöpfung aus dem Nichts, Die Entstehung der Lehre von der creatio ex nihilo,* Berlin/New York 1978
C.P. Mayer, *Die Zeichen in der geistigen Entwicklung in der Theologie des jungen Augustin I, II,* Würzburg 1969, 1974
M. Mellet et Th. Camelot, *Oeuvres de Saint Augustin, 15, La Trinité, Livres I-VIII,* Paris 1955
E.P. Meijering, *Orthodoxy and Platonism in Athanasius. Synthesis or Anti-*

thesis?, Leiden 1974[2]
E.P. Meijering, *God Being History, Studies in Patristic Philosophy*, Amsterdam/Oxford/New York 1975
E.P. Meijering, *Tertullian contra Marcion. Gotteslehre in der Polemik (Adversus Marcionem I-II)*, Leiden 1977
E.P. Meijering, *Theologische Urteile über die Dogmengeschichte. Ritschls Einfluss auf von Harnack*, Leiden 1978
E.P. Meijering, *Augustin über Schöpfung, Ewigkeit und Zeit. Das elfte Buch der Bekenntnisse*, Leiden 1979
E.P. Meijering, *Calvin wider die Neugierde. Ein Beitrag zum Vergleich zwischen reformatorischem und patristischem Denken*, Nieuwkoop 1980
E.P. Meijering, *Hilary of Poitiers on the Trinity. De Trinitate 1,1-19,2,3*, Leiden 1982 (in close cooperation with J.C.M. van Winden)
E.P. Meijering, *Der "ganze" und der "wahre" Luther. Hintergrund und Bedeutung der Lutherinterpretation Adolf von Harnacks*, Amsterdam/Oxford 1983
E.P. Meijering, *Melanchthon and Patristic Thought. The Doctrine of Christ and Grace, the Trinity and the Creation*, Leiden 1983
E.P. Meijering, *Athanasius: Contra Gentes. Introduction, Translation and Commentary*, Leiden 1984
E.P. Meijering, *Die Hellenisierung des Christentums im Urteil Adolf von Harnacks*, Amsterdam/Oxford/New York 1985
E.P. Meijering, *F.C. Baur als Patristiker. Die Bedeutung seiner Geschichtsphilosophie und Quellenforschung*, Amsterdam 1986
P. Munz, Ego sum qui sum, in: *Hibbert Journal* (50) 1950/51
K.A. Neuhausen, *De voluntarii notione platonica et aristotelea*, Wiesbaden 1967
A. Olivar, Sol intaminatus, in: *Analecta Tarraconensia* (25) 1952 and (29) 1956
J. Pépin, *Théologie cosmique et théologie chrétienne*, Paris 1964
M. Pohlenz, *Die Stoa. Geschichte einer geistigen Bewegung I- II*, Göttingen 1970/1972[4]
V. Pöschl-H. Gärtner-W. Heyke, *Bibliographie zur antiken Bildsprache*, Heidelberg 1964
G.-L. Prestige, *Dieu dans la pensée patristique* (transl.), Paris 1955
H.-C. Puech, *Le Manichéisme. Son fondateur- sa doctrine*, Paris 1949
J.M. Rist, Plotinus and Augustine on Evil, in: *Atti del Convegno internazionale sul tema: Plotino e il Neoplatonismo in Oriente e in Occidente*, Rome 1974
J. Rivière, *Oeuvres de Saint Augustin, 9, Exposés de la foi. De fide et symbolo-Enchiridion. Texte, Traduction, Notes*, Paris 1947
O. du Roy, *L'intelligence de la foi en la Trinité selon Saint Augustin, Genèse de*

sa théologie trinitaire jusqu' en 391, Paris 1966
O. Scheel, *Die Anschauung Augustins über Christi Person und Werk. Unter Berücksichtigung ihrer verschiedenen Entwicklungsstufen und ihrer dogmengeschichtlichen Stellung,* Tübingen 1901
C.E. Schützinger, Die augustinische Erkenntnislehre im Lichte neuerer Forschung, in: *Recherches Augustiniennes* (2) 1962
M. Simonetti, S. Agostino e gli Ariani, in: *Révue des études augustiniennes* (13) 1967
P. Smulders, *La doctrine trinitaire de S. Hilaire de Poitiers.* Rome 1944
A. Solignac, *Oeuvres de Saint Augustin, 14, Les Confessions VIII-XIII,* Paris 1962
M. Spanneut, Le Stoicisme et Saint Augustin, in: *Forma Futuri. Studi in onore del cardinale Michele Pellegrino,* Turino 1975
K. Staritz, *Augustins Schöpfungsglaube dargestellt nach seinen Genesisauslegungen,* Breslau 1931
G.C. Stead, The Platonism of Arius, in: *The Journal of Theological Studies* (15) 1964
G.C. Stead, Rhetorical Method in Athanasius, in: *Vigiliae Christianae* (30) 1976
G.C. Stead, *Divine Substance,* Oxford 1977
B. Studer, Le Christ, notre Justice, selon Saint Augustin, in: *Recherches augustiniennes* (15) 1980
M. Tetz, Zur Theologie des Markell von Ankyra I. Eine markellinische Schrift "De incarnatione et contra Arianos", in: *Zeitschrift für Kirchengeschichte* (75) 1964
W. Theiler, *Die Vorbereitung des Neuplatonismus,* Berlin/Zürich 1964[2]
W. Theiler, *Forschungen zum Neuplatonismus,* Berlin 1966
J. Tixeront, *Histoire des dogmes de l'antiquité chrétienne II,* Paris 1924[6]
C. Tresmontant, *La Métaphysique du christianisme et la naissance de la philosophie chrétienne. Problèmes de la création et de l'anthropologie des origines à Saint Augustin,* Paris 1961
W.C. van Unnik, Irenaeus en de Pax romana, in: *Kerk en vrede. Feestbundel voor Prof. dr J. de Graaf,* Baarn 1976
G. Verbeke, Augustin et le Stoicisme, in: *Recherches Augustiniennes* (1) 1958
J. Verhees, *God in beweging. Een onderzoek naar de pneumatologie van Augustinus,* Wageningen 1968
J. Verhees, Heiliger Geist und Inkarnation in der Theologie des Augustinus von Hippo, in: *Révue des études augustiniennes* (22) 1976
J. Verhees, Heiliger Geist und Gemeinschaft bei Augustinus von Hippo, in: *Révue des études augustiniennes* (23) 1977
C.J. de Vogel, *Greek Philosophy III. A Collection of Texts,* Leiden 1959

C. Walter, *Der Ertrag der Auseinandersetzung mit den Manichäern für das hermeneutische Problem bei Augustin,* München 1972
J.H. Waszink. *Q.S.F. Tertulliani De anima, Edited with Introduction and Commentary,* Amsterdam 1947
J.H. Waszink, Observations on Tertullian's Treatise against Hermogenes, in: *Vigiliae Christianae* (9) 1955
J.H. Waszink, *Tertullian, the Treatise against Hermogenes,* London 1956
J.H. Waszink, Bemerkungen zu Justins Lehre vom Logos Spermatikos, in: *Mullus, Festschrift für Theodor Klauser,* Münster i.W. 1964
J.H. Waszink, *Studien zum Timaioskommentar des Calcidius I,* Leiden 1964
J.H. Waszink, Bemerkungen zum Einfluss des Platonismus im frühen Christentum, in: *Vigiliae Christianae* (19) 1965
J. Whittaker, *God Time Being. Two Studies in the Transcendental Tradition in Greek Philosophy,* Oslo 1971
J.C.M. van Winden, *Calcidus on Matter,* Leiden 1959
J.C.M. van Winden, *An Early Christian Philosopher. Justin Martyr's Dialogue with Trypho. Chapters 1-9,* Leiden 1971
J.C.M. van Winden, The Early Christian Exegesis of "Heaven and Earth" in Genesis 1:1, in: *Romanitas et Christianitas. Studia J.H. Waszink . . . oblata,* Amsterdam/London 1973
A. Wlosok, *Laktanz und die philosphische Gnosis. Untersuchungen zu Geschichte und Terminologie der gnostischen Erlösungsvorstellung,* Heidelberg 1960
H.A. Wolfson, *The Philosophy of the Church Fathers,* Cambridge 1956

INDICES

I. INDEX OF QUOTATIONS FROM ANCIENT AUTHORS

II. INDEX OF SUBJECTS AND NAMES

III. INDEX OF MODERN AUTHORS